# Deafness and Child Development

# Deafness and Child Development

## Kathryn P. Meadow

# Edward Arnold

©1980 by
The Regents of the University of California

First published in Great Britain 1980 by
Edward Arnold (Publishers) Ltd.
41 Bedford Square, London WC1B 3DQ

**British Library Cataloguing in Publication Data**

Meadow, Kathryn Pendleton
  Deafness and child development.
  1. Children, Deaf—United States
  2. Child development—United States
  I. Title
155.4'5'120973    HV2545    80-49981

ISBN 0-7131-6325-9
Printed in the United States of America

For my parents
Wilma Karnes Pendleton
Orien A. Pendleton (1899–1975)
and my children
Lynn Elizabeth Meadow
Robert Keith Meadow

# Contents

Preface    ix

1. Introduction    1
2. Language Development in Deaf Children    17
3. Cognitive Development in Deaf Children    44
4. Social and Psychological Development
   in Deaf Children    74
5. Behavioral Problems of Deaf Children    98
6. The Developmental Environment    129
7. Policy Implications of the Research Findings    172

References    199
Index of Subjects    229
Index of Authors    233

# Preface

This book has been "in process" for more than five years. During that time many people have contributed, both directly and indirectly, to the ideas and information to be found in it. I would like to express my thanks to some of the people who helped me at various stages of the preparation. The support of Grant Barnes, Executive Editor at the University of California Press, was a major factor in the completion of the manuscript. He continued his good-humored encouragement long past the time when it could have been expected.

The idea for the book began with an invitation from the Society for Research in Child Development to contribute a chapter entitled "The Development of Deaf Children" to their *Review of Child Development Research*, Volume Five (1975). The editorial assistance and substantive suggestions of John W. Hagen were numerous throughout the writing of that chapter. Lynn Liben, Mavis Hetherington, and two anonymous reviewers contributed many helpful suggestions. Later, Roger Freeman read the book manuscript with great care and offered myriad comments that provided the basis for many changes and additions. Charlotte Baker, Anthony Bass, Evelyn Cherow Skalka, Iris Daigre, Carol Erting, Carolyn Ewoldt, Jean Moore, Jane Nunes, Harry Olsen, and Jan-Marie Sweeney helped with literature searches; Paula Mathieson provided skillful editorial assistance, as did Gene Tanke, Marjorie Hughes, and Susan

Peters. Mary Alliatta, Karen Dean, Gerri Frank, and Sylvia McAlester typed portions of the manuscript.

I owe a major debt of gratitude to Hilde Schlesinger, my long-time friend and colleague. Many of the ideas expressed here, and much of the work reported, was formulated and carried out in a collaboration that began more than ten years ago, and has been a source of gratification from the beginning. Other colleagues at the University of California, San Francisco, who have shared thoughts and ideas over the years are: Paul Brinich, Winifred DeVos, Holly Elliott, Roberta Farwell, Alice Nemon, Michael Stinson, Roger Van Craeynest, Charles and Connie Yannacone. John Clausen has been most supportive of my work, especially at the time when my interest in deafness was just beginning. I am grateful to all my friends at the Kendall Demonstration Elementary School, Gallaudet College, who have helped me to learn about deaf education, and most especially to Robert R. Davila, who has been an unfailing source of support.

*Kathryn P. Meadow*

# CHAPTER ONE

# Introduction

THE consequences of early childhood deafness are so far-reaching and varied that some rudimentary knowledge of the linguistic, cognitive, social, and psychological aspects of human development is necessary if an understanding of any one specialized area is to be possible. Demographic, medical, and audiological dimensions of deafness provide a necessary context for understanding the educational treatment of deafness. A developmental approach to the study of behavior in deaf children can provide a needed perspective for practitioners working with those children, because historically those professionals trained to work with deaf children have known little about deaf adults, and vice versa. An understanding of developmental stages throughout the life cycle may also help resolve the conflict that currently surrounds the formulation of educational policy for deaf children. In addition to providing an overview of key research results reported throughout the book, this chapter will provide basic information designed to help the non-specialist to evaluate published research in a more critical way.

The paucity of developmental research with deaf children is in part a reflection of the relatively low incidence of profound auditory loss. In the United States in 1976, approximately 45,000 children were enrolled in 671 special schools and classes for the deaf, with an additional 6,000 deaf children receiving education in regular classrooms (Craig and Craig, 1977, p. 138). The Bureau of Education for the Handicapped estimates that there are 52,000 deaf children and 350,000 hard-of-hearing children, of whom

1

80,000 are served in special education programs (Hobbs, 1975, p. 68). This compares with an estimated 875,000 children receiving special education for the mentally retarded (Hobbs, 1975, p. 51). Deaf children comprise less than 1 percent of the total school-age population, but the theoretical importance of this group is greater for an understanding of human development than numbers would indicate.

Even though the deaf population is numerically small, the diversity of its subgroups is great. Therefore, in conducting research into any aspect of the development of the deaf child it is necessary to consider a large number of variables in the selection of research subjects and in the treatment of data. Confounding influences contribute to misleading conclusions about results. The combination of the small number of available research subjects and the greater need for selectivity means that behavioral scientists must often compromise if they are to carry out research at all. One reason for the many areas of contradictory results from various studies is that researchers include different kinds of subgroups in their studies. The experimental group is labeled "deaf" when in actuality there may be as many differences *within* the deaf group as between the deaf group and the hearing control group. The sophisticated reader must be aware of the important differentiating variables if he is to have a basis for evaluating research findings.

*Background Variables*

DEGREE OF HEARING LOSS. Hearing, or sensitivity to sound, is assessed by means of an audiological evaluation that combines elements of pitch or frequency (measured in Hertz or cycles per second) and loudness or intensity (measured in decibels).* The results of an au-

---

*Some of the material in this section was extracted from the *Kendall Guide to Assessment*, portion on "Audiological Assessment," prepared by Kathleen Weiss. Jean Moore and Evelyn Skalka reviewed the content and made suggestions that were incorporated in successive revisions.

diological evaluation are recorded on a graph called an audiogram (see Figure 1).The numbers across the top of the audiogram represent pitch or frequency. The frequency range measured is from 125 Hertz, which would reflect a low-pitched sound such as a truck motor, through 8000 Hertz, which represents a high-pitched sound such as a whistle. The numbers down the side of the audiogram (0 to 120) represent the loudness or intensity of the sound. Zero decibel/hearing level represents the softest sound that can be heard by most young adults with normal hearing; whispered speech is about 20 to 30 decibels/hearing level; conversational speech is at the level of 60 to 70 decibels, and 120 decibels is extremely loud and may be painful to people with normal hearing. The most important frequencies for the understanding of speech are in the mid-frequency range of 500, 1000, and 2000 Hertz.

An understanding and appreciation of the functional range of performance for children with differing kinds of audiograms can be important to an interpretation of their communication skills, especially of their ability to comprehend and then to produce understandable speech. A method often used to summarize the information presented in an audiogram is to average decibel/hearing level over the three frequencies that represent the speech range. This summary, however, can cloud some significant differences between individuals with the same average. Figure 1 shows three audiograms, all of which reflect an average hearing level of approximately 95 decibels in the speech range. However, the functional hearing of three individuals with these audiograms would be quite different, as would be their amplification needs. Audiogram A represents the sound response of a person who has some usable hearing in the high frequencies. Because there is some measurable response to sound at each level, it is easier to fit such an individual with a hearing aid that would help him or her to function. Audiogram B, on the other hand,

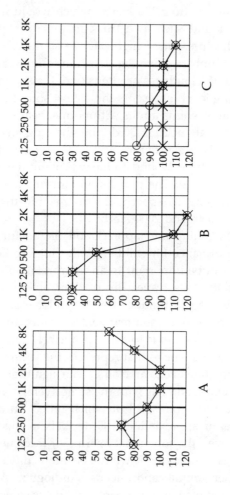

Figure I
Three Hypothetical Audiograms

represents the responses of an individual with a good deal of usable hearing in the low frequencies. This person would have considerable awareness of sound, even though he or she cannot understand the nuances of speech. Both individuals (A and B) might present puzzling pictures of variability in their everyday functioning. Sometimes each would respond to a sound and other times neither would. This variability in a young child is often interpreted as deliberate inattention, which can become a source of frustration to caretakers and resultant conflict with them (Ross and Matkin, 1967; Fry, 1966; Hirsh, 1966). Audiogram C represents an individual who would probably hear only loud sounds, even with a hearing aid, and would be considered to be profoundly deaf (Silverman, 1966). The pure tone audiograms illustrated in Figure 1 are only one way of defining auditory potential in a hearing-impaired individual. Speech discrimination measures are also necessary in order to complete the picture of that potential.

The consistent use of appropriate hearing aids from infancy onward, and training in the use of residual hearing, can influence a child's response to sound. Thus, not only the degree and configuration of hearing loss but also personal history make a difference to individual functioning. All of these nuances are important in deciding if children or adults who are grouped together as "deaf" or "hard of hearing" do indeed form homogeneous groups or if they vary from each other as much as they do from some control group.

TRAINING AND USE OF RESIDUAL HEARING. It is rare that deafness is total. Although there are few deaf children whose hearing level cannot be improved with proper amplification, it remains impossible to restore normal hearing by means of electronic aids. The gain from a hearing aid is usually about 30 decibels, although in some cases it may be as much as 60 decibels. The researcher should provide information on the hearing loss of his study population both with and without hearing aids. Ability to make use of residual hearing is determined by a complex interplay of hearing-loss pattern, proper fit and prescription of hearing aids, and educational, psychological, and social factors. Hearing aids and batteries must be checked and maintained if they are to continue to provide maximum benefit. Two different studies of the functioning of hearing aids worn by large groups of deaf children showed that more than half were not in working order (Zink, 1972; Porter, 1973). Some deaf children and adults refuse to wear a hearing aid (Schein, 1968). Early auditory training can help in the use of residual hearing, but delays in diagnosis and prescription frequently occur (Jackson and Fisch, 1958; Fellendorf and Harrow, 1970; Elliott and Armbruster, 1967). The importance of using existing hearing and the presence of early training are becoming especially important as control variables with the development of new techniques for early screening and identification (Downs and Sterritt, 1967; Glorig, 1971; Goldstein and Tait, 1971) and new developments in hearing aids (Ling, 1971 and 1975; Erber, 1971; Stein, 1973).

AGE AT ONSET OF DEAFNESS. Age at onset of deafness is an important research variable, because the later the onset the more likely it is that the child had acquired language before he lost his hearing. The ability to respond to sound in the early months of life is important to other aspects of human development as well. The human fetus responds to sound even *in utero*, and newborn babies can discriminate speech-like signals on the basis of frequency and intensity. Any human voice soothes a two-week-old infant; a female voice is preferred by three-week-old infants; the mother's voice is preferred as early as five weeks of age (Schlesinger, in press). Definition of the "critical" age has changed over the years. The 1920 Census definition included as deaf all persons who had lost their hearing before the age of eight (U.S. Bureau of the Census, 1928 and 1931). With earlier identification and remedial procedures, the critical definition has become "prelingual deafness." The cut-off is often defined as two years of age. There is increasing speculation that receptive language heard in the early months of an infant's life is a positive influence on his future language development and his use of residual hearing (Fry, 1966; Lenneberg, 1967).

The National Census of the Deaf, conducted in 1971, collected data indicating that 41 percent of those deafened before the age of 19 were born deaf. An additional 32 percent became deaf before the age of three (Schein and Delk, 1974, p. 114).

THE ETIOLOGY OF DEAFNESS. The etiology or cause of deafness is important to the selection and description of research subjects because it is related to age at onset, to possible additional handicaps, and to parental attitudes about the handicapped child. Epidemics and medical advances have produced changes in composition of the deaf population. Some conditions that cause deafness are relatively unlikely to do additional damage to the human organism; others may create wide-ranging physical and intellectual handicaps.

About one-third of the deaf children in the United States have at least one handicap in addition to deafness (Gentile and McCarthy, 1973; Schein, 1975). Emotional or behavioral problems, visual defects, and perceptual motor defects are the predominant additional handicapping conditions. The percentage of males among the deaf population with multiple handicaps is slightly higher than the percentage of males in the total deaf population, which is in turn slightly higher than the percentage of males in the general hearing population. The Annual Survey of Hearing-Impaired Students for 1970–1971 showed 54 percent to be boys and 46 percent to be girls, with 35 percent of the deaf boys having at least one additional handicap, compared to 30 percent of the deaf girls (Rawlings, 1973; Gentile and McCarthy, 1973).

Parents react differently to their deaf children in ways that may be related to the cause of deafness. Parents who are knowledgeable about the probable reason for a handicap seem to be more capable of coping with the guilt, shame, and sorrow that accompany the diagnosis (Meadow, 1968a; Davis, 1961 and 1963). However, in one-third to one-half of the cases of deafness, the cause is unknown (Rainer, Altshuler, and Kallmann, 1969; Vernon, 1968; Barton, Court, and Walker, 1962; Schein, 1968; Hicks, 1970). Of the adults responding to the National Census of the Deaf in 1971, about one-third did not specify the cause of their deafness; about one-third said they became deaf as a result of illness (Schein and Delk, 1974). For reasons that are not entirely clear, children whose deafness is of unknown origin are more likely to be identified as exhibiting problem behavior at school (Schlesinger and Meadow, 1972).

There are more than sixty types of hereditary hearing loss (Konigsmark, 1972). It was estimated, from the New York State survey, that about half of all early total deafness is inherited: about 10 percent accounted for by dominant genes, the remainder accounted for by recessive genes (Sank, 1969). (See also Kloepfer, Laguaite, and McLaurin, 1970.) Although some forms of hereditary deafness have associated anomalies (Fraser, 1964), it is fairly safe to assume that when there is presumptive evidence of hereditary deafness, there is less chance of additional damage to the central nervous system than there is in other etiologies of deafness.

Other kinds of damage often occur in children whose

deafness results from certain specific causes. About 70 percent of the Rh deaf children surveyed in one study had multiple handicaps, over half of these being cerebral palsy (Vernon, 1967c). Perinatal anoxia and traumatic instrumentation are also associated with multiple handicaps (Schlesinger, 1971). Prematurity is sometimes listed as the cause of deafness, usually because the premature infant also suffered anoxia. Almost one-fifth of Vernon's (1967b) large sample of deaf children were born prematurely.

Deafness resulting from maternal rubella can be particularly complicated. (Rubella is not reflected in statistics on the etiology of deafness in older groups because it was identified as a causative factor only in 1941.) Before the epidemic of 1963 to 1965, an estimated 10 percent of childhood deafness was caused by rubella (Vernon, 1967a). A later study found 40 percent of one population to be rubella-deaf (Hicks, 1970). Several studies have confirmed that there is a characteristic flat or basin-shaped audiological pattern in rubella-deaf children (Anderson, Barr, and Wedenberg, 1970; Fitzgerald, Sitton, and McConnell, 1970; Jackson and Fisch, 1958; Vernon, 1967a). In this type of loss, where there is some residual hearing in the high sound frequencies, the child gets more benefit from amplification than he does when his hearing loss follows a different pattern. Some observers believe that the rubella-deaf child is more likely to experience pain from the amplification of sound. However, this was not true of children studied by Hicks (1970) or by the Vanderbilt group (Fitzgerald, Sitton, and McConnell, 1970). Rubella-deaf children are believed to be more hyperactive, and atypical in a number of ways. Again, these anomalies have not been found in several research populations (Bindon, 1957; Hicks, 1970). Levine (1951) and Vernon (1967a), on the other hand, report that there were more signs of brain damage among their rubella children. Chess, Korn, and Fernandez (1971) challenge the assumption of an organically determined hyperkinetic syndrome, and assert that the behaviors displayed by children with cerebral dysfunction are extremely varied. Freeman and others (1975) warn against assignment of the label of "brain damage" without very careful assessment of children. Freeman uses this diagnosis only when precise tests yielding "hard signs" have been completed, and suggests that some of the findings showing more brain damage among rubella-deaf children were based on assessments completed before current procedures were perfected. Additional, more general references are available in this area (Rutter, Tizard, Yule, Graham, and Whitmore, 1976; Rutter, 1977; Seidel, Chadwick, and Rutter, 1975; Shaffer, McNamara, and Pincus, 1974; Shaffer, 1977).

Deafness occurring after birth due to inflammatory disease or its aftermath has shown the most drastic decrease of all causative factors. Many of the viral diseases once suspected of causing deafness have been eliminated by vaccines, or their consequences have been lessened through antibiotics (Schlesinger, 1971). One study showed that the proportion of children adventitiously deafened had decreased from 50 to 30 percent from 1929 to 1959 (Kent, 1962). However, more children who have birth defects or have suffered birth injuries survive today than formerly, with an attendant increase of damage to the central nervous system, including deafness.

The etiology of deafness is important in research related to the cognitive development of deaf children, because four of the five known leading causes of deafness (prematurity, meningitis, maternal rubella, and Rh incompatibility) are also major causes of brain damage (Vernon, 1968). The presence of multiple handicaps can affect all areas of development for the deaf child. The effect may be both direct, in terms of functional difficulties, educational treatment, and medical needs, and indirect, in terms of family, community, and societal reactions.

Introduction                                                    11

EDUCATIONAL SETTING. The two major educational settings in which deaf children are placed are state residential
schools and day classes located in regular public schools
for hearing children. Smaller numbers are found in private
residential or day schools and in public day schools attended only by deaf children. Both the reasons for the
various educational settings and their developmental consequences make research specification (and sometimes
sample separation) important. Most obvious is the far-
reaching effect of living at home within the family versus
living in a dormitory separated from the family unit. A
second important difference is the minority status of deaf
students in a day class compared to an entire school environment composed of other deaf pupils.

There are also traditional differences between public day
and residential schools in the use and acceptance of oral
and manual communication. The state residential schools
have long been a locus of the deaf subculture (Meadow,
1972), and most deaf parents with deaf children prefer to
send their children to these residential schools. Whereas
some teachers and counselors in the residential schools are
deaf, most teachers in day schools are hearing. The use of
sign language in the classroom, at least in the upper
grades, is accepted in most residential schools. Children
who are least able to learn through oral methods of speech
and lipreading because of more profound hearing loss, or
additional mental, physical, or emotional handicaps, may
be sent or transferred to the residential schools. Thus it is
not surprising that a number of studies have concluded
that deaf day-students perform at a higher level academically than comparison groups of residential students (Pintner and Reamer, 1920; Upshall, 1929; Barker, 1953; Quigley
and Frisina, 1961).

Meadow compared the academic achievement scores
and social-psychological adjustment ratings of pupils in
residential schools and day classes (Schlesinger and

Meadow, 1972). The residential school group was divided according to parents' hearing status. Comparisons where differences were statistically significant favored the residential students with deaf parents on the following dimensions: self-image, maturity, independence, sociability, popularity with peers and adults, adjustment to deafness, written language ability, communicative confidence, and use of intellectual potential. Comparisons favored the day-school students, all of whom had hearing parents, on the dimensions of appropriate sex-role behavior and speech. On almost all of the comparisons, the residential students with hearing parents scored or were rated lowest of the three groups. These findings suggest that there is an important interaction between school and family variables, and that perhaps the issue of residential versus day schooling cannot be evaluated meaningfully when only one factor is considered.

FAMILY CLIMATE. Both structural and affective variations of families with deaf children serve to differentiate subgroups in important ways. The hearing status of the deaf child's parents can summarize a large number of family differences. Deaf parents are less likely to define the diagnosis of deafness in their child as a tragic crisis (Meadow, 1967). Hearing parents, however, like the parents of children with other kinds of handicaps, often express feelings of incompetence, self-doubt, and sorrow (Meadow, 1968a; Mindel and Vernon, 1971; Zuk, 1962; Cummings, Bayley, and Rie, 1966). In some cases, the integration of the family is threatened, and the balance of previous relationships is destroyed (Farber, 1960; Jordan, 1962).

Deaf parents have usually communicated with their deaf children by means of sign language as a matter of course. Until recently, most hearing parents have used only oral means of communication (Meadow, 1967; Stuckless and Birch, 1966; Rainer, Altshuler, and Kallmann, 1969; Collins,

1969). Deaf children with hearing parents are more apt to receive early amplification, auditory training, and preschool education (Meadow, 1967). Because of their social, educational, and linguistic deprivation, deaf parents are likely to have fewer social and economic resources, compared to the hearing parents of deaf children. Perhaps for the same reason, it has been suggested that deaf children of deaf parents are more likely to come from "problem families" (Brill, 1960). Depending on the kind of research undertaken, the hearing status of deaf children's parents might influence the kinds of predictions that were made about their development.

Deaf children with hearing parents are much more numerous, comprising more than 90 percent of the total number of deaf children. Within this larger group, too, there are variables that separate families into important subgroups. It would seem likely that various racial and ethnic groups might view a child's handicap generally, and a communication handicap specifically, in differing ways. The social and economic resources that families can muster are of special importance for the consideration of the development of handicapped children. The additional financial burdens placed on these families can become a source of constant concern and frustration: the investment that parents of deaf children make in hearing aids is considerable, and ear molds, batteries, repairs, and audiological examinations all add to the drain on the family budget. Thus, the economic aspects of the handicap can become enmeshed in the emotional response and create tension, particularly within families whose financial resources are already limited. Also, parents from middle and upper social strata are more likely to have expectations for verbal and academic achievements that are difficult or impossible for deaf children to meet.

The parents' education can be an important factor in relation to a handicapped child also. Much of the information that can be helpful to the child is of a general nature. However, a major requirement for parents of handicapped children is that they be able to deal with various professionals who will become an important part of their child's life. Often, parents with less formal education feel, or are made to feel, that they are unable to provide the optimum environment and special help needed by the handicapped child. Although this often reflects a need for education on the part of the professional rather than on the part of the parent, it continues to be an important factor in assessing the total developmental environment of a deaf child. The child's position within the family can have an important influence on some variables that are likely to be of interest to developmental scientists (Clausen, 1966). The parents' treatment of the child, and their response to the diagnosis of a handicap, may well be related to his ordinal position or to his adoptive status.

No studies of adopted handicapped children and their families have yet been reported. Kirk (1964) has suggested that adoptive parents suffer from "role handicap" because they believe that adoptive parenthood is an inferior status. Parents of handicapped children also experience difficulties in perceiving themselves positively (Meadow and Meadow, 1971). Thus, the adoptive status of deaf children would seem to be an important variable for the description of research groups. However, this information is difficult to obtain from records, so it may not be a feasible criterion for selection.

Ordinal position within the family is of possible importance in understanding some facets of the development of handicapped children. Farber (1960) found that the handicapped child in a family was treated "as if" he were the youngest, regardless of his true ordinal position. Freeman and his colleagues (1975) report that mothers of only children who are deaf rated their behaviors as much worse than did the mothers of only children who are hearing, even though ratings of their school behavior did not differ from those of other deaf children.

*Summary*

1. The incidence of profound childhood deafness is relatively low. Approximately 45,000 deaf children are enrolled in special schools and classes in the United States, representing less than 1 percent of the total number of school children. In designing and evaluating developmental research with deaf children, it is important to consider the relevance of various subgroups to the possible range of findings.

2. Most important to consider is the degree of the child's hearing loss. A child whose hearing loss averages 80 decibels in the speech range is considered to be profoundly deaf. One with a hearing loss of from 60 to less than 80 decibels is considered to be severely deaf to hard-of-hearing. However, additional residual hearing at lower or higher frequencies may provide auditory clues leading to better functioning.

3. Proper amplification may raise the hearing threshold anywhere from 30 to 60 decibels. Early auditory training may increase the child's ability to use residual hearing. Information on both aided and unaided hearing loss should be included in the description of any research population.

4. Age at onset of deafness is a crucial variable in the selection of research subjects. Children who are deaf at birth and those who are deafened after the acquisition of language form two distinctly different subgroups.

5. The etiology or cause of deafness may tell us something about additional physical and mental handicaps and may help explain parental attitudes toward the child's handicap. Where the cause of deafness is unknown, for example, parental anxieties are greater.

6. The deaf child's placement in a residential or a day-school setting may be related to her degree of hearing loss and her school performance. It affects her interaction with her family, with deaf and hearing peers, and with deaf adults. Also associated with the educational setting are the relative use and acceptance of oral and manual communication, with most residential schools permitting or encouraging the use of sign language.

7. The hearing status of the deaf child's parents influences their acceptance of her deafness and their use of oral and manual communication with her. Other important subgroups within the total population of deaf children are created by racial, ethnic, socio-economic, and educational factors, and by adoptive status and the ordinal position of the child within the family.

It is very difficult indeed to consider every important variable when formulating a research design and planning the selection of deaf children as research subjects. Choices must be made, often between a representative sample and a more specialized, homogeneous group. Both the researcher and the reader need to be aware of the intricate interplay of all the variables in order to recognize those that are critical for any particular investigation.

# CHAPTER TWO

# Language Development In Deaf Children

T HE basic deprivation of profound congenital deafness is not the deprivation of sound; it is the deprivation of language. The deaf child cannot communicate clearly about her own needs, thoughts, and experiences, nor can her parents, teachers, and friends communicate easily with her. We take for granted the fact that a four-year-old hearing member of any culture has a complete working grasp and knowledge of her native language—a knowledge that she has absorbed, processed, and assimilated without formal teaching. For most deaf children, a limited grasp of oral communication can be acquired only at the cost of prolonged and intensive tutoring, with much attendant frustration. The efficacy of various methods of teaching language to deaf children has been hotly debated for over two hundred years (Bender, 1960; Schlesinger, 1969; Levine, 1969a). This controversy is an important part of the social and cultural context of the deaf child's development, because it influences all the developmental issues related to deafness. Wittgenstein's (1921) observation that the limits of one's language coincide with the limits of one's world has special meaning for language-deprived children and their parents.

Several previously published reviews of language development in deaf children can be useful for readers who wish to pursue the subject further (Cooper and Rosenstein, 1966; Rosenstein, 1961; Bonvillian, Charrow, and Nelson,

1973). In this chapter, research findings on language development and deafness are presented under four major headings: the acquisition of a first language; the acquisition of a second language; written language used by deaf children; and deaf children's linguistic environments.

*First Language Acquisition*

In considering the acquisition of a first language, we must examine the different linguistic input received by three groups of deaf children: (1) those whose deaf parents use American Sign Language as their preferred means of everyday communication, at least within the home, and whose socialization therefore takes place through manual communication; (2) those whose hearing or deaf parents use a simultaneous combination of signed and spoken English; (3) those whose hearing parents use spoken English as their only means of communication, in the hope that eventually the child's sole mode of communication will be oral English.

AMERICAN SIGN LANGUAGE (AMESLAN). Ameslan is used by approximately three-quarters of the deaf adults in the United States (Rainer, Altshuler, and Kallmann, 1969). It is an unspoken language comprised of combinations of symbolic gestures deriving meaning from the shape of the hand, the location of the hand in relation to the body of the signer, and the movement of the hand or hands. Many of the individual signs symbolize concepts rather than individual words. The derivation of many of the signs is iconic—that is, apparently based on natural pantomime gestures. Ameslan has long been a stigmatized language, and many have insisted that it is not a language at all. But linguists, who have only recently begun to study Ameslan seriously, have found that it does have all the characteristics of language, although there are some differences deriving from the crossing of modalities—that is, from sound and voice to sight and movement (Stokoe, 1960; Stokoe, Casterline, and Croneberg, 1965; McCall, 1965; Bellugi and Klima, 1972 and 1975; Klima and Bellugi, 1979). Parents who use Ameslan as their "native" or first language are with rare exception deaf themselves. Not all deaf parents use Ameslan to communicate with their deaf children, however. Some use only or mostly spoken English as their primary mode of communication. Other deaf parents use Ameslan with each other, but only spoken English with their deaf child (Stuckless and Birch, 1966). A special characteristic of Ameslan as a "native" or first language is that in most cases the deaf parents of deaf children acquired their own Ameslan from other deaf children in residential school sometime after the usual and perhaps optimum age of language acquisition. Their own experiences with early language, and with early family interaction, may have been sparse and even painful. Their ideas about parent-child interaction and linguistic socialization may be quite different from those of the hearing parents whose children were the subjects of previous linguistic studies. Only recently has the language acquisition of young deaf children received any systematic attention and analysis. Some features of Ameslan acquisition have been reported by Schlesinger (Schlesinger and Meadow, 1972), Bellugi (1972), Hoffmeister and Moores (1973), Todd (1971), and McIntire (1974).

Schlesinger studied two children of deaf parents. The first child, Ann, was observed periodically from 8 months to 22 months of age (Schlesinger and Meadow, 1972, pp. 54–68). Ann's mother, also the child of deaf parents, used English syntax in her written English and alternated between English and Ameslan syntax in her signed and spoken communications. Ann's father was more likely than her mother to use Ameslan syntax in all his communication.

At the age of 10 months, Ann first made some approxi-

mations of recognizable signs; at 12 months, she signed
*pretty* and *wrong;* at 14 months, she added *cat* and *sleep* to
her vocabulary and combined *bye sleep.* When Ann was 17
months old, nine two-sign combinations were recorded.
At the age of 19 months, she had a vocabulary of 117 signs
and five manual letters of the alphabet. Two weeks later,
her recorded vocabulary was 142 signs and 14 letters. Thus,
Ann had more than 100 signs at the age when Lenneberg
(1967) estimates that a normal hearing child will have acquired no more than 50 spoken words.

Numerous examples are cited in which Ann used one-
word utterances in holophrastic ways (to convey several
ideas), just as hearing children first use spoken words. For
example, at the age of 15 months, Ann used the sign for
smell to mean *I want to go to the bathroom,* or *I am soiled,*
*please change me,* or *I want the pretty smelling flower.*
Schlesinger observed a number of immature variations in
Ann's early signs, comparable to the baby talk found in the
early language of hearing children. The nonstandard variations were in the configuration, placement, or movement
of her hands. Thus, the immediate situational context plus
the remaining standard features were important in de-
ciphering the meaning of the signed utterances.

Schlesinger emphasizes that the style and feeling of the
linguistic input are as important as the content. The enjoyment apparent in the language interactions in which
Ann and her mother participated was a striking contrast to
the affect of many other deaf children and their mothers.
She suggests that the understanding of meaning, when
combined with an enjoyment of mother-child communicative events, may represent a necessary feature of normal
language development. This theme is elaborated in a later
paper on the language development of deaf children
(Schlesinger, 1972).

The language of Karen, the second child in the

Schlesinger study, was analyzed from a body of 200 combinations of two or more signs collected over a period of eight months, from age 2 years 10 months to age 3 years 6 months (Schlesinger and Meadow, 1972, pp. 70–74). The primary focus of this analysis was a comparison with previously published accounts of children's combinations of "open" and "pivot" words. Pivot words have been defined as the small group of words the young child uses frequently, presumably either first *or* last in two-word combinations, and combined with an unlimited number of open words. Pivot words are more like adult function words (such as prepositions), whereas open words are more like adult content words (such as nouns and verbs). For example, in the two-word utterances, "There boy," "There apple," "There doggy," "there" is a pivot word. "Boy," "apple," and "doggy" are open words. Schlesinger's data supported those of several other investigators who were beginning to question the strict definition of the pivot word in child language. Karen's pivot signs were found to occur alone as well as in combination with other open signs, in combinations with other pivots, and either first or last in two-sign combinations (Schlesinger and Meadow, 1972).

Bellugi, who was among the first to study the process of language acquisition among hearing children, has more recently looked at the sign-language acquisition of deaf children. A report based on these studies suggests that deaf children learning sign language are systematic, regular, and productive in their language, just as were the hearing children studied earlier (Bellugi and Klima, 1972). One child, Pola, provided their initial data on sign-language acquisition. Like hearing children, Pola appeared to overgeneralize linguistic rules at first, but later learned to apply appropriate restrictions. Before she was three years old, Pola spontaneously used the signs for *name, stay, tomorrow, will, where, who, what, how, dead, know, understand, none, nothing, don't know;* she could also fingerspell the letters of the manual alphabet. Pola's early sign combinations expressed the full range of concepts and semantic relations found in the expressions of hearing children of a comparable age. The increase in length of her signed expressions matched the increase in length of spoken communications by hearing children. Bellugi and Klima (1972) conclude that in spite of the difference in modality, the milestones of language development may be the same in the deaf child as in the hearing child.

Hoffmeister and Moores (1973) studied the initial language interaction of a child named Alice and her deaf mother at one-month intervals at the time Alice was 25 to 28 months old. Eight thirty-minute videotapes were analyzed to trace the development of Alice's use of "pointing action." The authors concluded that the pointing action is a separate linguistic unit, to be glossed as "that" or "this." As such, it was used in a way very similar to the demonstrative pronouns used by normal hearing children, but with more apparent precision of meaning. Although children with normal hearing use pointing as a gesture, Alice used pointing to indicate different meanings. From their observations of Alice, Hoffmeister and Moores concluded that referring to specific things by pointing is an initial stage of sign-language acquisition.

The exact differences between the pointing "sign" used by Alice and the pointing "gesture" used by hearing children would seem to be nebulous and difficult to decipher. Working on this problem with adult signers, Bellugi and Klima (1975) are attempting to develop criteria for differentiating between pantomime and sign. They have observed that certain elements must remain recognizable and constant if a gesture is to be considered a specific sign.

BIMODAL ENGLISH. Some children receive a simultaneous combination of signed and spoken English as their earliest language input.* Their parents, usually hearing, have chosen to learn manual communication in a form that allows for a precise translation of English. Until very recently, the use of sign language in any form was seen as an admission of failure on the part of the deaf child, his parents, and his teachers. Since manual communication was believed to interfere with the acquisition of speech and lipreading skills, parents feared using either nonsystematic gestures or systematic signs. The formal sign language to which deaf children are exposed today is quite different from the sign language known to deaf children in the past (Bornstein, 1973). The earlier introduction of sign language, and its use by teachers as well as by peers, are also major changes. Schroedel (1976) analyzed data from the 1971 National Census of the Deaf, and reported that 48 percent of the workers in his sub-sample had learned signs from school personnel, whereas only 9 percent had learned signs from their parents. (An additional 9 percent had never learned signs; the remainder learned from other sources.)

In recent years the term "total communication" has come to refer to a combination of speech, lipreading, amplification, and the simultaneous use of a manual sign system. The substitute term "bimodalism" has been suggested by Schlesinger (1978). The several manual sign systems are derived from the basic signs of American Sign Language. The variations in the different systems are designed to provide a means for signing a direct and precise

---

*This is a very precise use of the word "simultaneous" and is a somewhat different conceptualization of "Total Communication" than is used by some professionals in the field. It means that the spoken and the signed modes are used congruently and consistently. Some people in the field mean that either spoken or signed communication can be used with a deaf child at any particular time, but not necessarily simultaneously. It is this simultaneity that led Schlesinger to coin the term "bimodal" and to stress the importance of this aspect of the child's input.

gloss of spoken English, rather than using the non-English syntax of American Sign Language. The first efforts in this direction began in 1962 with the work of Anthony (1966). Bornstein (1973) summarized four major sign systems now being developed by research groups in different parts of the United States. These are called Signing Exact English, Seeing Essential English, Linguistics of Visual English, and Signed English (Gustason, Pfetzing, and Zawolkow, 1972; Kannapell, Hamilton, and Bornstein, 1969; O'Rourke, 1970). The four systems differ in several ways, primarily in the extent to which they incorporate traditional signs and in the method for forming the auxiliary verbs, pronouns, articles, and so forth that are not used in American Sign Language.

Two other systems should be mentioned here, because they could also be called "bimodal." One is the Rochester Method, characterized by the simultaneous use of spoken and fingerspelled language (Scouten, 1967). The other is Cued Speech; this system utilizes hand shapes representing specific sounds which are formed at the time spoken words are produced (Cornett, 1967).

Schlesinger followed the language development of two children, Ruth and Marie, whose hearing parents were using both signed and spoken English, as well as hearing aids and speech training. Ruth was observed and videotaped from the age of 2 years 8 months to 3 years 5 months. Her deafness had been diagnosed at the age of 9 months, and her parents began to learn and to use total communication when she was 15 months old. At 3 years of age, Ruth's vocabulary included a total of 348 words; at 3 years 4 months, she had a vocabulary of 604 words, including one or more in each form and structure class. On the basis of three tests of grammatical complexity administered when Ruth was 3, Schlesinger concluded that Ruth was following the same order of grammatical emergence in signed and spoken language that hearing children have demonstrated (Schlesinger and Meadow, 1972).

Marie was adopted by a hearing family at the age of 6.5 months and was diagnosed as deaf by the age of 12 months. Her parents began to use manual communication with her when she was 3 years 1 month old; she was followed by Schlesinger from the age of 3 years 4 months to 5 years 3 months (Schlesinger and Meadow, 1972, pp. 82–85). Data on Marie's language showed that she was incorporating English syntax and was appropriately using characteristics that are not a part of Ameslan, such as plurals and tense. (For example, she used the words *popped* and *broken* at 3 years 4 months, and the words *glasses, teachers, potatoes, shared, stabbed,* and *working* at 3 years 5.5 months.) Marie's mother played fingerspelling anagram games with her, and at the age of 4 years 5 months Marie demonstrated that she was able to transfer her learning from these to reading materials. Marie also gave evidence of the acquisition of negation (*I don't want,* for example) in the same sequence as has been observed in hearing children. An assessment of her lipreading skill at age 3 years 10.5 months showed that she was a more proficient lipreader than most 5-year-old deaf children.

Analysis of the early linguistic samples from these children demonstrates the similarities between their acquisition of bimodal language and the acquisition of spoken English by hearing children. Schlesinger's report of data collected somewhat later in the language acquisition process illustrates a fascinating difference between these bimodal deaf children and hearing children. Hearing children typically acquire the "ing" ending for the present progressive before they learn to use the accompanying auxiliary verb (for example, *girl running* is used before *girl is running*). Apparently, hearing children who use spoken language pay more attention to the endings of words. This principle did not apply as forcefully for some of the bimodal youngsters studied, and may be related to the different perceptual salience of various morphemes in the visual and the auditory modes. Perceptual salience appears to be directly related to the amount of residual hearing and to the precision and frequency with which the child's parents use the morphemic modulations in sign language. Thus, the child with the most usable residual hearing acquired the "ing" ending very much as hearing children do, although the auxiliary verb appeared earlier for the deaf child. Another child who was profoundly deaf acquired the "ing" and the auxiliary simultaneously. The third youngster, who was also profoundly deaf but whose linguistic input was less precise for the morphemic modulations, persisted in the use of the auxiliary alone, with no trace of the "ing" form, for a long period of time. Schlesinger relates these data to Brown's (1973) idea that the relatively late acquisition of the possessive form in hearing children may result from the indistinct and frequently slurred nature of the spoken form.

ORAL ENGLISH ONLY. By far the largest number of deaf children (practically all those with hearing parents, or more than 90 percent of the total number) have had their initial exposure to language through only spoken English. Most parents and educators have been committed to the "oral-only" approach to language acquisition for deaf children. There are several methods used. One, called acoupedics, places exclusive reliance on training the deaf child to use his residual hearing. This is a unisensory approach because all visual cues, including lipreading, are avoided. Mothers are counseled that they must not accept the idea that their children cannot hear because this implies resignation and will lead eventually to reliance on gestures. Proponents indicate that the program is designed for children who have an average aided hearing loss of less than 60 decibels

(Pollack, 1964). The Verbotonal approach, developed by Guberina in Yugoslavia, also emphasizes the use of residual hearing (Craig, Craig, and DiJohnson, 1972).

Most educators, however, include lipreading within their definition of "oral-only" approaches to language acquisition. There is a strong commitment to the belief in an exclusively oral environment, which means the conscious elimination of any meaningful gestures from the child's linguistic input during the critical period of language development (DiCarlo, 1964). The reasoning behind the oral-only approach is that the deaf child who is permitted to use an easier gesture communication system will not work to acquire the more difficult oral skills of lipreading and speech. Despite the firm convictions attached to what Furth (1966a) has called "the myth of least effort," it is only recently that any attempts have been made to test the theory empirically.

Of the many students of various aspects of the language development and deficiencies of deaf children, most have as their subjects children whose early linguistic input was largely unintelligible and therefore meaningless. Much is based on unsystematic observation and anecdotal material. There seems to be unanimous consensus that the young deaf child exposed to the difficult spoken English environment is extremely impoverished. DiCarlo (1964) comments that a 5-year-old deaf child probably has fewer than 25 words in his vocabulary unless he has had intensive language instruction. Hodgson (1953) believes that only the unusual 4- or 5-year-old deaf child knows as many as 200 words, whereas the hearing child at that age can be expected to know about 2,000 words.

Schlesinger and Meadow (1972) collected language data on 40 deaf and 20 hearing preschoolers. They found that 75 percent of the deaf children had a language age of 28 months or less, although their mean age was 44 months. All the hearing children scored at the expected age level.

The usual buzzing confusion of language is greatly increased for the deaf child. Because her verbalizations are usually grossly distorted and often misunderstood, she often receives inappropriate reactions and nonselective reinforcement from others. These inconsistent responses to her speech often produce bewilderment and may actually inhibit her future effort to produce spoken language. She finds it more difficult to generalize; she fails to develop linguistic discrimination; she lacks both primary and secondary reinforcement for her language. It is not surprising that her vocabulary and her language are grossly retarded (DiCarlo, 1964). The painfully laborious nature of language acquisition in these circumstances may help to explain not only the impoverished nature of the deaf child's language but also the absence of any systematic studies of deaf children whose input is spoken English. Furthermore, it has been suggested that discouraging the deaf child's attempts to communicate through the use of natural gestures may well dampen her curiosity about the world around her, thus impeding her formal cognitive development (Chess, Korn, and Fernandez, 1971).

McNeill (1965) has speculated about the possible effect of the delay experienced by deaf children in language acquisition. He suggests that the capacity to acquire language may be transitory, peaking between the ages of 2 and 4, and declining after that. Pointing also to the greater difficulty experienced in the acquisition of a second language after puberty, McNeill observes that early language acquisition is especially crucial for the deaf child.

The production of speech cannot be separated from the reception of speech. In discussions of deaf children, this is too often forgotten. There are three aspects of speech development: the learning of motor skills, the mastery of cues for recognition, and the building of linguistic knowledge that is basic to both production and reception (Fry, 1966).

Most available studies of the development of speech and speechreading skills in deaf children have been conducted with oral-only children as subjects, and therefore tend to equate speech development with language development. Physical disabilities, in addition to the hearing deficit, could be expected to influence and limit the development of language reception and production. Cerebral palsy, for example, can have a negative effect on the development of expressive language, either oral or manual. Severe visual defects can make the development of receptive language—especially lipreading, but also the understanding of signs and fingerspelling—more difficult for deaf children.

The earliest vocalizations of deaf infants appear to have the same tonal quality as those of hearing infants. Analyzing tape recordings of babies in deaf and in hearing homes, Lenneberg, Rebelsky, and Nichols (1965) concluded that crying and cooing depend upon maturational readiness rather than on environmental stimulation. (However, this study included only one *deaf* infant.) Anecdotal accounts indicate that while deaf babies cry and coo normally at birth, the cooing gradually lessens and is no longer heard after the age of about six months. Of seven children whose speech development was followed beginning when they were between the ages of 11 and 32 months, none was judged to have normal vocal quality at the beginning of their training (Lach, Ling, Ling, and Ship, 1970). After 12 months of training, five of the seven were judged to have normal voice quality, but none of them produced more than ten words during the year of training.

The interdependence of all linguistic skills is illustrated when studies of the speechreading skills of deaf children are evaluated. Speechreading has been found to correlate with both written language and reading ability, although these correlations have not been entirely consistent from one study to another. O'Neill and Davidson (1956) found no relationship to reading, but Craig (1964), Myklebust (1960), and Neyhus (1969) report significant positive correlations. Speechreading has received a great deal of attention from researchers attempting to unravel the mystery of the relative abilities of deaf persons to use this method. Of the many factors investigated, amount of residual hearing is the only one that continues to bear an unequivocal positive relationship to the ability to read lips (Farwell, 1976; Donnelly, 1969).

Conrad's studies in Great Britain (1977a, b, c) help to illuminate some of the questions around speechreading and its relationship to language skills generally. For example, he found that the lipreading abilities of hearing children, who have no special training or experience with this skill, received scores on speechreading tests that were as high or higher than those of deaf children.

Reported correlations between IQ test scores and speechreading ability vary greatly. Most researchers have reported positive but non-significant correlations (Reid, 1947; O'Neill and Davidson, 1956; Simmons, 1959; Butt and Chreist, 1968; Lewis, 1972). Some have considered the influence of visual synthesis, visual closure, visual memory, concept formation, and rhythm. Most studies report positive correlations between speechreading and chronological age. The fact that the correlations are generally low, however, indicates that speechreading is not a naturally developing compensatory phenomenon. Although the effects of training on speechreading ability are also unclear, training does not appear to have long-term positive effects on speechreading proficiency (Black, O'Reilly, and Peck, 1963; Craig, 1964; Heider and Heider, 1940). It may well be that the contradictory nature of the results of investigations is due to inconsistencies in the selection of research subjects in terms of some of the subtleties of audiological variables such as degree of residual hearing, early training, and the early prescription of appropriate amplification.

## Acquisition of a Second Language

Because of the atypical way in which most deaf children acquire a first language, the question of what constitutes a second language for them is somewhat murky. Despite the fact that most deaf children receive no signed linguistic input from their parents, most know at least some formal or recognizable signs by the time they are 11 years old. Apparently these signs are learned from peers, usually the deaf children of deaf parents. Whether these signs are a first or a second language is a moot point. In some cases the formal signs used within a specific group of deaf children appear to have evolved from natural gestures that are group-specific. A study of this kind of language was conducted by Tervoort (1961). He studied 24 American and 24 Dutch children, residential school students aged 7 through 12 years. Dyads of age-mates were filmed during ten-minute conversational units. These children apparently did not have access to a formal sign language system; that is, their language input from adult models was through oral language, but their peer-group communications were accomplished by means of gestures.

Tervoort observed that a natural gesture, which he calls a "motivated sign," is a concrete representation of some object within the visual field. It is based on true imitation and associative recognition on the part of all children, whether deaf or hearing. At first the gesture is strictly situation-bound. Later, however, it often develops into a formal sign, disconnected from the object that was the immediate stimulus for the motivated sign. Some signs formalize slowly because their imitative character stays so evident. Others are natural only to those to whom the motivation is known. Frequently gestures that seem natural are actually formal in use. Formality (freedom from association with a specific object) is a prerequisite of any language symbol and is a prerequisite for multidimensional use—that is, with abstract, metaphoric, or idiomatic meaning.

Tervoort's study is extremely interesting because it shows the ways in which deaf children develop their own formalized signs. Apparently this development is slower than it is when a formal language symbol is transmitted directly. Thus, Tervoort's subjects had signs that were disconnected from the stimulus object in meaning but were not yet at the stage of formality that permits or requires more subtle uses of language (such as metaphor or humor). Bellugi and Klima (Bellugi, 1972; Bellugi and Klima, 1972 and 1975) show that American Sign Language allows for the use of metaphor, humor, and abstraction in "rich profusion."

Charrow and Fletcher (1974) studied the acquisition of English as a second language by 13 deaf students of deaf parents matched for IQ and hearing loss with 13 deaf students of hearing parents. Mean age was 17 years 9 months, with the "hearing parent" group more than 12 months older, on the average, than the "deaf parent" group. The test of English as a Foreign Language (TOEFL) was administered to all the students. Significant differences favoring the students with deaf parents were computed on three of the four subtests and for the total scores. The researchers' assumption that the students with deaf parents were learning a second language (English) at school seems warranted because all of them had learned Ameslan earlier at home. However, it becomes difficult to evaluate the meaning of the results because there is no way of knowing from their data the extent to which English taught at school constituted a second language for the subjects with hearing parents.

*Written Language Used by Deaf Children*

The nature of the written language of deaf children has been the subject of several studies. These have often analyzed the type and number of errors made by deaf children in their written language productions. Since these errors are reported in terms of statistics, it may help to have some samples of the kind of language that may be expected. The examples given below were taken from papers written by deaf high-school students applying for admission to Gallaudet College in Washington, D.C., one of the few college programs for the deaf in the world (Fusfeld, 1958):

> I began to love it as to be my favorite sport now.
> She told him that there was a fitted place to put.
> To his disappointed, his wife disgusted of what he made.
> Many things find in Arkansas.
> She is good at sewing than she is at cooking.
> The doctor believes that a sickness woman would live within three or four weeks.
> The backfield players must follow the play what the captain say.
> This room was small and many furnitures lay crowdly.
> I was happy to kiss my parents because they letted my playing football.

The kinds of language errors illustrated above pervade the compositions of deaf children. Pintner and Paterson (1916) made one of the earliest studies of the practical consequences of linguistic deprivation among the deaf. They used a test called the Easy-Directions Test consisting of 20 simple printed directions, such as "Cross out the G in 'tiger,' " and "What comes next after D in the alphabet?" The investigators submit that these directions demand very little actual knowledge, but rather test the ability to comprehend simple language. The test was administered to 655 deaf pupils and 621 hearing pupils ranging in age from 9 to 20. From the age of 9 on, the hearing children achieved perfect scores with almost no exceptions. However, the average deaf child never reached that point. At the age of 9, the median score for deaf children was one correct response. This performance increased slowly to a median score of 7 for the 20-year-olds. Thus, the deaf child barely reached the median of the 8-year-old hearing child and never approximated the score of the 9-year-old.

The written language of deaf and hearing children was analyzed by Heider and Heider (1940) through 1,118 compositions based on a short motion picture. They summarized their conclusions as follows:

1. The sentences of the deaf are shorter than those of the hearing.

2. The deaf use more simple sentences.

3. No significant differences were found in the total length of compositions.

4. In general the compositions of the deaf resemble those of less mature hearing children.

5. If different forms of subordination in sentence structure are analyzed as to difficulty, it is found that the more difficult forms are used less by the deaf than by the hearing.

The simpler style of the compositions of the deaf students involved relatively rigid, unrelated language units following each other with little overlap of structure or meaning. The Heiders' research subjects were students at the Clarke School for the Deaf in Massachusetts, a highly selective private institution, so the performance level of these students was no doubt considerably above that of the majority of deaf children who attend public schools.

Myklebust (1960) reported a complex analysis of stories written for the Picture Story Language Test. He administered this instrument to 200 deaf children in residential and day schools and to 200 hearing children, matched for IQ score and age. He selected 40 children, 20 of each sex, at ages 7, 9, 11, 13, and 15. Every word in each of the 400 stories was counted and classified according to the parts of speech. The deaf children were found to use a higher proportion of nouns at all age levels (Myklebust, 1960, pp. 306–318). If noun usage is taken as the criterion, the language of the deaf students was substantially more concrete than that of the hearing students for both groups. Verbs were the second most commonly used, articles third, and pronouns fourth. Other parts of speech were used less frequently by deaf children than by hearing children, and deaf children began to use them at a later age than did hearing children. This was true for adjectives and prepositions. The deaf group used virtually no adverbs, while the hearing children began using them at age 9.

The "cloze" procedure, devised originally to measure the readability of textbooks, has been used to evaluate the linguistic ability and style of deaf children.* Moores (1970a) selected a group of deaf students with a mean age of 16.10 and a mean reading achievement score of 4.8. He then recruited a group of hearing fourth and fifth graders, with a mean age of 9.10, who also had a mean reading achievement score of 4.8. Three passages of 250 words each, selected from fourth, sixth, and eighth grade texts with every fifth word deleted, were presented to the two groups of students with instructions to fill in the missing words. The deaf students' scores for verbatim reproduction at the respective grade levels were 41 percent, 16 percent, and 15 percent. The hearing students' scores were 52 percent, 30 percent and 19 percent ($p < .001$). When the data were analyzed for form class reproduction rather than verbatim

---

*This is a procedure whereby every fifth (or seventh or eighth) word is deleted from a passage. The student is then asked to supply the deleted words so that the passage makes sense.

accuracy, the hearing students scored significantly higher than the deaf students for the fourth- and sixth-grade-level tests. Differences for the eighth-grade text passage were not significant. Moores concluded that even when the deaf students' language was grammatically correct, it was stereotyped and redundant; modes of expression were restricted and repetitive, and vocabulary was limited. He believes that the language of deaf students differs from that of hearing students both quantitatively and qualitatively. Not only does their language develop at a slower rate, but they develop constructions that produce sentences unlike those of hearing children.

One of the consequences of this "deviant" linguistic construction is that mental health professionals who are unfamiliar with the linguistic handicaps of deafness may diagnose a deaf person as mentally retarded or emotionally disturbed on the basis of their unusual language productions. Freeman (1977, pp. 287–288) suggests that grammatically incorrect language should not be considered to be a sign of thought disorder or mental retardation when deafness is involved, that the services of a highly skilled interpreter should be obtained for diagnostic testing and interviewing, and that information about behavior should always be collected from more than one setting.

Cohen (1967) also used the cloze technique to analyze the language abilities of deaf and hearing children matched for reading ability. Her subjects were instructed to restore deleted words to a story that had been paraphrased by a deaf child, and then to a paraphrase written by a hearing child. The hearing subjects found the deaf paraphrases significantly less predictable than either the original passage or the paraphrases of it written by the hearing subjects. The deaf subjects found the different types of material equally predictable. It was hypothesized that differences between the deaf and hearing performances were due to the fact that the hearing children were better users of English than the deaf children, and therefore showed greater ability to distinguish between good and poor language samples.

Odom and Blanton (1967) presented phrasal-defined language segments to groups of deaf and hearing fifth and twelfth graders. Some received eight verb phrases; some received eight noun phrases; some received the same words in scrambled (nonsense) order. As was expected from previous experiments, the hearing subjects recalled the verb phrases better than the nonphrasal segments containing the same words. The deaf students showed no difference in recall performance. The investigators made the tentative suggestion that deaf students do not have the same mental processes operating with regard to English structure.

Boothroyd (1971) conducted an exploratory investigation of eight young deaf children, students in the Lower School Program at the Clarke School for the Deaf. On the basis of their recall of meaningful and nonsense forms, he concluded that if one takes a child's apparent performance at face value, one is likely to overestimate his true language capacity and to expect a much higher level of functioning than that of which he is capable. He observed that whereas the children were working in their classrooms with complex syntactical forms, their spontaneous language would lead one to believe that their internal language model was still fairly rudimentary.

From most of the studies cited above, it seems possible to say that when the traditional formats for evaluating language are applied to deaf children, language levels are inflated beyond reality. Perhaps the spontaneous language examples quoted at the beginning of this section reflect the true impoverishment of the expressive language of deaf children. When given a task where the linguistic structure is already provided, as in the cloze procedure, they need not rely on their own grasp of syntactical principles.

*Evaluation of the Linguistic Environments of Deaf Children*

The data describing the language acquisition and linguistic achievements of deaf children leave no doubt that
most profoundly deaf children do not have a sufficient
command of language to enable them to function on a high
academic level. Few studies evaluate the various methods
and philosophies of language acquisition for deaf children,
even though this would seem to be one of the most critical
research areas in terms of implications for training and
education.

Three studies have been designed to evaluate, among
other variables, the language of deaf children exposed to
differing linguistic input in their school settings. Two of
these were conducted by Quigley (1968). In one, he was
able to incorporate random assignment of children to the
experimental classroom where the Rochester Method of
simultaneous speech and fingerspelling was used. Comparison subjects were exposed to the oral method of
speech only. Test instruments were administered to the 32
participating students at the end of each of five years.
Results varied somewhat from one year to another, and
differences were often directional rather than statistically
significant. Nevertheless, the children exposed to fingerspelling showed better speechreading ability and scored
higher on reading tests and on three of the five measures of
written language ability. Quigley's second evaluation study
included more than 200 subjects from six residential
schools. Experimental schools used speech plus fingerspelling; comparison schools used speech plus manual
signs. In this case also, the children exposed to fingerspelling achieved a generally higher language level than
those whose teachers used the sign combination.

The third evaluation study was conducted by Moores
and his associates (1972) with preschool children in seven
different programs using oral-only methods, fingerspelling

plus speech, or total communication. The results of the first two years of the study show that the children in three of the programs were performing relatively well in all areas of linguistic competence. These programs had five elements in common. All had a heavy cognitive or academic orientation; all used some form of manual as well as oral communication in the classroom; classroom activities tended to be structured and organized; auditory training activities were included in ongoing classroom events; the parents were comfortable with the combined oral and manual mode used by the school.

The few studies that exist do not support the view that the development of sign language will discourage the development of oral language. Montgomery (1966) reported positive significant correlations between the manual communication rating and the Donaldson Lipreading Test results for 59 Scottish students he tested. A number of studies comparing the language proficiency of the deaf children of deaf parents to that of the deaf children of hearing parents have shown that the deaf children of deaf parents have significantly better scores on reading and written language, with no statistical differences on tests of speech and lipreading skill (Stuckless and Birch, 1966; Meadow, 1968b; Quigley and Frisina, 1961; Vernon and Koh, 1970). Of course, there are factors in addition to the early communicative mode operating in the deaf and hearing families, so that it is impossible to assume that early manual communication is the only factor influencing the higher language achievements of the children with deaf parents.

A report of the language development of two deaf children exposed to both oral and manual communication during the critical early years of language acquisition provides evidence related to the educational issues under consideration (Schlesinger and Meadow, 1972, pp. 45–87). If the oral and manual systems of communication are competitive rather than mutually supportive, or if speech fails to develop in children exposed to signs, these children could be expected to reflect these theories.

Schlesinger made counts of the expressive language modes for the two deaf children of hearing parents whose language was studied intensively:

|        | Age   | Speech Only | Signs Only | Both |
|--------|-------|-------------|------------|------|
| Ruth   | 2–11  | 10%         | 22%        | 68%  |
|        | 3–1   | 24%         | 19%        | 57%  |
|        | 3–3   | 29%         | 4%         | 66%  |
| Marie  | 3–4   | 12%         | 79%        | 9%   |
|        | 3–10  | 4%          | 81%        | 14%  |
|        | 4–8   | 18%         | 58%        | 24%  |

At successive ages, Ruth's use of speech alone increased while her use of signs alone decreased. Her combined use of signs and speech remained approximately the same. Marie, on the other hand, increased her relative use of speech both alone and together with signs, while her use of signs alone decreased significantly. In comparing the two children, the differences in the relative usage of varying communicative modes is striking. Compared to Marie, Ruth consistently used a smaller proportion of signs only and a larger proportion of speech and signs together.

There are a number of possible explanations for the discrepancies. First, Ruth consistently had hearing-aid amplification more appropriate for her hearing loss than Marie had, and her parents were more conscientious about keeping her hearing aids in working order. Second, Ruth's parents were more committed than Marie's to the idea that the combination of speech and signs was the optimum communicative input. The differing viewpoints of the parents may well have been perceived by the children and influenced their linguistic modes. Third, Ruth's mother used a combination of speech and signs consistently with her, while Marie's mother slipped into the use of signs alone more often. These factors, and perhaps others too, helped form the linguistic environments of the two children. Emotional and attitudinal influences on the communicative modes and styles of deaf children have a special importance that is frequently ignored in discussions of communicative performance.

Greenberg (1978) studied 28 children ages 3 to 5. Half of the children were in oral-only preschool programs, half were in total communication preschool programs. Greenberg's theoretical interest was in the examination of attachment behavior as reflected in the child's reactions to separation from the mother. Greenberg found that all the children were able to accept separation. The mothers who used oral-only communication used some gesture (usually a raised forefinger) that signified "wait" or "I'll be back soon." Dividing the oral-only and the total communication dyads in two groups (those who were rated above and below the mean for "reciprocal understanding"), Greenberg found more differences between "high" and "low" communicators than between the "oral" and the "total" subgroups as a whole. There were almost no differences in communicative behavior between total and oral-only children. The oral-only mothers showed a higher frequency count of messages than did the total communication mothers, but this was a function of the former groups' repeating messages that bore the same meaning. When interactive behavior of the two groups of dyads was analyzed some important differences emerged. Total communication children showed a significantly higher percentage of spontaneous communications, touched their mothers more frequently, and avoided visual contact less frequently than did the oral-only children (Greenberg, 1978, pp. 60–62). Both mothers and children using total communication tended to smile and laugh more frequently than did the oral-only mothers and children (p. 62).

Greenberg presents data illustrating the importance of

early diagnosis and intervention, of parent education and involvement. His results show a disappointing degree of proficiency in sign language for the mothers whose children are enrolled in total communication programs, and suggests the need for ongoing sign-language instruction for families rather than time-limited courses.

*Summary*

1. The basic deprivation of deafness is the difficulty it produces for the process of normal language acquisition. This includes inner language development as well as the more superficial oral language skills of speech and speechreading.

2. Language acquisition was reviewed for three categories of deaf children whose linguistic environments and first language inputs differed according to the communicative modes of the parents and the kind of linguistic socialization taking place. The first group includes deaf children of deaf parents who use only American Sign Language (Ameslan) in communicating with their children. The few existing studies illustrate some of the variations that occur when linguistic socialization takes place in a visual rather than an auditory mode, relying on some features of visual salience. Similarities in the language acquisition of deaf and hearing children have been observed in initial holophrastic usage, and in overgeneralization of first-learned language rules.

3. Deaf children of deaf or hearing parents who use some simultaneous combination of signed and spoken English develop bimodal expressive language. Vocabulary growth, grammatical complexity, and syntactical structure all progress in the same way as for hearing children.

4. Deaf children whose parents use only oral English have not received systematic study in terms of the process of their language acquisition. Studies of the language proficiency of these children at various ages make it clear

that acquisition is painfully slow. Linguistic retardation continues through adolescence and remains a factor for most deaf adults.

5. Analyses of the written language of deaf children have shown that the vocabulary is limited, and the sentence structure is simpler and more rigid than for hearing children of the same ages or grade levels.

6. Analyses of studies that can be used for either direct or inferential evidence about the efficacy of various methods of linguistic socialization for deaf children show no reason to support continuing dedication to an oral-only approach. Children who are exposed to early manual or simultaneous manual-oral input appear to develop more adequate inner language, with no reduction in their abilities to use speech and speechreading for communication, than children who are not so exposed.

# CHAPTER THREE

# Cognitive Development in Deaf Children

**T**HE cognitive development of the deaf child has been a provocative and challenging area for study. The relationship between language and thought, problems related to the attainment of concepts, perceptual-motor processes, attributes of memory functioning, performance on tests of intelligence, and academic achievement have been considered in studies of deaf children. Rosenstein (1961) provides a good review and commentary on earlier studies of perception, cognition, and language development in deaf children, and concludes that there is no clear picture of the performance level of deaf children in the perceptual or cognitive domain. There continues to be uncertainty, even though much important research has been published in the last decade. Confusion of terms, reliance on research populations with characteristics that can well confound results, and difficulties in designing testing procedures that do not confuse linguistic and cognitive variables all add to the research problems. The naturally occurring "control" of deafness offers a unique opportunity to examine learning theories (Vernon and Rothstein, 1968).

Some of the problems attendant upon research with deaf children have special importance when cognitive development is under study. There are many difficulties in finding homogeneous subgroups and gathering background data that will enable the researcher to control statistically for important intervening variables. For example, it is apparent that we can now expect a higher prevalence of motor disturbances along with deafness in children because of the increased possibility of central nervous system damage. The nonverbal tasks the researcher may rely on often require gross or fine motor coordination, which may also be impaired in the deaf. Especially when questions related to memory and retention are being investigated, it is important to sort out difficulties of test administration, and of language availability and modality, from problems of information processing. Earlier studies particularly, but some contemporary ones as well, fail to acknowledge that sign language is available to many deaf children as a possible means of communication in a testing situation. For the most part, there has been little appreciation and less research investigation of the necessity for a different interpretation of responses to the combination of signed and spoken or written stimuli.

The general question of the degree to which deaf children constitute a group "without language" is an extremely complex one for studies of the cognitive domain. As discussed in the previous chapter, the assumption that sign language as used by the deaf community does not constitute a true language, and perhaps not even a complex symbolic system, is no longer tenable in view of current research. The degree to which deaf school children have achieved receptive and expressive proficiency in sign language varies tremendously in relation to age, school setting, and the hearing status of parents. Some measure of sign-language achievement needs to be available in evaluating the cognitive performance of deaf subjects. The degree to which deaf children acquire spoken language is also variable. In a discussion of some of these research issues, Blank (1965) has pointed out that most deaf children are exposed to intensive oral language training beginning as early as age 2 or 3. Some respond well and learn a good deal of language; but most do not.

The problems of developing materials that will allow for the assessment of cognitive development without the confounding factor of language sometimes appear insurmountable. Even if tasks are constructed that seem relatively independent of linguistic ability, the problem of administration remains. If the examiner must communicate instructions that are even slightly complicated, it is difficult to be certain that apparent understanding is real. Many deaf children have learned that they are rewarded in many ways for "agreeing" with adults. The compliance that is often found can be a dangerous trap for a researcher.

The difficulties inherent in communicating complex tasks to deaf children have led, perhaps inevitably, to the design of tasks that seem too simplistic for the measurement of complex concepts, particularly when research with deaf children is designed to investigate issues of the relationship between language and thought. Sigel (1964) has raised the question of the level of difficulty of tasks. In Piagetian research with hearing children, he suggests that comprehension of a principle should be tested by the introduction of a series of tasks graduated in level of difficulty, in order to gain an understanding of individual differences between children. This problem is perhaps even more important when deaf children are research subjects.

The research on cognitive development in deaf children will be considered under five headings: intelligence as measured on IQ tests; academic achievement; attainment of concepts; memory; and finally, perceptual and motor functioning and sensory compensation (the substitution of one sensory mode for another) in information processing.

*Intelligence as Measured by IQ tests*

The traditional way of assessing the level of cognitive development is to evaluate performance on standardized tests purporting to reflect intellectual ability. An early review of studies done with deaf school children between 1900 and 1930 concluded that these children were retarded by three to four years in comparison with hearing children, and that they usually scored in the low 90's when tested with performance IQ scales (Pintner, Eisenson, and Stanton, 1941). Vernon (1969b) reviewed a large number of studies and concluded that deaf and hard-of-hearing children have essentially the same distribution of intelligence as the general population, even though the mean score for deaf children may be slightly below that for hearing children.

There is an extensive body of literature available on the special characteristics of particular tests and the problems of the administration of these tests to deaf children (Myklebust, 1960; Levine, 1960 and 1969b; Levine and Wagner, 1974; Hiskey, 1956; Mira, 1962; Vernon and Brown, 1964). Some of the tests used frequently include the Leiter International Performance Scale, the Ontario School Ability Examination, and the Nebraska Test of Learning Aptitude (also referred to as the Hiskey-Nebraska test). One study (Mira, 1962) indicated that the Hiskey-Nebraska test yielded consistently inflated scores, compared to the Leiter. It is apparent from several of these studies that the scores of young deaf children are highly unreliable.

The most widely used IQ test for deaf children is the Performance Scale of the Wechsler Intelligence Scale for Children (WISC), now available as the WISC-R. This is considered to yield fairly valid IQ scores for deaf children ages 9 to 16. Because of the difficulties of administering verbal tests, the Verbal Scale is usually omitted from the battery, and an IQ score is calculated on the basis of the Performance Scale alone. The wide use of this scale, both for assessing the intelligence of deaf children and for equating research samples, gives special importance to a study reported by Graham and Shapiro (1953). These researchers evaluated the effect of pantomimed (nonverbal) instructions on children's scores on the WISC Performance Scale. They selected three groups of 20 children each, ages 6 to 12. In one group the children had a marked hearing loss (60 dB or greater); the other two groups included only children with normal hearing. The deaf children and one group of hearing children received pantomimed instructions. The other group of hearing children received standard verbal instructions. The three groups were matched on several demographic characteristics and were equated for intelligence as measured by the Goodenough Draw-a-Man Test.

The hearing children who received standard instructions performed at a significantly higher level on the overall performance scale and on three of the subtests: Picture Arrangement, Coding, and Mazes. The scores of the hearing children who received pantomimed instructions were significantly higher than the scores of the deaf children for Picture Arrangement, Coding, and Mazes, but the deaf group scored higher on Object Assembly. Therefore, the use of pantomimed instructions, even on a test that is supposedly nonverbal, appears to place children at a disadvantage. This finding has two significant implications for the testing of deaf children. First, deaf children generally will be at a disadvantage, compared to hearing children, because less information is conveyed by pantomimed versus verbalized instructions. Even on performance subtests, deaf children will not have an equal opportunity to demonstrate their potential. Second, if deaf children know sign language but do not have the advantage of the test being administered in this mode, the pantomimed instructions may place them at an even greater disadvantage because some gestures might be misinterpreted as codified signs.

Patterns of subtest scores obtained by deaf children on the WISC have also been described by Levine (1956), Goetzinger and Rousey (1957), and Vonderhaar and Chambers (1975). Using the WISC with children ranging from age 6 through late adolescence, all the investigators consistently found that the highest subtest scores were earned on Object Assembly, a task that requires the subjects to assemble puzzle pieces into a coherent whole. It has been theorized that emphasis on visual training and perception in the activities of the deaf may foster achievement on this subtest. As with Object Assembly, the Block Design subtest, on which deaf subjects have been found to score high relative to the other subtests (Hess, 1960), more manual manipulation is required than with other WISC performance subtests. Agreement on the lowest-scoring subtest of the WISC is less great; the two most often cited as falling farthest below the mean performance score are the Picture Arrangement subtest and the Coding subtest.

In 1974, a revised version of the WISC (WISC-R) was published (Wechsler, 1974). Using this version, Anderson and Sisco (1977) collected data on 1228 deaf students that enabled them to establish norms on the Performance Scale for deaf students. Generally speaking, they found that deaf children performed in a manner similar to that of hearing children on all the performance subtests except for Coding and Picture Arrangement. On these two subtests, the deaf children performed significantly below their hearing peers. They also found more variance within the scores of deaf children than in comparable groups of hearing children.

In summary, it can be said that deaf children usually score within the normal range on the performance scales of intelligence tests, although their mean scores are somewhat lower than those of hearing children. This is true provided that the tests administered are nonverbal and do

not require a high level of language either in input (instruction) or output (response). Considering the problems inherent in test administration, as well as the fact that
many deaf children can be expected to have additional
difficulties that interfere with intellectual development,
this conclusion is noteworthy. The apparently normal intellectual capacity of most deaf children is not reflected in
their academic achievement, however.

*Academic Achievement*

Two large-scale testing efforts have been undertaken to
evaluate the academic achievement levels of deaf students.
The 1959 survey (Wrightstone, Aronow, and Moskowitz,
1963) was designed to develop reading norms for deaf
pupils. The Metropolitan Achievement Test, Elementary
Level, Form B, was administered to 5,307 deaf students in
73 special schools or classes for the deaf in the United
States and Canada. Students were between the ages of 10.5
and 16.5 years at the time of test; 52 percent were boys,
48 percent were girls. Mean hearing loss was 84 dB. Selecting grade level 4.9 as a minimum functional reflection of
literacy, Furth calculated that a score of 4.9 or better was
attained by 1 percent of the deaf children ages 10.5 to 11.5, 7
percent of those 13.5 to 14.5, and 12 percent of those 15.5 to
16.5 (Furth, 1966b, p. 461).

The most recent nationwide achievement testing effort
was conducted by the Office of Demographic Studies
of Gallaudet College in 1969 and 1971 (Gentile and
DiFrancesca, 1969; DiFrancesca and Carey, 1972; Di-
Francesca, 1972; Trybus, Buchanan, and DiFrancesca, 1973;
Ries, Trybus, Sepielli, and Buchanan, 1973). Stanford
Achievement Tests were administered to 19,000 students in
288 programs for hearing-impaired children. Analysis of
about 17,000 scores indicated that these children showed
better achievement in reading than in other academic areas
during the first three years of schooling. Beyond grade

three, achievement in spelling and in arithmetic was better than achievement in reading. The age of the children tested was about 12.5 years, which places their median grade level at 6.5. However, the average achievement level on arithmetic computation subtests was grade 4.1; average achievement level on the paragraph-meaning subtest was grade 3.0. The highest scores on these two subtests, achieved by the 19-year-olds in both cases, were 4.4 and 6.7 respectively. These findings illustrate the exceedingly slow increment of achievement between ages 12 and 19. Also, it is evident that in the decade between these two major surveys of educational achievement among deaf children, there was no apparent improvement in their overall attainment of a functionally useful ability to read.

A follow-up testing effort conducted by the Office of Demographic Studies (O.D.S.) gives longitudinal data on educational achievement in addition to the cross-sectional data summarized above (Trybus and Karchmer, 1977). In 1974, the O.D.S. retested 1,543 deaf children tested initially in 1971. These data showed the mean increment in reading achievement to be slightly less than 0.3 grade equivalents per year. This low increment level was found despite the fact that the students who remained in the same school programs over the three-year time span could be expected to score at a higher level than deaf students in other situations. Gains in reading comprehension scores were analyzed for subgroups of deaf children as well. These data can be summarized as follows: Girls tended to demonstrate more gain than boys; increment in reading achievement is inversely related to hearing loss; students with no handicaps in addition to deafness show more reading gain than those with multiple handicaps; early school entrance is related to accelerated reading gains; neither ethnicity nor parental hearing status is related to achievement gain. However, whites score higher than Spanish-Americans or blacks, and students with two deaf parents score higher than those with either one deaf parent or with two normal-hearing parents (Trybus and Karchmer, 1977, p. 65).

Conrad (1977b) has reported a major effort to assess the reading achievement of deaf students in England and Wales. All deaf students ages 15 to 16.5 receiving special education were tested by means of Brimer's Wide-Span Reading Test. Intelligence was assessed by means of Raven's Progressive Matrices. Excluding 86 students for a variety of reasons, Conrad analyzed the test performances of the remaining 355. He found that reading ability depends significantly on degree of hearing loss, and that there was no significant relationship between hearing loss and nonverbal intelligence. Fifty percent of the students with a hearing loss greater than 85 dB were found "to have no reading comprehension at all." Twenty-five percent of those whose hearing losses were less profound also showed no prose comprehension, so far as the Wide-Span Reading Test was concerned. (This test has a "floor" of 84 months of age.) "Taking the entire population of children of school-leaving age in schools for the deaf (in England and Wales), it can be seen that some 40 percent are totally illiterate for prose comprehension" (p. 142).

Smaller studies of special populations of deaf children can add dimensions to our understanding of educational achievement. Fiedler (1969) studied students at the Clarke School in Massachusetts. Although only 20 students were involved, the longitudinal nature of the study, conducted over a ten-year period, the careful individual testing, and the prestige of the school in educational circles make this an important study. The subjects were the 20 children entering the three youngest classes at the school in 1951. Their ages ranged from 4–5 to 5–7 at that time. When these students were tested ten years later, three of the girls (27 percent) and six of the boys (67 percent) were found to be educationally retarded by five years or more. Only three of the 20 students "were not retarded academically" (p. 13).

"In addition to the three extremely poor learners, three girls and three boys, 16 years old, were educationally retarded from 5 to 5.5 years on achievement tests, as compared with the mean retardation of four years for the entire group. Thus, they were functioning at the fifth to sixth grade level according to median test scores, but at only the fourth grade level on subtests of paragraph (meaning) and word meaning" (p. 65). The students' scores on the WISC Performance Scale ranged from 90 to 142.

Jones' (1976) study of educational achievement of 27 matched pairs of rubella and non-rubella students at the Clarke School showed no significant differences between the two groups on SAT subtests for Vocabulary, Reading Comprehension, or Arithmetic Computation. However, there were significant differences between the two groups on the Clarke School Speech Intelligibility Test, differences favoring the rubella children. Jones suggests that perhaps the rubella group had hearing losses which were less severe at birth but then became rapidly worse over the first two years of life.

The achievement of deaf children in spelling is illuminated by a study conducted by Hoemann and his colleagues. This study was conducted in a school making extensive use of fingerspelling to supplement oral communication. The data showed that the deaf subjects' performance was equal to or exceeded hearing norms, and that phonetic errors were infrequent. Hoemann expands these findings to suggest that "there is a functional relationship between the accessibility of language rules in the deaf child's linguistic environment and the linguistic or psycholinguistic abilities developed" (Hoemann and others, 1976, p. 493).

A number of studies comparing the deaf children of deaf parents to those of hearing parents include comparisons of academic achievement. These studies are important as a group as well as individually, because of the consistently higher scores achieved by the students with deaf parents. In each study, attempts were made to control for intelligence, as measured by IQ tests.

In a study of graduates from the California School for the Deaf at Riverside from 1956 to 1971, it was concluded that mean grade level scores were 7.0 for students with hearing parents, compared to 8.4 for students of deaf parents (Balow and Brill, 1972). In one study (Stuckless and Birch, 1966) using matched pairs of students, when differences in Metropolitan Achievement Test reading scores were computed, the students with deaf parents were found to score higher than the students with hearing parents. In another matched pair study (Meadow, 1968b) the mean differences between the two groups on the Stanford Achievement Test were 2.1 years for reading, 1.3 years for arithmetic, and 1.3 years for overall grade level scores, with the differences in each case favoring the students with deaf parents. A third study (Vernon and Koh, 1970) also used a matched pair design but included children with hearing parents only when there was presumptive evidence of hereditary deafness. This criterion effectively controlled for the possibility of differences due to the etiological basis of deafness. Significant differences favoring the deaf children with deaf parents were found on the following subtests of the Stanford Achievement Test: Paragraph Meaning, Word Meaning, Reading Average, and General Average.

The design of a study by Brasel and Quigley (1977) permits the examination of another variable in assessing the influence of early language environment on educational achievement. These investigators compared the achievement scores of four groups of deaf children: those whose deaf parents used American Sign Language (and "whose written language showed gross deviations from Standard English," p. 98); those whose deaf parents had a good command of English and who used manual communication in the form of Manual English; those whose hearing parents used oral methods with them "exclusively and intensively"; and those whose hearing parents "received no formal training in oral methodology and did not attempt any special training of their children before enrolling them in school." Performances on the following subtests from the Stanford Achievement Tests were analyzed: Language, Paragraph Meaning, Word Meaning, and Spelling. The manual English group performed significantly better than the other three groups on all four subtests. The two manual groups performed significantly better than the two oral groups on every test measure. Thus, the authors conclude, not only the mode of communication but also the form of the manual communication influences the linguistic competence and eventually the educational performance of deaf children.

It is clear that the poor reading achievement of deaf children has been documented time and time again. Even when subgroups of deaf children are examined and differences found among those with varying characteristics, the students performing at a higher level still do not score at levels equivalent to their hearing peers. In the research reported, however, a unitary approach has been taken to the evaluation of reading, reflecting a traditional view of the reading process. Ewoldt (1977) has applied a psycholinguistic approach to reading in an exploratory descriptive study of deaf children, and has reported data that may provide a new direction both for research and for the teaching of reading to the deaf. She describes this psycholinguistic approach to reading as follows: "Reading is viewed as a receptive language process in which readers actively search for meaning. Because readers do not always have productive control over appropriate labels for concepts, psycholinguistic research looks beyond the production of labels for other evidence that a concept has been grasped" (pp. 3–4). Using the model and the methodology (Miscue Analysis) developed by Goodman (1976) and

Goodman and Burke (1970), Ewoldt analyzed the reading strategies of four profoundly deaf students ranging in age from 7 to 17 years.

This approach emphasized the students' strengths rather than their weaknesses. Compared to the standardized test approach to the evaluation of reading level, it enables the investigator (or the teacher) to view the possible progressive understanding of material by the reader from the beginning to the end of a particular passage. Ewoldt analyzed a total of twenty-five story retellings from her four deaf subjects. (These stories were transcribed from videotapes by three independent coders. Differences in interpretation were resolved by a native signer.) Ewoldt reported that the students did acquire meaning through reading, in spite of the high percentage of actual semantic and syntactic errors. "Retelling scores were fairly high for these readers. All readers produced inferences and misconceptions, showing that they were interacting with the information in the total story" (Ewoldt, 1977, p. 3). Other findings with importance for researchers and educators include the following: the students produced the kinds of errors that indicated they assigned ASL deep structure to English sentences; the errors made were frequently semantically and/or syntactically acceptable; they were capable of making both syntactic and semantic predictions, and their control of syntactic patterns seemed to increase through repetition of the patterns.

*Attainment of Concepts*

The research described in the two previous sections shows that deaf children apparently have normal intellectual potential, but that their school achievement is acutely subnormal. In this section we shall review research that may help explain this discrepancy by examining the *process* by which deaf children attain concepts that enable them to engage in logical thought.

Among the results of one study (Schlesinger and

Meadow, 1976) was the finding that although the hearing children consistently outperformed the deaf children on three major intelligence tests, there was no striking difference in the *pattern* of performance demonstrated by the two groups of children. The generalized deficit was not distributed differentially over the range of skills tapped by the various subtests. That is, for the performance measures used, no cognitive "holes" were observed among the deaf children, despite their generally lowered IQ ratings.

At least two hypotheses can be invoked to explain the observed differences. The first is that the "deficit" reflects the special communicative difficulties the deaf children encounter in the testing situation. Such communicative difficulties, resulting from the generally low verbal language level seen in deaf children, can and do interact with the testing process both at the input (instruction) and output (response) stage. (This difficulty also appears in the test records of children who speak nonstandard English.) A number of researchers who have studied deaf children believe that it is this communicative difficulty which produces the classic performance deficit seen in deaf children (for example, Furth, 1966a, 1971; Vernon, 1967a). A second hypothesis is that deaf children who lack good linguistic skills lack one of the important tools of thinking; thus the cognitive processes underlying test performance are seen to be affected by the linguistic deficit. A basic question remains: Are the difficulties in communication incidental to thinking or crucially related to it? It does not appear possible to separate language from thought, and therefore it is not possible to determine precisely whether the difficulties in communication interfere with the performance aspects or with the central processing procedures of intellectual functioning.

Much of the recent research on cognitive development in children has been based on the work of Jean Piaget. Hans Furth has used a Piagetian approach in his extensive research on the cognitive development of deaf children.

Furth's reviews (1964, 1971) and his classic book, *Thinking Without Language* (1966a), are important references. His basic conclusion is summarized in the title of his book: logical, intelligent thinking does not need the support of a linguistic symbol system; intelligence is not dependent on language, but language is dependent on the structure of intelligence (Furth, 1966a, p. 228).

Furth and others have investigated a large number of concepts necessary to logical thinking in their attempts to understand how and when these operations, or thought processes, develop. Some of the operations identified and investigated are outlined briefly below.

The *concept of classification* summarizes the process that results in the logical combination of items that are similar or the same into homogeneous groups. For example, a child might be given a group of six objects that differ in shape and color, or in size and texture, and asked to "put together the things that go together." If he can consistently group the objects that are the same color, or the same shape, or the same shape *and* color, he is beginning to attain the concept of classification. The *concept of seriation* refers to the ability to combine items in logical order on the basis of differences between them. For example, the child might be presented with a number of forms that are shaped identically but are of varying sizes. If the child can consistently order the forms serially in ascending or descending order, he is discovering the concept of seriation. The *concept of conservation* refers to the idea that the weight, or volume, or quantity of a given amount of liquid or mass does not change as long as nothing is either added or subtracted to the substance. For example, a child might be shown a tall narrow glass filled with water. While he watches, the experimenter pours the water into a short wide glass. If the child consistently asserts that the quantity of water has remained the same, he has fulfilled one of the requirements for mastery of the concept of conservation.

An overview of studies comparing the performance of deaf children to hearing children on tasks reflecting concept attainment indicates that deaf children perform as well as hearing children during the earlier ages and stages of cognitive development. In Piaget's framework, children progress from the pre-operational stage, in which they are unable to use concepts consistently to draw logical conclusions, to the stage of concrete operations in which they are able to engage in logical thought about nonsymbolic materials. Finally, at the most advanced stage of formal operations they are able to utilize abstract, symbolic logic for the solution of problems. For example, Templin (1950) found that the scores of the deaf and the hearing children whom she studied did not differ significantly for any of her subtests related to classification. However, the scores of the hearing children on the subtests related to analogy were significantly higher than the scores of the deaf children. Templin suggests that analogies are less likely to be discerned concretely in daily life, and that this fact may explain the differences in the scores for the deaf and the hearing children. Rosenstein's (1960) study also shows the same equality between deaf and hearing children. He compared 60 deaf children with 60 hearing children, ages 8 to 12, on nonverbal tasks requiring classification abilities and found no differences between the two groups. Essentially the same results were reported by Kates, Yudin, and Tiffany (1962), who investigated concept attainment in deaf and hearing adolescents.

In one of Furth's first published studies (1961b), the classification behavior of 180 deaf and 180 hearing subjects, ages 7 through 12, was examined. The children were presented with three kinds of classification tasks. One required classification of objects that were the same, another of objects that were similar, and a third of objects that had opposite characteristics. The deaf children and the hearing children performed equally well on the first two kinds of tasks, reflecting an ability to manipulate the concepts

of sameness and similarity. However, while 96 percent of
the hearing children were able to complete successfully
the task reflecting mastery of the concept of "opposite,"
only 78 percent of the deaf children were able to do so.
Furth suggests that the hearing subjects did not "truly"
understand the concept of opposition any more completely than the deaf subjects did, but that their mastery
of language enabled them to give the impression that they
did. This explanation would seem to be weak, particularly
when the whole thrust of Furth's investigations, and
the eventual conclusion that he drew, was that language
in and of itself has little influence on the development of
logical thought.

An alternative explanation is suggested from the
framework of Blank's (1974) paper on the cognitive functions of language in the preschool years. Blank found that
the tasks with which deaf children had the greatest difficulty were those with instructions which could not be
communicated by means of gestures. In her experiments,
Blank found ways of training the deaf children to grasp
what they were to do. However, she reports that it took
only a few seconds to communicate the information to the
hearing children, whereas five minutes were required to
train the deaf children in the correct procedures.* Thus,
one of the functions of language is seen to be to communicate requests that have no visible referent. Another is the
reverse ability of the experimenter to comprehend what his
subjects are communicating. Unless both of these language
functions can be performed, the experimenter is unable
to say whether the deaf child has or has not grasped a
concept.

*In this context, it is interesting to note the results of Jordan's experi-
mental study of the rate of communication for speaking and for signing
college students. He reports that "while the communications of the deaf
subjects were significantly shorter than those of the normal hearing subjects, they were also much faster, and thus, deaf subjects managed to say
more in a short time than did normal hearing subjects" (Jordan, 1975,
p. 91).

Additional evidence supporting the notion of the equivalence of deaf and hearing children during the earlier stages of cognitive development, with a widening gap at later ages, is derived from another of Furth's studies (1963a). Deaf and hearing college students were tested in this study, in which tasks were administered requiring the mastery of the more difficult *concept of transfer*—that is, the subject is required to extrapolate his knowledge from one situation to another. The deaf students participating in the experiment did not perform as well as the hearing students on these tasks. Furth suggests the absence of verbal or language ability in the deaf subjects was not related *directly* to mastery of the concept, but rather that their deficient language produced an inability to use a prior set or piece of knowledge. The implication remains that if the linguistic abilities of the two groups were equivalent, their cognitive attainment might be equivalent as well.

Both Silverman and Best report results suggesting that a greater grasp of language allows for a higher standard of performance on cognitive tasks on the part of deaf children. Silverman (1967) matched deaf and hearing children on the basis of reading achievement scores, and found that this procedure eliminated differences in their abilities to engage in more complex abstract reasoning. Best (1970) compared the performance of three groups of deaf children with varying exposure to signed and spoken language with the performance of a group of hearing children on a variety of classification tasks. Generally speaking, performance correlated with exposure to language. The hearing children performed most effectively. Those deaf children with most exposure to both oral and manual language performed better than the other deaf children. Of additional interest is Best's finding that all groups were found to progress through the same stages of cognitive development, and to use the same strategies for problem solving, although the progress of the hearing children appeared to be more rapid than that of the deaf children. Also, correct verbal reasoning usually accompanied correct performance on the tasks, but there was no evidence that this relationship was a causal one. It is necessary to be very cautious in making causal inferences from correlational results. The relation is almost certainly reciprocal—the more intelligent the child, as measured by IQ score, the better the child will be at learning to communicate, and the more proficiency the child has in communication, the higher the IQ score will appear.

In a study by Schlesinger and Meadow (1976), language deficit was shown to have a strikingly adverse effect on the aspect of cognition measured by intelligence test performance. The deaf children who had better communication skills were found to perform at an appreciably higher level than the deaf children whose communication skills were less well developed. Even though every attempt was made to reduce the verbal skills necessary for understanding and responding to the tasks, skill in receiving and producing understandable language was found to correlate highly with the IQ measure. Tentative evidence suggested the priority of language in the relationship between language and intelligence or cognitive process. Deaf children who were exposed to two different modes of language input from their parents did not have significantly different IQ test scores as measured on the Stanford-Binet in 1970. However, in 1972, IQ test scores were significantly different: Children who had received early and consistent bimodal language input (that is, Total Communication) ranked first with mean IQ scores of 111; children who had received early and consistent oral-only language input ranked second with mean IQ scores of 107.5; children who had received mixed and less effective language input ranked third with mean IQ scores of 97.7. Thus, the deaf children who appeared to have similar intellectual potentials in 1970 were seen to differ in their IQ scores two years later. The immediately identifiable difference between them was the kind of language input they had received during the intervening years. A high level of communication skills seemed necessary for a high level of performance on the cognitive tasks. The researchers conclude that linguistic competence is an intervening variable mediating between IQ and a number of indexes of cognitive performance.

Of the cognitive tasks studied, the concept of conservation is generally seen as one of the more difficult, and one that is mastered later. In three studies of conservation (Oleron and Herren, 1961; Furth, 1966a; Templin, 1967), deaf children were found to be retarded in mastery of this concept when compared to hearing children. However, other results of these studies differed in some important respects. Studying the conservation of weight and volume, Oleron and Herren found deaf subjects to be retarded by approximately six years in comparison to the hearing controls. Furth studied the conservation of weight concept in deaf children with a mean age of 8.5. He found that the performance of the deaf children was similar to that of hearing first graders with a mean age of 6.10—a retardation among the deaf of less than two years. Templin reported different findings at a first and second administration of tasks measuring the conservation of weight. At the initial testing, 12- and 14-year-old deaf subjects were retarded by about two years compared to the hearing subjects; the second administration of the materials revealed about a six-year retardation of the 14-year-old deaf subjects.

A suggested explanation for the differences in the results points again to the importance of the administrative procedures used with deaf children. Templin observes that kinesthetic cues were built into the procedures designed by Furth but were not included in the other studies. There is a possibility that by requiring the subjects to actually handle the clay, Furth emphasized the kinesthetic as well as the cognitive aspect of the conservation of weight task.

The way in which *experience* may serve as an intervening variable, helping to determine the relationship of language and cognitive development, presents another important issue. In Best's (1970) study described above, the degree of language exposure of the deaf subjects was varied by selecting children with differing experiences both at school and within the family. Templin (1950) used a similar though less complex design by choosing two groups of deaf children and two groups of hearing children, with one group of each population attending day schools and the other attending residential schools. Templin was interested in testing the hypothesis that environmental restrictions on experience would be related to restrictions on the ability to perform abstract reasoning. Environmental restrictions were seen either as internally imposed (the limitation of deafness) or as externally imposed (the limitation of a residential institution). Several tests of abstract reasoning were administered to pairs of residential and day students matched for age, grade placement, IQ score, and sex. The mean hearing loss of the deaf residential students, however, was greater than that of the deaf day students. When subgroups who had compatible hearing levels were compared, scores of the residential and the day students did not differ significantly. Thus, it seems that the apparent relationship between attendance at a residential school and poor reasoning ability is spurious. The important explanatory variable is, rather, the extent of the hearing loss. The ability to reason declines as the extent of the hearing loss increases.

The scores of the deaf and the hearing children did not differ significantly for any of the subtests related to classification. However, the scores of the hearing children on the subtests related to analogy were significantly higher than the scores of the deaf children. Templin's suggested explanation of the differences in the scores—that analogies are less likely to be experienced in daily life—agrees with Furth's suggestion that *experience* is the intervening variable between language and cognition. There are at least two difficulties with this explanation. First, the validity of the results is based upon the assumption that children in a residential institution might be expected to have a narrower range of experience than children living at home and attending a day school. Second, if language deprivation leads to experiential deprivation, which in turn leads to deficient or retarded cognitive development, this would seem to be evidence that thinking is influenced by language, although in an indirect manner.

In spite of the many studies that have investigated the attainment of concepts by deaf children, it is obvious that there are still many unanswered questions and unresolved problems.

*Memory*

Memory has been used as an indicator of cognitive ability in a number of studies reported with deaf children as subjects. Again, many of the results seem contradictory. Goetzinger and Huber (1964) found that their hearing subjects performed better than the deaf on delayed recall, but only equally well on immediate recall. Doehring and Rosenstein (1960) found no differences between deaf and hearing children in their ability to recognize and reproduce letters, trigrams, and four-letter words that were exposed briefly. Furth (1961a) found no differences between deaf and hearing children in visual memory at ages 7 to 10, but found marked differences favoring 11- and 12-year-old hearing children.

A number of studies suggest the conditions under which deaf children are deficient or equivalent in comparison to their hearing peers. Blair (1957) matched groups of deaf and hearing children for IQ, age, and sex, and then administered several visual memory tests to the 53 pairs of children. The deaf children performed significantly better than the hearing children on the Knox Cube Test and on the Memory-for-Designs Test. The hearing children had consistently higher scores on all four of the memory-span tests. Blair suggests that the memory-span tasks require greater mental abstraction and conceptualization, and that these areas are more difficult for deaf children. However, Furth (1966a), comparing deaf and hearing adolescents and adults on memory-span tasks, found that the deaf subjects differed minimally from the hearing subjects when the task involved memory for forms, but that their performance was at a significantly lower level when the task involved digits. This relatively better ability to remember forms leads to a consideration of a study by Odom, Blanton, and McIntyre (1970), who found that deaf children were more likely to remember words for which there were sign-language equivalents than words for which there were no sign-language equivalents. Words in the two groups were equated for length and for frequency as judged by the Thorndike-Lorge list. These several studies indicate that there are a number of factors to be considered in evaluating the memory skills of deaf and hearing children. Among these are the available symbol systems; divergent motor, kinesthetic, visual, and auditory cues in the stimulus materials; and differing levels of experience related to language exposure.

These factors are illustrated in a study by Blanton, Nunnally, and Odom (1967). They found that deaf subjects were more likely than hearing subjects to remember the graphemically related words—that is, words similar in visual appearance. Hearing subjects were more likely than deaf subjects to remember the words that are related phonetically. Similarly, a study on retention of words judged to be easy or difficult to pronounce (Blanton and

Nunnally, 1967) showed that hearing children were significantly better able than deaf children to retain the difficult words. This finding illustrates again the factor of auditory deprivation, and the fact that material related to the experiences of deaf children is retained better than material that is divorced from their experiences.

An important question is whether cues presented simultaneously in different modalities have a distracting or a facilitating influence on retention and recall. Bruininks and Clark (1970) experimented with groups of hearing first graders classified as disadvantaged retarded, disadvantaged normal, and advantaged normal. To control for differences in reading ability, pictures were used as stimuli in the presentation of lists of noun-pairs. The performance of all groups under visual and combined auditory-visual conditions was significantly higher (p<.01) than that attained under the auditory condition alone. Most of the previous research studies reviewed by these authors indicated that a visual presentation is superior to an auditory presentation of verbal materials when nonmeaningful materials are employed. In a study by Ross, Kessler, Phillips, and Lerman (1972), the lipreading scores of 20 of 29 deaf children were higher when combined visual-auditory modalities were used than when either modality was used alone, in the administration of the Word Intelligibility by Picture Identification Test.

Erber (1975) has reviewed almost fifty papers relevant to the question of auditory versus visual presentation of speech, and has concluded that "numerous clinical and laboratory studies on the auditory-visual performance of normal-hearing and hearing-impaired children and adults demonstrate that combined auditory-visual perception is superior to perception through either audition or vision alone" (p. 481).

Another possible clue to an explanation of deaf children's differential responses to bimodal presentations is provided by Conrad's research results. In his first studies, Conrad (1970) analyzed the errors of deaf boys in the immediate written recall of letters when these were read silently and when they were recited aloud. Conrad concluded that one group relied primarily on articulatory coding, whereas another group relied on visual coding. In an extension of this research, Conrad (1971) found that the subjects who had been classified as relying on articulatory coding scored higher in a test of reading comprehension when they read the test material aloud. Those who had been classified as relying on visual coding scored higher when they read the material silently. Conrad does not speculate about the basis for this difference in coding modalities, but his findings that relate learning or performance to the "fit" between the presentation of materials and the ability to learn from them suggest that the same kind of presentation may not be efficient for all deaf children. Some may benefit more from one mode, some from another.

## Perceptual and Motor Functioning

Studies of the perceptual and motor functioning of deaf children have been designed to investigate the bases for their different levels of cognitive achievement, to learn about the cognitive results of sensory deprivation, and to explore the human capacity for modal compensation or the substitution of one sensory modality for another.

Several investigators have used the Bender Gestalt Test with deaf children. Gilbert and Levee (1967) found that deaf children produced more errors than hearing children of a similar age and intelligence. They interpret this finding to suggest a higher incidence of brain damage in deaf children. However, the results of Keogh, Vernon, and Smith (1970) indicate that the Bender Gestalt Test may have limited accuracy in determining brain damage in individual deaf children. Disturbances in the motor functioning of deaf children have been measured by a balance board (Pintner, Eisenson, and Stanton, 1941); and locomotor co-ordination has been evaluated by the Heath Railwalking Test (Myklebust, Neyhus, and Mulholland, 1962). A study (Boyd, 1967) that used the Oseretsky Scale for Evaluation of equilibrium, coordination, and speed found significant differences favoring the hearing children over the deaf children. Also, a larger proportion of the deaf children was found to be left-handed.

Research based on perceptual-motor evidence might help answer questions about whether the presentation of material to deaf children in a variety of modes would enhance or hinder learning, and it might resolve some of the educational controversies about cross-modal teaching techniques. MacDougall and Rabinovitch (1971b) conducted an experiment to determine the role of auditory and kinesthetic cues produced by overt verbalizations in a learning situation. The group of hearing children and one of the two groups of deaf children used speech to learn lists of pictures, words, and nonsense syllables. The second deaf group used signing and fingerspelling as the verbalization method. Verbalization in neither the auditory nor the kinesthetic modality resulted in an improvement in the performance of any of the three groups.

A different approach to this question is represented in two animal studies (MacDougall and Rabinovitch, 1971a; 1972). These experiments resulted from a study (Rosenzweig, 1966) that reopened the "sensory-compensation hypothesis" when it was found that the weight and biochemical activity of nonvisual areas of the cortex of blinded or visually deprived animals were greater than in the sighted control animals. The effect was particularly pronounced when the animals were raised in an enriched environment. MacDougall and Rabinovitch studied *behavioral* weight and tissue culture differences in mice deafened by ototoxic drugs, congenitally deaf mice, and normally hearing littermates. No differences were found in the simple or complex learning of any of the mice in either normal or enriched environments. "These results suggest that early auditory deprivation does not lead to the development of increased visual perceptual ability. This may mean that the anatomical and physiological changes found (Rosenzweig) are not manifested at the behavioral level, or, different effects may be produced when the deprivation is in the auditory rather than the visual modality" (Mac-Dougall and Rabinovitch, 1971a).

The second study reported by these researchers dealt with the effect of early auditory deprivation on the exploratory behavior of mice. At two months of age the deaf and hearing mice, raised in an enriched environment, showed no difference in their patterns of exploratory behavior. However, when tested at maturity, they showed different patterns. These findings suggest to the investigators that the deaf mice learned to use their intact senses in a unique way to obtain information and stimulation from the environment.

Findings reported by Sterritt, Camp, and Lipman (1966), comparing the auditory and the visual information processing of nine deaf and nine hearing children, disprove the thesis that children with a hearing loss compensate by achieving superior visual skills. Compared to the hearing subjects, the deaf children were inferior in their discrimination of visual temporal patterns.

Most of the research evaluating sensory compensation has concentrated on auditory versus visual stimuli. A few studies have evaluated possible tactile (touch) compensation; none has evaluated the possibility of haptic (movement) compensation. This might be a meaningful approach because it has been pointed out (Schlesinger and Meadow, 1972) that the cortical areas controlling vocal and hand movements are adjacent in the brain. It has been reported (Rosenstein, 1957) that a group of blind children performed better in the tactile perception of rhythmic patterns than did the deaf, normal, and aphasic groups. Also, the blind and normal children improved on successive trials, whereas the deaf and aphasic children did not (see also Warren, 1977). Schiff and Dytell (1971) report that deaf and hearing subjects performed similarly on a battery of tactual perception tests and concluded that acoustical storage of information does not necessarily have to precede cross-modal identification. In a study of the transfer of a concept from visual to tactile modalities, deaf children were found to be more proficient at using tactile cues than were the hearing children with whom they were compared (Blank and Bridger, 1966). This appears to be still another area where additional research would be useful to the understanding of the cognitive development of deaf children.

*Summary*

1. Studies of the cognitive development of deaf children are particularly liable to the pitfalls of research methodology. Special attention must be given to the possibility of central nervous system impairments with related built-in deficits in perceptual-motor abilities. Baseline data on language ability, spoken and signed, should be accumulated for deaf subjects and used in designing and administering test instruments, and in interpreting the test performance results. Inattention to these methodological details undoubtedly contributes to the picture of conflicting results and consequent differences in assessing the manner of cognitive development and level of achievement in deaf children.

2. Deaf children usually score within the normal range on intelligence tests, although their mean scores are somewhat lower than those of hearing children. This finding, however, is true only when tests are administered with nonverbal instructions and do not depend on spoken responses.

3. The general level of academic achievement in deaf children is much below that which could be expected from performance on tests of cognitive development. The most recent nationwide assessment of academic achievement showed that the highest achievement by any deaf age group on paragraph meaning was at grade level 4.4; the highest average achievement by any deaf age group on arithmetic computation was at grade level 6.7. Deaf children of deaf parents consistently perform at a higher level on tests of academic achievement than the deaf children of hearing parents.

4. Considerable evidence indicates that deaf children learn concepts in the same sequence and in the same manner as hearing children do. However, these processes occur at later ages than with normally hearing children. The influence of innate intellectual ability on the attainment of concepts is an open question, particularly since the question is confounded by the possibility that secondary effects of auditory and experiential deprivation may depress the ability to perform on tests of intelligence.

5. Deaf children appear to have particular difficulty in attaining the concept of opposition, but they show relatively little retardation in attaining the concepts of sameness and symmetry. Tasks related to classification skills are easier for deaf children to perform than tasks related to analogy. Superordinate reasoning, allowing a number of concepts to be combined parsimoniously for the solution of problems, appears to be more difficult for deaf children than for hearing children. The question of the relationship between language and thought has been explored by interpreting comparative performances of deaf and hearing children on conceptual tasks. Linguistic competence appears to be associated with cognitive performance. Some researchers argue that the relatively high performance of deaf children demonstrates that thought develops independently of language. Others suggest that thought is

influenced by language and that both are mediated by experience.

6. Studies of the performance of deaf children on memory tasks show conflicting results, often seemingly related to the type of test material used. For example, deaf children are more likely to retain words that have a sign equivalent than words that do not, and compared to hearing children are more likely to remember geometric forms than digits. The patterns of their word associations are similar to those of hearing children of a younger age.

7. Deaf children are more likely than hearing children to have problems with equilibrium and balance, stemming from the same etiological basis as their hearing handicap. Disturbances in lateral preference (handedness) are also more likely among deaf than among hearing children.

8. A few efforts have been made to evaluate the comparative efficacy of unimodal auditory and visual cues and of bimodal cues on comprehension. The results have been contradictory, but the direction of the effect seems related to the degree of hearing loss. Ability to attend to one or another presentation mode may be related to an inherent or learned "set" that differs idiosyncratically from one individual to another.

9. The hypothesis that deprivation in one sensory modality leads to compensation through improved functioning in another modality has been investigated in some animal studies. Although blind animals appeared to compensate in nonvisual areas of the brain, the same did not hold true for deaf animals. But although the deaf animals did not seem to be more sensitive in other perceptual areas, they did use their intact senses in unique ways to obtain information and stimulation from the environment.

CHAPTER FOUR

# Social
# and Psychological
# Development
# in Deaf Children

**T**HE difficulties that deaf children experience in linguistic and cognitive development are reflected in their social and psychological development as well. In this chapter, social development, self-concept, and personality development are reviewed.

## Social Development

SOCIAL MATURITY. The concept of social maturity is difficult to define and to study. It is concerned with behavior that is appropriate for particular ages and stages of development. However, when a child is handicapped, "significant others" in his environment may scale down their expectations for his social achievements. One way of viewing social development in younger children is to evaluate their ability to care for their own needs as they move toward greater independence and self-reliance. The Vineland Social Maturity Scale was designed to measure increasing ability in the areas of self-help, self-direction, locomotion, occupation, communication, and social relations (Doll, 1965). This scale was used in several early studies of deaf children. Many of these early studies have been reviewed by DiCarlo and Dolphin (1952).

Streng and Kirk (1938), Avery (1948), Burchard and Myklebust (1942), and Myklebust (1960) all found that deaf children received lower scores on this scale than hearing children of comparable ages. In many of the studies reported before 1950, children with varying degrees of hearing impairment were included in the same groups. Changing pictures of etiology, early educational treatment, and audiological advances make these earlier studies less meaningful in terms of predicting the kinds of behavioral responses that could be expected from deaf children today. However, the basic theoretical issues remain much the same.

Schlesinger and Meadow (1971) used the Vineland Scale in a study of 40 deaf preschoolers. They found a strong positive relationship between the Vineland score and an index of communicative competence. (This index included the Mecham Language Development Scale score, teachers' ratings for expressive and receptive communication, speech, and lipreading, and two communication ratings devised from videotaped mother-child interaction.) The results were that 65 percent of the children who scored below the median on the Vineland also scored below the median for communicative competence, and 75 percent scoring above the Vineland median also scored above the median for communication.

Myklebust (1960) reports a study using the Vineland Scale with results that are similar to those of Burchard and Myklebust (1942). He surveyed 150 deaf children from 10 to 21 years of age, in a public residential school. The mean social quotient (with a norm of 100) was 85.8. On the basis of these data, plus additional data collected independently from preschool deaf children, Myklebust concluded that the gap between the social maturity of deaf and hearing children widens with increasing age. The social quotient for the preschool group and for the other age groups up to 15 years was slightly above 90. For the age groups from 15 to 21, there was a gradual decline in social quotient: at 15 it was 82.2; at 17 it was 80.4; and at 19 it was 76.2. Myklebust's conclusion should be regarded with caution because of the special nature of his older population. Furthermore, those who were older than 18 and still remaining in school may also constitute a special group. Barker and his colleagues (1953) have hypothesized that the social immaturity seemingly characterizing deaf children and adults may result from the high proportion attending residential schools, where the development of independence and responsibility may be stifled.

Meadow's studies of different subgroups of deaf children allow some inferences about the various factors that contribute to the low level of social maturity found in many studies of deaf children. On the basis of teachers' ratings of 54 matched pairs of deaf children in a residential school, the deaf children of deaf parents were rated significantly higher than the deaf children of hearing parents on dimensions of maturity, independence, and ability to take responsibility (Meadow, 1972); deaf students living at home and attending day schools or classes received ratings intermediate to those of the two residential school groups. That is, the deaf children of deaf parents in the residential setting were rated highest; the deaf children of hearing parents in non-residential school settings received intermediate ratings; and deaf children of hearing parents in residential settings were rated significantly below the other two groups.

It is suggested by these findings that parents' attitudes and child-rearing practices may contribute most to the slow development of social maturity in deaf children, but that residential living, with the absence of family contact and the close supervision leading to few opportunities for independence, also presents a negative causative factor. It must be noted that a true test of the effect of the residential setting would have required the inclusion of a fourth group of children in Meadow's design: deaf children of deaf parents attending a *day school*. This group, however, was insubstantial: in the day schools contacted, only about 1 percent of the deaf children had deaf parents.

A number of studies give some insight into the dynamics of how the protectiveness most families have for their deaf children probably contributes to their retarded social development.

Chess, Korn, and Fernandez (1971) collected material on levels of self-help functioning from mothers of 243 rubella children. Although 30 percent of these children had no hearing loss, and some had no other identifiable handicap, their data are important because it appears that the parents' *definition* of the child's fragility may be a major critical variable regardless of the actual limit of the child's abilities. The most striking finding is the discrepancy between the children's actual capabilities and the self-help tasks that they performed on a regular basis. Half the children for whom information was obtained were able to do at least 80 percent of the activities necessary for dressing themselves; however, fewer than half regularly performed as many as 25 percent of these activities.

This finding is elaborated by Gordon's (1959) attempt to relate maternal attitudes toward independence to deaf children's social maturity. He studied nineteen mothers and their deaf children, ages 2.5 to 6. Gordon used the discrepancy between scores on the Merrill-Palmer (a performance IQ test) and the Vineland Social Maturity Scale as the measure for maturity level, and McClelland's Thematic Apperception Test plus Winterbottom's Independence Training Attitude Questionnaire to reflect maternal attitudes. He concluded that the more important influences on the handicapped child are not the maternal attitudes toward the handicap in particular, but rather the mother's attitude toward children in general. It was reported that (1) attitudes favoring early independence in normal children were found among the mothers of deaf children whose scores showed relatively large discrepancies; (2) independence training attitudes toward deaf children and discrepancies between attitudes toward deaf and normal children were not associated with the child's maturity level; (3) mothers with low need achievement tended to be moderate in their independence training attitudes toward normal children, while mothers with high need achievement tended toward the extreme positions of favoring very early or very late independence; (4) high need achievement mothers favored significantly later independence in deaf children than did low need achievement mothers. It was suggested that the mother who encourages early independence in her hearing child is free to devote more interest in her handicapped child. Gordon's results raise a general question about the roots of achievement motivation in mothers for their children. Possibly it is those mothers whose children are not progressing at an optimum developmental rate who begin to concentrate on encouraging the child in areas where he has difficulty. Parents of deaf children are sometimes made more anxious by teachers who try to encourage them to work harder for the children to achieve.

Meadow (1967) interviewed deaf parents and hearing parents about various practices that might reflect the encouragement of independence in deaf children. Almost half of the deaf parents and only 15 percent of the hearing parents stated that a deaf child should be allowed to play independently in the immediate neighborhood before the age of five. The hearing parents were more reluctant than the deaf parents to grant neighborhood independence to *both* deaf and hearing children. Meadow suggests that the hearing parent, in eagerness to "treat the deaf and hearing child alike," may achieve this goal by scaling down expectations for the hearing child rather than by giving the deaf child the same degree of independence.

Gregory found, in her interview study of 122 English families, that more than half of the mothers reported that they made concessions to their deaf children that were not made to hearing siblings (Gregory, 1976, p. 184). "Far fewer mothers of deaf children felt able to make no concessions than mothers of cerebral palsied children interviewed in a similar study." The siblings of deaf children were reported to experience more jealousy than was the case of the siblings of other children. The form taken for punishment of the deaf children was different, as reported by the English mothers: 69 percent of parents of normal 4-year-olds deprived the children of candy or TV as a form of punishment, compared to 5 percent of the mothers of deaf children. "Presumably this is because such deprivations lose much of their point if you cannot explain to the child why they are taking place" (Gregory, 1976, p. 88). Another area in the treatment of deaf and hearing children that can be seen as affecting "mature" or age-appropriate behavior is treatment of children at bedtime. Gregory reports that four times as many deaf children as hearing children had "indulgent bedtimes" (p. 69).

Stinson (1974, 1978) compared the attitudes of 31 mothers of hearing impaired boys to those of 33 mothers of boys with normal hearing. He found that the mothers of the hearing subjects tended to react to the pressures, burdens, and restrictions of child-rearing by increasing their demands on their children, while the mothers of the hearing impaired subjects responded by relaxing demands. He also studied maternal and child behavior in task situations designed to reflect verbal and nonverbal achievement orientation and motivation. Whereas intense demands were optimal for the hearing subjects to acquire nonverbal achievement motivation, moderate demands for the attainment of verbal skills worked more effectively with the hearing impaired subjects. Too early or too late expectations for language appeared to limit acquisition of the achievement motive in the hearing impaired subjects. Instituting demands of appropriate intensity may be difficult, especially because different standards must be used in judging the progress of deaf and hearing children in their acquisition of verbal skills.

There is a good deal of pressure on parents to provide their deaf children with early training and education. One study found that 80 percent of the deaf sample had received some form of early preschool education (Meadow, 1967). Traditionally, the deaf child has been viewed in an educational context. His mother is trained by educators to be his teacher. Added to the strain of communicative frustration is the strain of extended demands on the mother's time and attention. Studies of interaction between mothers and deaf children illustrate the outcome of this thrust. Schlesinger and Meadow (1972) found the mothers of deaf preschool children to be significantly less permissive, more intrusive, more didactic, less creative, less flexible, and as showing less approval of their children in comparison with the mothers of hearing preschool children. No significant differences were observed between the two groups of mothers in terms of their enjoyment of their children, their effectiveness in achieving their children's cooperation, and the degree to which they appeared to be relaxed and comfortable in the study situation.

Some of the ways in which child-rearing practices differ in families with young deaf children are illustrated in Schlesinger and Meadow's (1972) interviews with parents of preschool children. The parents of deaf children reported the children's need, or their own felt need, for more constant supervision in order to protect them from accidents. These parents reported a narrower range of disciplinary techniques, a heavier reliance on spanking, and more areas of expressed frustration around child-rearing generally than the parents of hearing children reported. The parents of the deaf children were constantly concerned about whether they were expecting too much or too little from their deaf children and about whether they were being overprotective or underprotective.

When the behavior of the deaf and the hearing children was compared, the deaf children were rated as appearing significantly less buoyant or happy, less compliant, less creative or imaginative, and as showing less pride in mastery and less enjoyment in the interaction with their mothers. No significant differences were found in attentiveness, curiosity, independence, apparent comfort in the situation, or frequency of body movement. When the deaf children were divided into two groups according to their scores on an index of communicative competence, it was found that the deaf children with better communicative skills were rated very close to the hearing children with respect to buoyancy and enjoyment of the interaction; they also were evaluated more positively than the deaf children with inferior communicative skills on degree of compliance, pride in mastery, and creativity.

Schlesinger and Meadow conclude that mothers of deaf children are significantly more intrusive than mothers of hearing children. Collins (1969) classified 40 percent of the behavior of the mothers of deaf children as "directing." Goss (1970) found the mothers of deaf children to give directions significantly more often than the control mothers of hearing children. Bell (1964) reviewed five studies of families containing children with various kinds of handicaps. In each of the five studies, the mothers of handicapped children scored higher than the control mothers for intrusiveness as measured by the Parental Attitude Research Inventory. Bell suggests that an intrusive attitude may be induced in a mother as an effect of a limitation in her child's ability to cope with situations.

The reciprocal nature of mother-child interaction is clarified and its importance magnified when the deaf child and his mother are the focus. The mother's dilemma in

finding a balance between withholding appropriate opportunities for her child to develop independence and
exposing him unnecessarily to the dangers imposed by
his handicap is one that has major implications for
socialization and child development theory. The role of
the father in families with deaf children has been studied
very little. There is some evidence that fathers may interact less frequently than mothers with their handicapped
children (Jordan, 1962). Fathers of deaf children seem to
experience more difficulty in learning sign language. Also,
the meaning of a physical handicap differs for mothers and
fathers, depending partly on the sex of the child (Schlesinger and Meadow, 1972).

SOCIAL INTERACTION. Social development and language
acquisition are intertwined. It is to be expected that deaf
children whose language development is retarded will
have fewer opportunities for social interaction, both within
and outside the family. The feelings of others about aborted
attempts at communication are negative and lead to frustration, creating a spiral leading the deaf children to seek
increasing isolation from the fabric of social interaction.

Appropriate and satisfying social interaction is based, at
least to some degree, on the ability of an individual to
"take the role of the other." The response of the other
member of the dyad to one's actions and reactions, and the
correct interpretation of that response, is necessary if a
child can modify his or her actions to accommodate successfully to a particular situation. In a recent review of the
research literature on role-taking among exceptional children (Kitano, Stiehl, and Cole, 1978), the authors conclude
that these children have a generally decreased role-taking
ability, essentially unrelated to general intelligence (p. 66).
They note that handicapped children exhibit developmental delays in these role-taking abilities, contributing
to early inappropriate responses to others. For example,

their "awkward bids for friendship (for example, gaining attention through aggressive behavior) only alienate potential playmates. One contributing factor may be a failure to role take—that is, an inability to perceive that other children dislike their aggressive tactics" (Kitano, Stiehl and Cole, 1978, p. 66).

The deaf child with little language must rely more on facial and gestural impressions for interpreting others' responses. Bryan (1974) reported that learning-disabled children have difficulty in understanding subtle affective cues. Odom, Blanton, and Laukhuf (1973) studied seven- and eight-year-old deaf children and concluded that they were less accurate than hearing peers in the interpretation of emotions reflected in facial expressions. "This finding, apparently, is not due to some perceptual difficulty in recognizing the facial expression since deaf and hearing subjects performed comparably in the expression sorting task" (p. 150).

The authors suggest that the decreased abilities of the deaf children may well be related to their lessened opportunities to receive interpretations and verbal explanations of the emotions of others. "Verbalizations of feelings and attributes of a situation may serve to focus (orient) a child's attention on its salient and relevant aspects" (p. 150).

The effects of the child's inability to understand or to empathize with the subtleties of a situation influence the responses that significant others have to him. Parents interviewed by Schlesinger and Meadow (1972) reported some sense of frustration about their inability to communicate with their children. Most stated that the child's inability to understand them was more frustrating than their own inability to understand the child. Of the 16 mothers studied by Collins (1969), 13 reported that they could communicate with their preschool deaf children only about things or events that were present in time or space. Only one mother said that her child communicated about absent things or events; the others indicated that immediacy was a prerequisite for the children to be able to communicate.

Research conducted by Heider and Heider (1940) at the Clarke School illustrates some of the specific ways in which imperfect language interferes with social interaction. They observed 53 pairs of deaf preschool children during periods of unrestricted play and compared these observations with those of 22 pairs of hearing children. Additional data were collected on film. A striking feature of the interactions was the difference in the ability of the two groups of children to use references to future time in organizing and coordinating their activities. The researchers felt that the ability of the hearing children to refer to future activities or expectations of future events played a major role in their definition of the present. In contrast to the interaction of the hearing children, the deaf children's play had a global, nonspecific, amorphous character. The deaf children were able to announce only in a very general way the meaning and intent of their ongoing activity.

The limitation to present actions creates the possibility for much anxiety in deaf children. If their parents are unable to communicate to them the probable course of future events, and to reassure them about the outcome of current disturbing happenings, the children may develop doubt and distrust. Expectations may be shaken and events assume a more hostile meaning. The Heiders point out from their observational data that deaf children are handicapped in dealing with the qualities of objects or situations beyond what is immediately perceived. In the face of communicative deficits, it is difficult to know whether this handicap is only apparent or also real. That it is apparent is evidenced by other data (Schlesinger, 1972) showing that 95 percent of the deaf children and their parents limited communication to topics with a visual reference. In comparison, 45 percent of the hearing children in the study made at least a passing comment referring to a nonvisible object and 15 percent had a prolonged conversation about something outside the visual range.

The inability to refer to linguistically complex meanings may also handicap the development of imaginary play requiring fantasy and role-taking. Heider and Heider remark that their deaf subjects' imaginary play was restricted by the possible level of action, because elaborate pantomime was needed to communicate a role that a single word could have expressed. Possibility, which the hearing child uses to indicate what he is able to do, can be implied by the deaf child in a far less specific way. Evaluating and qualifying statements are difficult to express, as are statements of approval and necessity. Another block to the development of positive patterns of social interaction is the difficulty of referring specifically to internal events. References to thinking, knowing, guessing, watching, looking, or wanting can be expressed in only very general ways by the deaf child.

In a later study, Heider (1948) compared the personal relationships of 66 pairs of hearing and 48 pairs of deaf children. Each pair was offered a game which only one child could use at a time. The interaction of the hearing pairs was found to be more highly organized and to have greater continuity of structure. The ways in which language was used to enable one child to gain control of the situation without arousing either aggression or withdrawal on the part of the other gave fresh appreciation of its function in social relationships. At the same time, these data brought into sharp focus the question of the effect of the more diffused, less structured, less sharply oriented social relations of the younger deaf child on the development of his personality.

In connection with their evaluation research, Moores, McIntyre, and Weiss (1972) observed the communication patterns among preschool deaf children. These children depended primarily on gestures when communicating with each other unless they were in preschool programs using standardized sign language.

A study completed by Herren and Colin (1972) illustrates the greater difficulty deaf children had in progressing from competition to cooperation when confronted with a task requiring cooperation. They state that the delayed progression from competition to cooperation shown by the deaf is bound to an intellectual handicap secondary to language deprivation.

Van Lieshout (1973) studied the peer interaction of 34 prelingually profoundly deaf children and 34 hearing children with ages of 60 months and 61 months respectively. Observations of social interactions in small groups were conducted under a time-sample scheme on two occasions six months apart. Teacher ratings were also collected. The hearing children were rated as more sociable than the deaf children and were observed to have more social interactions than the deaf children, especially in the categories of verbal interaction and mutual attention. However, during both periods of measurement, the deaf children exhibited more social interactions of an expressive kind—more physical contact, approval, and negative interactions—and spent more time in non-interaction than the hearing children. These differences in the interaction experienced by deaf and hearing children as they relate to peers undoubtedly contribute to the findings about the deaf child's self-concept.

## Self-Concept

Social development and self-concept go hand in hand. As a child begins to be an object to himself and sees himself reflected in the appraisals of others, he begins to understand both their behavior and his own. The importance of the development of self-boundaries, of distinguishing oneself as having an identity separate from that of others, is a basic psychoanalytic concept. In spite of general agreement among behavioral scientists that the concept of identify is of great significance and that positive self-image is essential to mental health, there is no consensus about how to define, study, or measure self-concept. When the subjects of interest are deaf children, the problems of definition, interpretation, and research methodology are magnified.

Several investigators have compared the self-concept or self-image of deaf children with that of hearing children. Brunschwig (1936) used a sentence completion test to gather data on the self-image of deaf and hearing children; Craig (1965) used drawings to elicit sociometric choice data from which she extrapolated summaries of self-evaluation; Gillies (1968) collected drawings of the child and of another person and interpreted them for a self-image rating. All three of these researchers concluded that the deaf children rated themselves much more positively than the hearing children with whom they were compared.

Because of the language difficulties encountered in administering written sentence completion tests to profoundly deaf children, the data collected by Brunschwig are questionable. If her subjects were indeed able to provide adequate sentences, it is likely that they were postlingually deaf or that they were hard-of-hearing rather than deaf. The early date of the research makes this a good possibility, for reasons discussed previously. In a more recent study (Titus, 1965), it was concluded that the sentence completion technique was unsuitable for eliciting self-image data from a group of profoundly deaf students in a residential school. Meadow (1969) attempted the same technique in pre-test efforts to develop a self-image test, with equally negative results.

Craig's population of 48 subjects consisted of three groups: a deaf group from a residential school; a deaf group attending a day school; and a hearing group attending regular public school. The children (aged 9.5 to 12) were asked to decide which members of their class they would choose to sit near or to go to the beach with, and which they thought would choose them. Scores were derived for accuracy of self-perception, direction of errors of self-perception, and self-acceptance and sociability. The deaf children, in both day and residential schools, rated themselves significantly more positively than did the children in the other two groups.

Meadow's research on self-image (Meadow, 1969; Schlesinger and Meadow, 1972) provides an interpretation for the studies of Brunschwig, Craig, and Gillies, primarily because her research design permitted an analysis of various subgroups of deaf children. A disadvantage is that no comparable data were collected from hearing children. Meadow (1969) originally studied 58 pairs of deaf children attending a residential school. Pairs were matched for age, sex, hearing loss, and IQ score. One member of each pair had deaf parents, the other member had hearing parents. A graphic cartoon-like test was developed using written adjectives plus illustrations of the manual signs for the adjectives. For the older children, the test was administered in small groups; for the younger children, testing was individual. A combination of signs and speech was used for all. The deaf children with deaf parents (all of whom had used manual communication with the children from an early age) had significantly higher, more positive scores than did the deaf children of hearing parents.

Later this study was expanded to include a group of 74 deaf students attending day schools (Schlesinger and Meadow, 1972). The age of the children in the study ranged from 6 to 18. All of these children had hearing parents. (Too few students with deaf parents were available in the day schools to include this logical fourth group in the research design.) The average self-image test scores for the day pupils were almost identical to those of the residential school pupils with hearing parents—significantly less positive than the scores of the residential pupils with deaf parents. None of the hearing parents had used manual communication in any form when their children were young. Only a few hearing parents of the teenage children either used or approved the use of sign language.

The differences in apparent level of self-image between the deaf children with deaf and hearing parents can be interpreted in a variety of ways. The identity-match in terms of handicap, providing the deaf child with a positive role model, is one possible contributing factor. The (early) availability of sign language as a communicative mode is another. The symbolic value and role-modeling function of sign language is a third possible factor.

In his interpretation of Brunschwig's findings of the apparent self-judgments of superiority on the part of deaf children, Barker (1953) suggests that if these responses do indeed reflect real feelings of well-being, they may result from the fact that children in schools for the deaf are praised frequently for relatively minor accomplishments. He notes, too, that the full force of cultural restraints and coercions associated with physical handicap is not felt until adulthood.

Craig's subjects were no older than 12 years of age. It may be that the cultural restraints had not yet affected them, thus accounting for the high level of self-image of the deaf children compared to the hearing children in her study. Another factor of possible importance is related to the frequent transfer of deaf children from day schools to residential schools at or about the age of 13. If a number of her subjects had indeed transferred from a day-school setting, where they had been a distinct minority among a large population of hearing peers, to a residential school setting, where they could identify with all their classmates and with some of their teachers on the dimension of deafness, their self-image might well shoot upward, thus accounting for the sharp discrepancy between the older and the younger students of hearing parents in the residential school. It is also possible that those deaf students who remain in day schools during the critical transitional adolescent years feel their minority status even more sharply, with the resultant decline in self-image reflected in the lower scores of the older day students.

Other variables investigated by Meadow in relation to the self-image scores include family climate, school achievement scores, and communication scores. Positive relationships were reported between each of these three variables and self-image. In addition, the self-image scores were significantly more positive for those children whose deaf parents were particularly active in the deaf community. The parents' interaction with other deaf persons may have had a direct positive effect on their children. Also, the parents who formed associations within the deaf community may have felt more positive about their own identity and communicated these positive feelings about themselves to their children. Another possibility is that the support of the community was a positive influence independent of the family (Meadow, 1967).

*Personality Development*

Research on personality characteristics of deaf children has most often been conducted through the use of personality inventories. One of the major reasons for using these instruments is that they seem simpler to administer than some other kinds of test instruments. However, their simplicity is more apparent than real. Another type of instrument is the rating scale, completed by teachers or others in direct contact with the deaf child. It, too, has limitations for personality assessment. Early studies of personality development using inventories and rating scales, such as the Bernreuter Personality Inventory (Welles, 1932; Pintner, 1933) and the Haggerty-Olson-Wickman Behavior Rating Scale (Burchard and Myklebust,

1942; Springer, 1938; Getz, 1953), showed with few exceptions that deaf children displayed more adjustment problems than hearing children.

Levine (1956) used a projective technique, the Rorschach Test, for an in-depth study of personality characteristics of 31 girls, aged 15 through 18. All the subjects were students at the Lexington School for the Deaf in New York City, had a hearing loss greater than 70 dB in the better ear, and had hearing parents. All were rated as "normal deaf students" by three different teachers. That is, they were without any severe behavioral problems and were not considered unusual. Levine found few indications of anxiety, depression, or inner tension in their records, although many records were characterized by indications of conscious control and respect for reality. The most outstanding points of the test results were the singular absence or sparseness of signs of emotional disturbance and the adequate range of scoring factors in the responses; however, the incidence of egocentric and immature responses (indicating such behavior as impulsiveness, easy irritability, and suggestibility) was very high. Levine concluded that there was evidence of an impoverished capacity for inner creation, a meagerness of inner life, and an absence of the inner controls that should develop from it.

Levine's findings have been supported in a variety of ways by the projective tests administered to other groups of deaf children by several investigators. For example, Hess (1960) describes his 28 deaf subjects, between 8 and 10 years of age, as being more rigid in new situations and less aware of the individuality of others. They were seen as being more impulsive and more egocentric, and as having more superficial interpersonal contacts in comparison to 48 "well adjusted" and 49 "maladjusted" hearing children.

The Make-A-Picture-Story Test (Schneidman, 1952) used in the Hess study was also used by Bindon (1957) and by Neyhus (1964), with results that support those of Levine and Hess in a number of respects. Bindon administered the test to groups of rubella-deaf, non-rubella-deaf, and normal-hearing 15-year-olds. She found no differences between the rubella and non-rubella groups. However, when she compared the records of the rubella-deaf to those of the normal-hearing group, the responses of these deaf children were rated inferior in terms of maturity; they were typical of the responses of much younger children. Analyzing the Make-A-Picture-Story Test responses of 80 deaf adults, aged 18 to 65 (37 years average) Neyhus (1964) concluded that the personality pattern that emerged was one reflecting restriction in breadth of experience, rigidity and confusion in thought processes, and an inability to integrate experiences in meaningful ways. He also found evidence of feelings of social isolation and difficulties in forming interpersonal relationships. However, Neyhus and the other authors who have studied personality in deaf persons stated that there was little or no evidence of overt mental illness.

Three more recent studies of personality development of deaf subjects have been reported, and all make some use of projective tests (Levine and Wagner, 1974; Harris, 1975; Altshuler and others, 1976). The research projects reported by Harris and by the Altshuler group were designed specifically to investigate impulsivity in deaf individuals; the research of Levine and Wagner is more general in nature but has important implications for the understanding of impulse control. Harris summarizes the concept of impulse control as "an ability to plan ahead in a careful and organized manner, tolerate frustration, sublimate aggressive and libidinal impulses into socially acceptable outlets, delay one's needs and wishes for a more rewarding long-term plan, and utilize intellectual energies to enhance coping." Altshuler (1974) has characterized the deaf patients seen in clinical settings as more impulsive generally than hearing patients, exhibiting a good deal of "short-sighted action and a relative lack of internalized controls."

Altshuler and his colleagues studied 450 adolescents, almost evenly divided among Yugoslav and American high school students, profoundly deaf and with normal hearing. Several indicators of impulsivity were derived from a battery of tests including the Porteus Maze Test, the Draw-a-Line Test, the Id-Ego-Superego Test, and the Rorschach Test. The authors used a sophisticated but unconventional method for the quantitative analysis of their data, and concluded that both American and Yugoslav deaf groups were "more impulsive" than their hearing counterparts. Score levels across the two countries were "remarkably consistent," "with the Yugoslavs starting in each case from a higher baseline of impulsivity than the Americans" (Altshuler and others, 1976, p. 341). In the introduction to this paper, the authors state that their study was designed to decide "whether greater impulsivity is an unavoidable accompaniment of early total deafness." We would assume that their conclusion leads them to answer this question in the affirmative. However, the study reported by Harris, and the work reported by Levine and Wagner, would lead us to a less sweeping conclusion, and suggest that there are important reservations about the impact of auditory deprivation on personality development.

Harris designed a project to investigate impulsivity, using four indicators derived from the Draw-a-Man and the Matching Familiar Figures Test to compare 50 deaf children with deaf parents to 274 children from hearing parents. With age, socioeconomic status, and IQ test scores controlled, the deaf children with deaf parents consistently had scores reflecting greater impulse control than the deaf children of hearing parents. (Regardless of parental hearing status, these scores were positively correlated with scores on tests of academic achievement.) Harris suggests that his results may reflect the early communication experienced by the children with deaf parents, helping them to "develop cognitive and syntactic structures that lead to an ability to modulate impulses more constructively."

The third study in this group (Levine and Wagner, 1974) was designed to study personality development in deaf persons by means of the Hand Test (Wagner, 1962). This is a projective test consisting of 9 drawings of hands in ambiguous positions, about which subjects are asked to respond by telling the examiner what the hands appear to be doing. Four groups of young deaf adults were selected, representing a variety of adjustment modes: (1) exceptional linguistic and educational attainment; (2) marginal attainment (functionally illiterate); (3) typical attainment (6.9 was the mean grade level achievement for reading); and (4) hospitalized mental patients diagnosed as psychotic. Nineteen categories are used for scoring responses to the Hand Test, plus five categories derived from these, or scored from the total protocol. There were highly significant differences between the four subgroups on 20 of the 24 variables. "The vast differences among the four groups would seem to corroborate what workers with the deaf have known all along: personalities of 'the deaf' are divergent and deaf persons should not be lumped together solely on the basis of their auditory handicap" (Levine and Wagner, 1974, p. 1203). The authors conclude that the scores for the group classified as "exceptional" are remarkably consistent with the teenage norms for the test. The protocols of the psychotic deaf group resemble those of hearing schizophrenic and organic patients tested at a state mental hospital. The deaf group classified as illiterate produced almost twice the number of responses as any of the normative groups, possibly reflecting a "compulsive need to structure every facet of the environment" or denoting an "obsessive flow of ideas." "It therefore seems possible to conceptualize the illiterate deaf as a group of people who, seriously handicapped by difficulties in verbal communication, have been forced to forsake inner development and have been driven to compulsive attempts to establish and maintain 'facade' or book-of-etiquette contact with their external surroundings."

One variable that did *not* differentiate the four groups of deaf subjects in this study was a derived or combination variable called Acting Out Score. This means that there were no significant differences between any two of the four groups. Since acting-out could be equated with impulsivity, it bears additional attention, in view of the findings in the Harris and Altshuler studies discussed above. Wagner and Levine interpret this as suggesting that deaf people as a whole are not prone to strike out aggressively against others. However, their scoring category labeled "aggression," and taken directly from the test responses, differentiates among the four subgroups at the .00001 level of significance (p. 1202). The acting-out score is a complex one, derived by dividing the sum of three separate scoring categories by the sum of an additional two. It could be that this process yields a composite that has a meaning different from that labeled acting-out for the normative population.

In their monograph, Levine and Wagner stress again and again the interdependence of communication and personality development:

> The deaf no less than the non-deaf need to have all the languages that humans use in social encounters, and these include the whole range of levels of language from bodily contacts and movements to gestures and speech. It can be reasoned, therefore, that those deaf persons whose language abilities suffice for and are used to effect enculturation are, through this circumstance, enabled to overcome the potential adaptive handicaps of deafness; and that those at the other end of the language range, the illiterate deaf, who it must be stressed are aurally as well as linguistically illiterate, are only lightly touched by the culture

in which they live, and will thereby be severely marred psychologically by the deprivations thus experienced. These assumptions appear to be borne out by the Hand Test findings (Levine and Wagner, 1974, p. 1231).

*Summary*

1. Many independent studies, conducted over a period of 40 years, have found deaf children to be less socially mature than hearing children. Deaf children of deaf parents have been found to be relatively more mature than the deaf children of hearing parents with whom they were compared. Residential school life appears to be related to social immaturity as well. A number of findings indicate that parents of handicapped children generally, and deaf children specifically, are reluctant to grant them the freedom and independence that would encourage independence and consequent maturity. These attitudes are often coupled with strong pressures for achievement, as in the area of speech training, which is particularly difficult for the deaf child. The didactic and intrusive nature of the mothers' interactions with their deaf children may be induced by a realistic assessment of reduced coping ability in the child. These interaction patterns may then lead to exacerbated dependence and even more retarded social maturity in the deaf child.

2. Delayed language acquisition experienced by most deaf children leads to more limited opportunities for social interaction and to frustration for them and their parents. An inability to communicate future plans limits the child, his parents, and his peers in structuring social life. They are handicapped in dealing with the qualities of objects and with abstract relationships. Imaginary play is limited; reference to internal events and the expression of necessity and possibility are difficult. These linguistic features contribute to the reduced and constrained nature of the social interactions of deaf children.

3. Studies comparing the self-concept or self-image of deaf children to that of hearing peers indicate that the deaf children's ideas about themselves are perhaps inaccurate; they have inflated ideas about their capabilities and the opinions others have of them. Self-image studies of subgroups of deaf children have shown that the deaf children of deaf parents feel more positively about themselves than the deaf children of hearing parents with whom they were compared. Deaf children with hearing parents who attend residential schools have less positive self-concepts than their cohorts who attend day schools. This suggests that the opportunity to use adult deaf teachers and dormitory counselors as models may be important for the deaf children to develop positive feelings about themselves.

4. Personality inventories have consistently shown that deaf children have more adjustment problems than hearing children. When deaf children without overt or serious problems have been studied, they have been found to exhibit characteristics of rigidity, egocentricity, absence of inner controls, impulsiveness, and suggestibility.

5. In spite of consistencies in findings of personality studies, it would be a mistake to conclude that there is a single "deaf personality type." There is much diversity among deaf people, and it is related to education, communication, and experience.

# CHAPTER FIVE

# Behavioral Problems of Deaf Children

**T**HE relative psychological and social adjustment of deaf children is an area of great theoretical interest and tremendous practical importance. Theoretically, our questions revolve around a concern with environmental influences on deaf children that may lead to differences in their emotional development reflected in problematic behavior. A theoretical understanding is important for effective intervention, whether preventive or ameliorative. In this chapter, studies of the prevalence and the type of behavioral problems of deaf children are reviewed. They will show that there are many difficulties of definition inherent in any effort to estimate or to specify the extent to which any population group is subject to emotional or behavioral problems.

Mental health and mental illness can be seen as two ends of a continuum that can be defined in terms of gradations of emotional problems reflected in behavior. The diagnosis, the description, the label, or the definition of a behavioral problem is influenced greatly by the professional discipline of the person describing or defining the behavior. A child may be considered to be "mentally ill" by a psychiatrist, "emotionally disturbed" by a psychologist, or "behavior disordered" by a special educator (Hobbs, 1975, p. 57). That same child may be regarded by a sociologist as stigmatized and handicapped further by the very labels applied by helping professionals. Each of the diagnostic terms implies assumptions about the cause of the problem, about the kind of treatment to be applied, and about the prognosis for improvement. For example, "mental illness" is a term more likely to be utilized by professionals whose training concentrated within the medical sciences and who are more likely to prescribe drugs for the treatment of the difficulty.

The process of identifying and classifying the behavioral symptoms of both children and adults has long been recognized as a serious business with important implications for treatment and cure. Professionals have studied different systems and their consequences over a long period. A useful review of the existing systems of classification of emotional disorders in children has been written by Prugh, Engel, and Morse (1975). A study of the definitions and rates of prevalence for a wide variety of children's handicapping conditions was undertaken and recently published as a two-volume study. Classification of the various conditions was considered to be so important that the set was entitled *The Futures of Children* (Hobbs, 1975). According to estimates made by the Joint Commission on Mental Health, there are 1,400,000 children in the United States in need of psychiatric care. Of these children, 100,000 are receiving treatment in residential centers; over 500,000 are receiving special education because of their emotional or behavioral difficulties. Hobbs (1975, p. 58) points out that emotional disturbance is most difficult to diagnose in its mild and moderate forms. While professionals and lay persons alike may agree in the identification of a seriously disturbed child, there will still be a considerable difference of opinion on what his condition should be called.

CLASSIFICATION OF BEHAVIOR PROBLEMS. A specific diagnostic label, in and of itself, can be detrimental to a child. Thus, the practice of attaching any formal classification has been attacked by some who have concern for the possible violation of human rights. Even though there is much disagreement among professionals about the specific meaning of particular diagnostic categories, once a label has been attached to a child, it usually remains in his files or records that follow him from one school or treatment center to another. The danger of attaching diagnostic labels to children applies not only to those with extreme problems but perhaps even more to children with mild and moderate problems. Mild and moderate problems may represent short-term responses to immediate situations; when the child's situation improves, the problematic behavior may also improve. However, if a label has been attached to his behavior, the label itself may influence the responses others make to the child, thereby reinforcing his troublesome ways of dealing with difficult situations.

The classification of behavior problems of children encourages a static view of a behavior that may be tied to different rates of development or maturity. The traditional approach to the classification of childhood mental disorders was derived from and is associated with the classification of adult disorders. Professionals may be tempted to view the child as a miniature adult, thereby ignoring developmental patterns that reflect maturational lags. This approach may also encourage the fallacy that disturbance in childhood leads inevitably to disturbance in adulthood (Phillips, Draguns, and Bartlett, 1975, p. 40).

While there are dangers inherent in labeling or classifying behavior as "problematic," "abnormal," "deviant," or "exceptional," there are some positive reasons for classification. If services are to be provided for children who need them, it is necessary to know who the children are, what kinds of problems they have, and what kinds of special treatment can help them. Teachers and school administrators, the professionals who have most direct contact with the children and are most familiar with their special problems, can inform legislators and administrators of state and federal agencies about the kinds of attention needed by these special children.

Those most often concerned with the classification of children are those whose motivation is grounded in an ideology of help and service rather than of punishment (Rains and others, 1975, p. 90). This is in contrast with other kinds of classification of persons who are seen as deviant (for example, the sexual psychopath, the vagrant, and the drug addict). However, in both cases, the interests of the persons who perform the classification are sometimes served by defining larger numbers of exceptional children as needing services and larger numbers of deviant adults as warranting punishment. A system of checks and balances is needed to insure that the judgment of the diagnosticians is not influenced by self-interest in the eventual provision of services and correctional systems.

One criticism often made of classifying or labeling those who are "different" is that attaching a label can be the first step to confinement of an individual in an institution. Once the person is officially designated by a label that defines him as unmanageable within the community, he is placed on a track that channels him to a setting where his behavior can be managed. For the criminal, the managing institution is the jail; for the mentally ill, it is the mental hospital. A proper and humane concern for the rights of individuals, therefore, centers on the eventual result of having applied a label.

A possible, and unintended, consequence of attaching a label to an individual is the reduction in the possible alternatives for special services. This can happen to a young child—especially to a young deaf child—who is diagnosed as "emotionally disturbed." The application of this label may be the signal for his exclusion from school, the most significant institution outside his family that is available to him. Once a deaf child has been labeled as emotionally disturbed and excluded from school, the burden for his further care becomes exclusively the concern of his family. The emotionally disturbed deaf child becomes so exceptional that he fits into no existing program. There are very few alternatives for him. Deaf children with emotional problems are disqualified from most established educational programs. They are excluded from programs for deaf children because of their behavioral difficulties; they are excluded from programs for emotionally disturbed children because of their deafness. Their exclusion from both kinds of programs may stem from a complex mixture of objective and subjective, rational and irrational reasons. Specialists in the education of emotionally disturbed children may be frightened of deafness. A major tool in the treatment of emotional disturbance is language or communication. A child who is unable to communicate because of a physical condition represents a dual threat to a professional whose basic skills are based on language. On the other hand, it is unreasonable to expect a teacher to absorb a child with special needs into a group that already makes unusual demands on energy and skill.

The pattern of delivery of services is firmly entrenched in governmental units no larger than a single state. Parents of these doubly special children are widely dispersed geographically. Their abilities to form cohesive groups for purposes of advocacy are therefore more limited. It is a sad fact that most new programs for handicapped children have been developed as a result of pressure from parents rather than from action by professionals, administrators, or legislators. Parents are often forced to spend much of their time approaching administrators to beg for the kinds of opportunities that should be guaranteed. All children with special needs within already special groups have difficulty receiving equal opportunity. These children are among those who will benefit most from a new law passed by Congress in 1975 (P.L. 94–142). This law is to ensure free appropriate public education for every handicapped child.

One reason for passage of the law was the finding that of eight million handicapped children in the United States, four million were not receiving appropriate education, and one million were found to be excluded completely from educational or treatment programs (Rosen, Skinski, and Pimentel, 1977). Those most likely to be excluded are those with combinations of severe handicaps—for example, severely emotionally disturbed children who are also profoundly deaf.

In this discussion of the difficulties that face the emotionally disturbed deaf child and his parents, the ironies of the pros and cons of labeling are illustrated clearly. If a child is not defined as "extra special," he has no chance to receive the extra special services he needs. However, if he is defined as "extra special," some existing but less specialized resources may be removed. Often the only workable answer in this double-bind situation evolves from the creative application of definitions by administrators who combine expertise with compassion.

The behavior of the child who is likely to be labeled either to his detriment or for his benefit has importance in consideration of the classification of disorders. The child who is active, impulsive, and aggressive is more likely to be labeled as emotionally disturbed than the one who is shy, withdrawn, and uncommunicative. Our culture values and encourages behavior that is quiet, polite, and easy to manage. If a child says nothing and bothers no one, he may be considered a model of good behavior.

This cultural attitude is reflected in the differential rates of emotional disturbance and behavioral problems that are reported for boys and for girls. Consistently, higher rates are shown for males than for females. Parents expect, or permit, or encourage their sons to be more active and more aggressive than their daughters. If this heightened activity goes beyond the bounds permitted at school, teachers are then more likely to label boys as behavioral problems.

The kinds of behavior labeled as disturbed may be related to specific expectations, preferences, temperaments, and abilities of *individual* teachers and parents. As children's disorders are more likely to be defined in terms of social relations than in terms of intrapsychic symptoms, the perception of the "deviant child" almost always occurs in a context of adult expectations of acceptable patterns of behavior. These expectations may be idiosyncratic to a particular adult, and may reflect a judgmental evaluation of a child's behavior that might not be considered justified by everyone (Phillips, Draguns, and Bartlett, 1975). An active, responsive child may fulfill the expectations of one adult whereas another adult might find the same child unmanageable. The judgments of children's behavior made by both teachers and parents agree with those made by mental health professionals (Berlin, 1967; Bower, 1958). It has been shown that parents are good diagnosticians of their children's developmental lags (Knobloch, cited in Hobbs, 1975), as well as of their children's deafness (Fellendorf and Harrow, 1970; Freeman, 1977).

## Studies of the Prevalence of Behavioral Problems of Deaf Children

In reviewing prevalence studies of behavior problems in deaf children, it is essential to know both the definitions of problematic behavior that are used and the identities of those making the assessments. Although Rainer, Altshuler, Kallmann, and their colleagues at the New York Psychiatric Institute (1966, 1969, 1971) and Vernon (1969b, 1969c) have documented the prevalence of extreme behavioral disorders in a deaf population, only scattered attempts have been made to enumerate the hearing impaired children who are institutionalized because of mental illness (Goulder and Trybus, 1977). The dearth of information reflects the relative lack of interest in, knowledge about, and provisions for emotionally disturbed deaf children. It is generally agreed that there is a large number of children who could legitimately be classified in this way. Schein (1975, p. 93) states that the "high rate of emotional problems has been described as being of 'epidemic proportions.' " The few studies that have been reported have been conducted on children who are enrolled in schools for the deaf. Thus those children who have been excluded from schools precisely because they are emotionally disturbed were not included in the studies. Schein (1975) reported that in one suburban county nearly 10 percent of school-age deaf children were not enrolled in an educational program because they had emotional or behavioral problems too severe to be managed in existing classrooms. Vernon (1969a) reported that 9 percent of the students enrolled in the school that he studied had been dropped because of severe emotional problems. These two sources would indicate that the prevalence studies to be discussed probably show rates that are below the true prevalence of behavioral problems in deaf children.

Five sources of data yielding estimates of the prevalence of behavioral problems in deaf children will now be summarized. These studies indicate rates of behavioral disturbance ranging from about 8 percent to more than 22 percent. A review of the individual studies illustrates a number of problems concerning the base population surveyed, the definitions and methods of assessing problematic behavior, and the identity of the person making the determination about any particular child.

1. ANNUAL SURVEY OF HEARING IMPAIRED CHILDREN AND YOUTH. This survey is conducted as part of a continuing research and statistical program at Gallaudet College. All programs in the United States known to be providing special education and related services to hearing impaired children are contacted annually and asked to submit a variety of information on enrolled children. Participation in the

Survey is voluntary, and data are received on about 80 percent of the target population in any one year.

Schools are asked to report, among other items, whether the child has an "educationally significant emotional-behavioral problem." (In the first two years of the Survey, these two items were listed separately, resulting in double-counting of some children.) In the school years 1970–1971 through 1975–1976, the proportion of children listed as having emotional or behavioral problems declined slightly: the percentage of the total was 9.6 percent in 1970–1971 (Gentile and McCarthy, 1973), compared to 8.4 percent in 1975–1976 (Meadow and Trybus, 1979).

It is important to remember that the Annual Survey data are obtained from schools, and represent an educational view of emotional disturbance, based on the need to provide special accommodations and services for the children so labeled. This educational orientation is evident in the fact that the determination of the emotional-behavioral disturbance was usually made by the child's teacher (43 percent) or by a psychologist (37 percent). The diagnosis was made by a physician in the remaining 20 percent of the cases in which the diagnostician was known.

Two of the studies of deaf children from which prevalence rates for behavioral problems can be computed were conducted at state residential schools for the deaf (Vernon, 1969a; Schlesinger and Meadow, 1972). The focus of Vernon's study was an investigation of the causes of deafness and the prevalence of additional handicaps as these are related to measures of the functional abilities of deaf children. The study reported by Schlesinger and Meadow was designed specifically to provide an estimate of the prevalence of behavioral disorders in students at a particular residential school for the purpose of planning to meet mental health needs.

Both these studies are subject to the advantages and the limitations imposed by the selective nature of the population of deaf children enrolled in state residential schools. One advantage stems from the fact that there is a fairly large population base on which prevalence rates can be computed. Vernon used school records pertaining to all children who were admitted or evaluated by school personnel over an 11-year period (N = 1,468). This enabled him to select the 358 children whose deafness was caused by one of five specific conditions (maternal rubella, meningitis, prematurity, complications from Rh factor, or heredity). The enrollment at the school in the Schlesinger and Meadow study was 516.

Some of the characteristics of residential schools may lead to overestimates of the prevalence of behavioral problems in deaf students; others may lead to underestimates. The fact that these schools are public schools means that they are less selective in their enrollment criteria than most private schools. In spite of the mandate to provide educational services for all, most public schools still exclude children whose physical or emotional problems are severe, or whose intellectual potential makes the educational program inappropriate for them. Compared to day schools and classes, residential schools probably have more students whose parents are deaf. State residential schools may also have a disproportionate number of children from rural areas and from unstable families or broken homes. (This is because a residential school placement may be viewed more positively by single parents who have the entire responsibility of caring for a handicapped child.) These factors might influence the prevalence rate for behavioral problems. The point here is that whenever rates are reported based on a single school population, or on a population with a known selective bias, the data must be interpreted with caution.

The two studies conducted in residential schools made use of teachers for evaluating the students' behavior. In addition, the Schlesinger-Meadow study used dormitory counselors' evaluations. Vernon used school records and also administered psychological tests.

2. THE SCHLESINGER-MEADOW SURVEY. This survey was designed specifically for the purpose of identifying those children at a state residential school who were considered by their teachers or dormitory counselors to be severely emotionally disturbed and in need of psychiatric treatment. This particular definition was selected because the survey was to be used as one basis for defining the extent of the need for mental health services and as justification for a request for funding these services. The survey form that was used gave school personnel the choice of identifying children either as severely disturbed and in need of psychiatric help or as "not severely disturbed, but whose behavior necessitates a disproportionate share of the teacher's time or requires other special attention." There were two reasons for this choice: (1) By giving raters an option for identifying less severely disturbed children, it was believed that more confidence could be placed in the judgments on the more severely disturbed children. (2) By using the same format that had been used previously in a mental health survey conducted in Los Angeles County (State of California, 1960), a comparative base for this survey was provided. Teachers and counselors were not asked to attach specific behaviors to individual children. However, the survey forms included some suggestions about the kinds of behaviors that might lead school personnel to identify a child needing treatment or disproportionate care. Behaviors included being withdrawn from peers, overly dependent, hyperactive, accident prone, overly aggressive, and having truancy records, nervous habits such as tics, and chronic illnesses without identifiable physical causes.

Of the 516 students in the school, 11.6 percent were considered to be severely disturbed and in need of psychiatric treatment. An additional 19.6 percent were considered to have behavioral problems leading to disproportionate demands on teachers' and counselors' time. Of all school children in Los Angeles County, 2.4 percent were identified as severely disturbed and an additional 7.3 percent as needing disproportionate time in the classroom. Thus the survey at the school for the deaf showed a prevalence of behavioral problems five and three times greater than the respective rates for the children in the Los Angeles County School system.

3. THE VERNON STUDY. Vernon (1969a) studied the relationship between the etiology of deafness and the nature of secondary disabilities in children who attended or who received preadmission evaluations at one state residential school for the deaf from 1953 until 1964. This study included assessments of the psychological adjustment of some of the children. Most of Vernon's data are based on children for whom there was firm evidence that their deafness resulted from one of the following causes: heredity, Rh factor complications, prematurity, meningitis, or maternal rubella. Thus he eliminated from his data all children whose deafness was caused by other factors (32 percent of the total school population) or by unknown factors (30 percent of the total). Of the 413 students evaluated for admission at the school by a psychologist, 93 or 22.5 percent were classified as having severe emotional problems. Twenty-one of this number (5.1 percent) were diagnosed as psychotic. Teachers rated 358 current students for psychological adjustment (superior-above average-average-below average-poor). Twenty-one percent were given the rating of "poor." There was wide variation by etiology, however: hereditary, 10 percent; Rh factor, 15 percent; premature, 27 percent; meningitic, 12 percent; rubella, 31 percent.

The last two studies to be discussed in detail were both conducted outside the United States. One was done as part of a larger study of the education, health, and behavior of school-age children living on the Isle of Wight; the other was concerned specifically with deaf children living in the Greater Vancouver area, British Columbia.

4. DEAF CHILDREN ON THE ISLE OF WIGHT. The Isle of Wight, situated four miles off the coast of England, was selected for a comprehensive study of handicapping conditions of all children living there (Rutter, Tizard, and Whitmore, 1970). This is an extremely important study for all those interested in any aspect of physical, intellectual, or emotional deficiencies in children because of the completeness of the survey and the care with which the research was conducted. A series of surveys carried out in 1964 and 1965 examined the relationship between various kinds of handicapping conditions. Elaborate case-finding and testing techniques were developed to investigate each of several questions.

In the study of organic brain dysfunction and child psychiatric disorder (Graham and Rutter, 1968), subgroups were selected from within the total population of 11,685 children aged 5 to 14. These subgroups included: (1) children with brain disorders (epilepsy, cerebral palsy, and other disorders indicating "lesions above the brain stem"); (2) children with physical disorders not involving the brain; and (3) a random sample of the general population of 10- and 11-year-olds without any physical handicaps. These groups of children were carefully screened and examined by medical teams for their physical condition. The psychiatric status of the children was studied by means of (1) behavioral questionnaires completed by teachers; (2) similar questionnaires completed by parents; (3) interviews with parents about the children's behavior, relationships, and emotions; and (4) a psychiatric examination of the children. Based on these data, a determination was made of the presence or absence of psychiatric disorder in each child.

The rate of psychiatric disorder in the Isle of Wight children ranged from 6.6 percent for the general population of nonhandicapped children to a high of 58.3 percent for children who had signs of brain disorder that included fits. Deaf children showed a rate of 15.4 percent, more than twice as high as that shown by the nonhandicapped children. It should be noted, however, that this rate is based only on the 13 deaf children included in the study population. This is a drawback of this particular study for those specifically interested in the relationship of sensory disability and psychiatric disorder. Large general populations will include only a few deaf or blind children because of the low incidence of these handicaps. The approach used by the Vancouver group, discussed below, is more useful for our purposes because the initial criterion for including a child in the study was the existence of a profound hearing loss.

5. THE VANCOUVER STUDY. One of the most important studies for assessing the prevalence of behavioral problems in deaf children is the one conducted by Freeman, Malkin, and Hastings (1975) of all deaf children living in the Greater Vancouver area. The results of this study have special credence for the following reasons. (1) All deaf children between the ages of 5 and 15, representing a number of different schools, were included as subjects. The authors believe that only a few cases "escaped their net" (p. 392); therefore, the danger of bias from the elimination of subjects with specifically behavioral problems is less severe. (2) The number of children (N = 120) is large enough for figures to have relatively good reliability. (3) The investigators are specialists in problems of deafness, and thus sophisticated about the kinds of information that are critical and about the methodological pitfalls to be avoided.

(4) The identification of children with behavioral problems was done by combining the judgments of parents, teachers, and medical records, and thereby avoids the danger of idiosyncratic bias in the identification of individual children. (5) A control group of children with normal hearing, matched with the deaf children for age, sex, and neighborhood, was included.

A behavioral rating scale completed by parents and teachers was used as a major source for the global ratings reported as psychiatric disorders. This scale was a slightly modified version of the one used by Rutter and his associates in the Isle of Wight study. Some of the items included on this scale were: frequency of temper tantrums, toileting accidents, truancy, stealing, eating problems, restlessness, fighting, disobedience, excessive fearfulness, and bullying (Rutter, Tizard, and Whitmore, 1970, pp. 419–421).

On the global ratings that incorporated scales completed by parents and teachers, 22.6 percent of the Vancouver deaf children were judged to have a psychiatric disorder of moderate or severe degree. Those with a major impairment (6.1 percent) included children who had no social relations, exhibited bizarre behavior, were extremely anxious, or who were persistently involved in major delinquency (Freeman and others, 1975, p. 396).

## Comparisons of Prevalence Rates for Deaf and for Hearing Children

How do the rates of psychiatric disturbance or emotional-behavioral problems among the deaf children in these five studies compare to the prevalence of behavioral problems among children in the general population?

The Joint Commission on Mental Health of Children (1970) estimated that 2 percent of young people under 25 "are severely disturbed and need immediate psychiatric care. Another 8 to 10 percent are in need of help from mental health workers." The Schlesinger-Meadow report reflects a rate of severe emotional disturbance that is about five times that of the estimate of the Joint Commission and of the Los Angeles County public schools; the rate of less severe behavioral problems is two to three times as high as the comparative estimates for the general population. Freeman, Malkin, and Hastings give no specific comparative rates of psychiatric disturbance for the deaf and hearing children who participated in their study. However, they remark that their results on the type and frequency of behavioral problems are "generally in keeping" with other findings reviewed, including the Schlesinger-Meadow survey (p. 402). They report: "As compared with the hearing children, the deaf children were significantly more likely to be rated by their mothers as restless, possessive, overly dependent, disobedient, overly particular or fussy, showing distressing habits, destroying belongings of others, and having stolen things" (p. 396).

The only source that shows rates somewhat lower than the others is the Office of Demographic Studies, Annual Survey of Hearing-Impaired Children and Youth. The Annual Survey conducted in 1972–1973 was the basis for a separate report on emotional-behavioral problems among the children enrolled in the surveyed schools (Jensema and Trybus, 1975). About 3,400 (7.9 percent) of the 44,000 children included in this report were identified as exhibiting emotional-behavioral problems. Altshuler (1975) had the opportunity to check the reporting that was done by one school to the Office of Demographic Studies. As psychiatric consultant, he had been asked to evaluate 40 children from the school during the course of nine months. Only one-third of those referred children had been designated as emotionally-behaviorally disturbed in the report that the school had sent to the O.D.S. "Extrapolating nationwide we can be reasonably sure that the 8 percent estimate is a marked underrepresentation" (p. 4). This discrepancy may indicate that teachers and school administrators are more

reluctant to "label" a child when they assume that the
labeling is solely for research purposes than when they
believe that this procedure may lead to some actual help in
the management of a child with behavioral difficulties in
the classroom.

This point of view differs from that taken by Furth (1973)
in his discussion of the high rates of behavioral disorders
reported by Schlesinger and Meadow. Furth believes that
teachers in schools for the deaf tend to exaggerate the severity of the behavioral problems of their pupils and that
the high prevalence rates reflect the "attitudes of hearing
adults rather than the disturbed personalities of the deaf
children" (p. 82). Even considering the possibility of such a
bias, the evidence available in the surveys and studies
conducted to date would seem sufficient to conclude that
the rate of behavioral problems among deaf children is significantly higher than in the general population of school-
age children.

## Types of Behavior Problems
## Observed in Deaf Children

It is common for deaf children and deaf adults to be
described as lacking in social and emotional maturity.
Levine (1956) has described emotional immaturity in deaf
adolescent girls as being characterized by "egocentricity,
easy irritability, impulsiveness, and suggestibility." Hess
(1960) had similar findings in a group of 8- to 10-year-old
children. Myklebust (1960) found that deaf persons were
immature in "caring for others." Altshuler (1974) and
Rainer and others (1969) characterized deaf patients as
demonstrating "egocentricity, a lack of empathy, depen-
dency." Lewis (1968) summarized current opinions and
findings on the "personality traits" of deaf children by
noting that they are often described as immature in self-
awareness, egocentric, lacking in self-confidence and initiative, and tending to be rigid. Some of these and other

descriptions resulted from clinicians' experiences with deaf patients; others resulted from inventories such as the Vineland Social Maturity Scale (Doll, 1965). Streng and Kirk (1938), Avery (1948), Burchard and Myklebust (1942), and Schlesinger and Meadow (1972) all found that deaf children scored lower than hearing children of comparable ages on scales that equate maturity with self-help skills.

Behavioral symptom checklists that parents and teachers complete are also used to describe behavioral problems in deaf children. Such ratings were the basis for most of the prevalence studies cited in previous sections of this chapter. Reivich and Rothrock (1972) analyzed one set of behavioral ratings completed by teachers in a state residential school for the deaf in an effort to summarize the kinds of behavior most often checked by teachers to describe their deaf students. By using a computer they were able to complete a minute analysis of the traits that were considered to be present in at least 10 percent of the 327 students rated. The three groupings of traits which seemed to account for most of the disturbed behavior were traits related to unacceptable conduct and usually labeled as hyperactive lack of control, as traits related to personality and labeled as "anxious inhibition," or as traits related to immaturity and labeled as "preoccupation." Hyperactive lack of control was further described as behavior that was impulsive, unreflective, and uninhibited.

Another method of evaluating personality is by means of psychological tests. Levine (1956) used the Rorschach test with a group of adolescent deaf girls. More recently, she used the Hand Test in an effort to describe personality patterns in a group of deaf persons (Levine and Wagner, 1974).

One measure of the presence of serious behavioral problems that has considerable face validity is the child's referral to a mental health professional for treatment. If the mental health professional concurs in the recommendation and the parent agrees to cooperate in the treatment plan, there are, in effect, three persons familiar with the child who believe that his problems are severe enough to require intervention. This measure is possible only when appropriate care is available in the community where the child lives. Also, another difficulty is created in attempting to use the criterion of psychiatric referral with large survey populations. Deaf people do not have equal access to mental health treatment facilities, because of the geographical distribution of their relatively small population and because of the almost total absence of programs for training specialists to work with deaf persons of any age. However, it seemed a reasonable index of the presence of serious behavioral problems in a recent study by Meadow (1976a). Interviews were conducted with the parents of deaf and hearing children participating in a longitudinal study. Data were generated from information on referrals for psychiatric treatment, reflecting a global judgment of several persons familiar with the child, and from a Behavior Symptom Checklist, reflecting the parents' assessment of their child's behavior in a series of 19 discrete items.

Of the forty deaf children included in the study, eight, or 20 percent, were either receiving psychiatric treatment or had been referred for treatment. By contrast, only one of the twenty hearing children (5 percent) was receiving psychiatric treatment. Three additional deaf children (7.5 percent) had received psychiatric treatment in the past.

On the Behavior Symptom Checklist scores, however, there were no significant differences between the deaf and the hearing children. Fewer than 10 percentage points separated the deaf from the hearing children on ten of the nineteen items. These included the child's classroom participation, presence of nervous habits, failure to cooperate at home (more than half of the children were viewed as uncooperative by their parents), unacceptable ways of gaining attention, frequent illnesses, fits of temper, short attention span, sleep disturbances, and eating too much.

The deaf and the hearing children were separated by 10 or more percentage points on nine of the items. The deaf children were viewed as having more difficulties in peer friendships than the hearing children. Forty percent of the hearing children were seen as too anxious to please others, compared to 25 percent of the deaf children. Thirty percent of the hearing children had some problem with physical aggressiveness, compared to 20 percent of the deaf children. Forty-five percent of the parents with hearing children saw them as often tense or anxious, compared to 25 percent for the deaf children. On the two items dealing with finicky eating habits, the deaf children were much more likely to be seen as problematic by their parents: 60 percent of the deaf children were considered by their parents as too particular about the kinds of food they would eat, compared to 35 percent of the hearing children.

An explanation for this discrepancy in the prevalence of problem behavior in deaf and hearing children, as measured by the checklist scores and as reflected in the referrals for treatment, evolves from a global assessment of the content of the parent interviews. Generally speaking, the mothers of the hearing children seemed to express more concern for problematic behavior patterns in their children, to take the teachers' and mental health professionals' suggestions more seriously, and to worry more about their children's mental health. The mothers of the deaf children, by contrast, appeared to minimize the extent and the meaning of behavior that might reflect emotional problems in their children. A further explanation for the discrepancy is contained in a comparison of the ratings given to boys and to girls in the deaf and hearing groups. Mean scores were highest (indicating the greatest number of problem behaviors) for the hearing boys, with the deaf boys second, the deaf girls third, and the hearing girls fourth.

The larger numbers of behavior problems exhibited by

both the deaf and the hearing boys, compared to the girls, is a familiar finding, bearing out many other studies. The differing score distributions of the deaf and the hearing boys is of some interest, however. When scores were split so that three nearly equal groups were formed, it was seen that the deaf boys scored in either the high or the low group, with very few in the middle group. The hearing boys were concentrated in the high-score category, where three-quarters were found, with one-quarter in the low-score category. The deaf girls were evenly divided in the high, the medium, and the low categories. The hearing girls were concentrated around the median, with one-third in the low category and none in the high, most problematic, group.

Three items included on the Behavior Symptom Checklist were considered relevant for deaf children but not for children with normal hearing. These items related to avoidance of eye contact, noisy screeching or shrieking, and the production of other kinds of noises potentially disturbing to others. Only seven of the forty deaf children (18 percent) were seen by their parents as having a problem with eye contact avoidance. However, the mean Behavior Symptom Checklist scores for these seven children were a full 10 points higher than those for children with no problem of eye contact avoidance ($p < .001$). Four of these seven children were receiving psychiatric treatment, and a fifth had been evaluated for treatment earlier. More than half the deaf children were seen as having a problem with the production of disturbing noises and noisy shrieking. The overall mean for those children having some problem with noisy shrieking was 10 points higher than that for the others. Seven of the eight deaf children currently referred for or receiving psychiatric treatment were seen as having problems with noise-making. This is an especially interesting kind of symptom for deaf children, since it might be felt that they would be unable to control their noise-making because they are less likely to be aware of it. The fact that it could be defined as a psychiatric symptom indicates that it is perhaps an index of the process of socialization. Two sources, from special populations, illustrate the distribution of kinds of behavioral disorders that are reflected in psychiatric diagnoses. One is Williams' (1970) classification of 51 children who were either students in or applicants to a school for emotionally disturbed deaf children in England. Williams points out that those children who are referred for admission are more likely to be those "whose maladjustment is disturbing to their environment" (Williams, 1970, p. 3). The psychiatric diagnosis with the largest proportion of children (43 percent) was that of "antisocial disorder." The next largest category was "childhood psychosis," accounting for about 20 percent of the group.

The second special group of deaf children for whom psychiatric diagnoses are available consists of 65 rubella children, subjects of a study conducted at the New York University Medical Center (Chess, Korn, and Fernandez, 1971). Psychiatric disorders were diagnosed in 3 of the 4 children who had a hearing loss of unspecified severity, in 7 of the 14 who had a moderate hearing loss, and in 16 of the 47 who had a severe hearing loss. Degree of hearing loss has seemed to be a factor in the symptoms displayed in other deaf populations. Vernon noted that "paranoid behavior or suspiciousness is probably somewhat more common among the deaf mentally ill than corresponding hearing populations. This seems especially true of the hard of hearing and the adventitiously deafened" (1969c, p.27).

The diagnosis of the largest single group of children in the Chess, Korn, and Fernandez study was "reactive behavior disorder." Some degree of mental retardation was found in 12 of these children, and 5 were found to be autistic. The authors point out that these rates are high relative to the general population (pp. 145–149). They also comment on the fact that children with multiple physical handicaps are more likely to receive a psychiatric diagnosis as well. In their study of a group of 243 rubella children, 73 percent of whom had a hearing defect, either alone or in combination with a visual, neurological, or cardiac defect, they found that 41.7 percent of the children with hearing defects alone had psychiatric disorders. This contrasted with 81.8 percent of those rubella children who had visual defects either alone or combined with neurological or cardiac defects. Of the children with both hearing and visual defects, 76.2 percent were diagnosed as having psychiatric disorders (Chess, Korn, and Fernandez, 1971, p. 52).

Rainer and Altshuler (1966 and 1971) had extensive experience in outpatient treatment of deaf adolescents and adults. Their descriptions of typical clusters of symptoms found in their deaf patients include a general lack of understanding and empathy for others, egocentricity, coercive demands to have their own wishes gratified, and a lack of awareness of the effect their behavior has on other people. There were many instances of impulsive "acting-out" kinds of behavior, with few instances of self-imposed restraint. The kinds of problems observed in adolescent students referred for treatment in a residential school for the deaf were characterized as "primary behavior disorders of childhood" and "adjustment reactions of adolescence." The boys aged 13 to 16 years seemed exceedingly preoccupied with violence and fears. Girls seemed somewhat more mature than the boys. Both boys and girls displayed wide lack of knowledge about relationships with the opposite sex and sexual functioning.

## The Genesis of Behavior Problems in Deaf Children

Ideas about the bases of behavioral problems and of mental illness depend to some extent on the training, experience, and general orientation of the individuals performing the diagnosis. Theories range from almost complete reliance on physiological or biochemical explanations to almost complete reliance on psychological or experiential explanations. However, most professionals would agree that some combination or interaction of physical, biological, social, and psychological factors is usually necessary to arrive at an understanding of abnormal behavior. The question of etiology is particularly confusing when deafness is involved, because some of the diseases or conditions that cause deafness may also cause other problems that result in behavioral disorders. For example, there are genetic syndromes in which deafness is combined with a complex of difficulties; high fevers that accompany diseases such as meningitis may cause both deafness and brain damage; complications in addition to deafness may result from incompatibility of blood types in parents and from maternal rubella (Vernon, 1969a; Mindel and Vernon, 1971). Furthermore, the interaction of physiological and psychological factors in the creation of conditions often described as "neurological impairment," "minimal brain dysfunction," or "hyperkinesis" is not fully understood. These terms have become catch phrases disguised as diagnoses and have been used to describe impairments in language, motor or sensory functioning, and intellectual abilities, all supposedly related to impairment of the central nervous system. Hobbs (1975, p. 75) remarks, "In the sense of a unitary syndrome, the concept of brain damage or neurological impairment is virtually useless."

Several authors of the prevalence studies described make it clear that they exercised extreme caution in ascribing the label or diagnosis of "brain damage" to children included in their study groups. Chess, Korn, and Fernandez (1971) question the basic assumption of an organically determined hyperkinetic syndrome, and they relate this specifically to their research with rubella children. In evaluating the deaf children in the Greater Vancouver area, Freeman, Malkin, and Hastings (1975, p. 396) avoided analyzing their data in terms of etiology as an indicator of cerebral dysfunction. They preferred to use hard signs of neurological dysfunction "including, for example, current motor handicap of central nervous system origin, epilepsy, gross incoordination, and persistent drooling." Even using these criteria, "The association between cerebral dysfunction and behavior is not as marked as might be expected. It is more apparent in school ratings than in parental ratings, where only a trend is obvious."

One danger of attributing a child's behavioral problems to brain damage is the possibility that parents and professionals will give up their efforts to make situational changes that might help alter the unacceptable behavior. Altshuler points out (1974, p. 372) that symptoms such as hyperactivity, irritability, withdrawal, aggression, and sleeping and eating problems can result from a variety of causes: "The symptoms are final common pathways through which tensions engendered by conflicts are expressed. Rarely are symptoms specific for a particular underlying cause and the entire repertory may be brought into effect by a wide gamut of tension-evoking circumstances."

Uncertainty about the etiology of deafness can be a source of anxiety reflected in the parents' attitudes about and treatment of their deaf child. Meadow (1968a) showed that lack of knowledge about the cause of deafness was a source of great concern to parents of deaf children. A study of parents with orthopedically handicapped children suggested that the absence of etiological information increased the parents' guilt and subsequent anxiety regarding their responsibility for the child's condition (Davis, 1963). The relationship between lack of information and behavioral problems is shown in the 1976 study of Schlesinger and Meadow. All six of the children classified as "etiology unknown" had been referred at some time for psychiatric treatment. This finding confirms the one reported previously by Meadow and Schlesinger (1971). In their survey of a residential school, 55 percent of the students considered to be emotionally disturbed were listed as "etiology unknown" in the school records, compared to 16 percent of a randomly selected comparison group.

The tensions to which deaf children and their families are subjected are numerous. They are related to the general stress experienced by families with handicapped children and to the specific stress that accompanies the reduced ability to communicate (Meadow, 1968a; Mindel and Vernon, 1971). Schlesinger and Meadow (1972) suggest that absence of communication in the global sense leads to behavior problems, which in turn lead to even greater communicative deficits. Thus there is a spiraling effect, with difficulties in communication and in behavior reinforcing each other.

Stokoe and Battison (1975) report that the prevalence of emotional-behavioral disturbance among deaf children is almost twice as high among children with hearing parents as among those with deaf parents. Compared to hearing parents, deaf parents of deaf children are considered to have fewer problems both in ability to communicate and in psychological adjustment.

Schlesinger (Schlesinger and Meadow, 1972) has analyzed the development of deaf children from the perspective of Erik Erikson's eight stages of man, pinpointing the areas where communication and responses to the diagnosis are most likely to have an influence. Least is known about the deaf child's development in the earliest stage—infancy—when basic trust and attachment to the maternal figure are being established. Because the diagnosis of deafness is very often delayed until after the first year of life has passed, very little is known about what happens to the deaf child during his first twelve months and whether he responds differently to persons and objects in his environment.

Retrospective developmental data were collected from parents of deaf children upon their application to a school for emotionally disturbed deaf children (Williams, 1970, pp. 12–13). Ten of the 51 children Williams examined were diagnosed as "psychotic." Of the eight children on whom he had data, half were said to have shown excessive sleep patterns in the first year of life, a failure to anticipate being picked up, and negativism; six were described as excessively placid and indifferent; six showed gaze avoidance. From the data available for 22 of the nonpsychotic children, parents' complaints were of excessive wakefulness (6 cases), excessive crying (7 cases), feeding difficulties (5 cases), irritability (4 cases), and gaze avoidance (5 cases). Erikson suggests that during the period from 18 months to 3 years of age the basic developmental task is the establishment of autonomy—the sense of existence as a separate human being with control over one's own body and environment. The period from 3 to 6 years is seen as especially important for the development of initiative—a feeling of the purposefulness of life and of one's self. The child with hearing has increasing command of linguistic symbols during these two periods from 18 months to 6 years. The deaf child not only fails to understand the rules and restrictions but also fails to make himself understood. Children who do not understand what is expected of them, and why, are at a major disadvantage. It is not surprising that they are found to have more than their share of psychological problems.

The behavioral problems identified by parents, teachers, and mental health professionals alike are tied to the kinds of developmental expectations that caretakers have for children at differing ages. Following the development of five congenitally deaf girls, all rubella babies, Freedman, Cannady, and Robinson (1971, p. 769) state, "It is characteristic of all these little girls that they tend to translate their wishes into action more readily than might be anticipated from the observation of children of similar age with normal hearing."

In the study of rubella children aged 2.5 to 4 years, the

areas of "behavioral deviation" defined were: sleep problems, 46 percent; feeding and eating problems, 53 percent; elimination problems, 37 percent; mood difficulties (separation anxiety, withdrawn behavior, temper tantrums), 72 percent; discipline problems, 64 percent; deviant motor activity (hyperactivity), 55 percent; peculiar habits and rituals, 67 percent (Chess, Korn, and Fernandez, 1971, pp. 58–63). However, as noted previously, there was a marked discrepancy between the ability of the rubella children to perform self-help activities and their actual performance of them. A child's performance can be dramatically influenced by different definitions of his handicap and capabilities.

Parents of deaf children often feel they do not have the command of communication necessary to explain complicated events. Thus, children's worlds may change drastically from one day to the next with no explanation for a move from one house to another or from one city to another, for a trip to the hospital with frightening and painful procedures to be performed, or for the disappearance of a grandparent or parent. The following excerpt from a case history illustrates the possible consequences of such an experience:

> Alice's overall development and her use of language were not atypical until her father was hospitalized when she was 38 months old. An only child, she was left in the care of her grandparents. Mother made no effort to prepare the child for her departure, left the home secretly, and was gone for several days. Alice was extremely disturbed at the time. Following this event, she showed a marked regression in her use of language. Although her hearing loss is relatively mild (50 dB), she still uses little language (Freedman, Cannady and Robinson, 1971, p. 768).

Lesser and Easser (1972, p. 462) suggest that "the impulsivity of the deaf child is closely connected with his lack of adequate communicative modalities to express his needs and feelings. . . . We believe that impulsivity is directly related to the organization of emotions for the self and the understanding, the naming, if one likes, of the emotions by the self. Once an affect can be named, it can come under the sway of ego control. . . . This delay in organizing the 'emotional self' is clearly related to the deaf child's difficulty with empathic responses."

These are some of the many ways in which physical, psychological, familial, experiential, and linguistic factors interact to contribute to the creation, the treatment, and the outcome of behavioral problems of deaf children.

## Treatment and Prevention
## of Mental Health Problems in Deaf Children

The problems involved in establishing mental health services either for deaf children or for deaf adults are myriad. Treatment demands both skill in mental health practice and an intimate knowledge of the developmental exigencies of deafness. Sign language skill is desirable. Mental health professionals are accustomed to relying on communication skills with which they are familiar. When faced with a person who communicates differently or not at all, they may respond with "shock," "withdrawal," or "paralysis" (Schlesinger and Meadow, 1972). Thus it is not surprising that mental health services for the deaf were initiated for the first time only in 1963, with the involvement of the New York Psychiatric Institute (Rainer, Altshuler, and Kallmann, 1969), followed by a program for the deaf at St. Elizabeth's Hospital in Washington, D.C., shortly afterwards, and then at the Langley Porter Institute in San Francisco and Michael Reese Hospital in Chicago in 1968. It was not until 1973 that most of the presently existing programs opened their doors (Goulder, 1977, p. 14). Even with these existing programs, the majority of deaf children with emotional problems still remain without specific treatment (Edelstein, 1977).

The provision of treatment, both on in-patient and out-patient bases, is of great importance. However, the preventive mental health services for deaf children and their families can be even more important, over the long run. As Sussman has stated (1977, p. 108), these services should be available for deaf people "with everyday problems, with mild neuroses, situational reaction problems, children having difficulty relating to their parents, and so on. The idea is to nip these problems in the bud, before they erupt into more serious disorders."

> Prevention and treatment of disturbances are crucial for the deaf child in a school setting. Preventive maneuvers stress the relationship between the child and his environment. Support given at a time of crisis can prevent the occurrence of future disorder. Additional stresses imposed by deafness may require additional support for the deaf child and those in contact with him. Differences in the communicative stance between the deaf child and his environment require special communicative expertise. In decreasing hazardous circumstances and enhancing life experiences, communication can be made more reciprocal and less ambiguous and identities more inclusive. Early intervention both lessens the need for treatment and increases the opportunities for deaf children to find ways toward greater achievement and happiness (Schlesinger, 1977, p. 104).

*Summary*

1. There are dangers inherent in any classification system that attaches labels to children without regard for the independent consequences of the labeling process. Too often labels become catch phrases and shortcuts to diagnoses rather than thoughtful descriptions of behavioral

symptoms. A positive reason for attaching diagnostic classification terms to handicapped children is to procure better services for them. However, those who use the classification system need to be aware of its dangers as well as its benefits.

2. Each of the five prevalence studies discussed has methodological problems pointing up some of the difficulties in collecting adequate data on deaf children. These studies indicate that the rate of emotional or behavioral disturbance ranges from about 9 percent to more than 20 percent depending on the population included in the survey, the definition used for identifying disturbed children, and the identity of the individuals responsible for diagnosing the children. These rates appear to be from three to ten times higher than for comparable groups of children with normal hearing.

3. Deaf children are more likely to be described as "immature," "hyperactive," and "aggressive" than are children with normal hearing. Deaf children with additional physical handicaps are more likely to exhibit psychiatric problems. This fact illustrates and further strengthens the conclusion that physical and emotional handicaps interact with environmental factors in very complex ways. The complexity of the interrelated physiological and psychological bases of behavioral problems in deaf children is illustrated by the possible explanations given for the high prevalence of problem behavior in the cited studies.

4. Recognition of the high levels of behavioral disturbance in deaf children is a first step toward the provision of mental health services to treat the problems. Provision of services is a first step in the prevention of future problems. Parents and children can be helped by mental health professionals and by sensitive teachers to communicate in more effective ways and to give and to accept additional responsibility for the performance of developmental tasks.

# CHAPTER SIX

# The Developmental Environment

In the preceding chapters we have focused on the impact that auditory loss makes on a developing human being. Here, we shift our focus to the deaf child's significant others—those individuals and institutions that both affect the deaf child's development and are affected by his inadequate auditory contact with those around him.

We will look at parents of deaf children and at the institution of the family; at teachers of deaf children and at the institution of the school; at people in the community and at the social institutions and cultural traditions that continue to influence the deaf individual as he develops from birth through maturity. These relationships are exceedingly complex, because parental responses to the deaf child are influenced simultaneously by societal provisions for dealing with deafness and by cultural attitudes regarding handicap. Likewise, professional educators respond to the child and to the parents in terms of their previously formulated and perhaps half-understood feelings and experiences with handicap, the professional training they have received, and the legal prescriptions and proscriptions through which social institutions make their impact on the developmental process. The community at large—individuals unrelated to the deaf person but with whom he comes in contact—is subject to the sometimes primitive notions and fears about handicaps, and to competing pressures for attention and for the resources that the society provides—often reluctantly—to those defined as "less fortunate" or "deserving." Thus, economic, social, cultural, educational, and familial institutions all play on the deaf individual, affect his growth, and contribute to his developmental environment. An understanding of this environment is necessary for an understanding of the development of the deaf child. All of these elements form a kaleidoscope, constantly shifting, changing, revolving. In successive pages, we shall focus in turn on the family, the school, and the community, attempting to stop the kaleidoscope long enough to gain an integrated understanding of some of these forces as they interact with the deaf individual.

## The Deaf Child and the Family

In considering the relationship between the deaf child and the family unit, we shall look specifically at those families where both the parents have normal hearing. The picture in families where one or both parents is deaf is quite different. However, since more than 90 percent of deaf children are born to hearing parents, we shall deal more extensively with this set. Furthermore, we shall concentrate on those families where the deaf child is deaf from birth or shortly afterwards. Again, this is the situation in most cases, and it is also the situation creating the most dramatic and far-reaching effect on subsequent development.

ESTABLISHING THE DIAGNOSIS OF DEAFNESS. The diagnostic process itself is frequently traumatic for parents, and may influence their response to the deaf child for many years. Some of the elements in the diagnostic process are related to the ambiguous nature of childhood deafness, and to the fact that it is, medically speaking, a rare occurrence. Deafness is difficult to recognize in a very young child, and pediatricians usually have little or no experience in recognizing the symptoms when they are confronted with a small patient who exhibits them. This combination of circumstances produces even more trauma for parents who must live through the diagnostic experience.

Deafness is an "invisible" handicap. This makes it more difficult to detect than some other handicaps that are accompanied by obvious, visible stigma. The ambiguous nature of the symptoms of deafness include the changing and idiosyncratic responses to sound that are often present in a deaf infant. If parents are puzzled by these seemingly unexplained differences in response, they may delay reporting the behavior to a pediatrician. Sometimes, when the behavior is reported during a routine medical check-up, a pediatrician inexperienced in the condition makes a gross "test" of hearing loss such as clapping the hands behind the child's back. If the child "passes" this test, parents receive false reassurances but continue to feel uneasy. They may feel that their own observational skills have been negated, and that their parenting abilities have been questioned. They perceive (often accurately) that the doctor has labeled them as "overanxious parents."

Another factor adding to the ambiguity surrounding the diagnosis of deafness is that symptoms are sometimes confused with those of mental retardation, emotional disturbance, and perceptual difficulties. These mistaken diagnoses create anxiety and false kinds of prescriptions and guilt on the part of parents.

One study (Meadow, 1967) reported that over 60 percent of the parents of deaf children interviewed had experienced four or more medical consultations related to establishing a diagnosis. One-third of the parents reported that the first doctor consulted had assured them that the child was not deaf. These "false negative" diagnostic results are difficult for parents. However, it is important to remember that there undoubtedly are some "false positive" diagnoses, or at least that some of the families who suspect deafness in their child are wrong. We have no information on these families. The Vancouver group reported that many of the physicians seen initially "rejected parental suspicions, apparently believing their cursory tests to be of greater validity than countless parental observations, and about a third refused to refer to a specialist" (Freeman, 1977, p. 283). The delay in diagnosis, or time lag between suspicion and confirmation, averaged 9.7 months for the profoundly deaf children and 16.4 months for the severely deaf children (Freeman, 1977, p. 284). Also, the impact of a diagnosis of deafness varies in its traumatic impact. If parents believe initially that their child is either mentally retarded or emotionally disturbed but learn that these diagnoses are erroneous, deafness can seem "a lesser evil."

Typically, middle class families in the United States visit at least one pediatrician, an ear-nose-throat specialist, and an audiologist before a diagnosis of deafness is confirmed. None of these specialists are trained to deal with the feelings and emotions of parents in difficult diagnostic situations. The reluctance to be a "bearer of bad tidings," discomfort, and real sympathy for the family can produce an awkward and abrupt revelation of the diagnosis that sometimes creates lasting bitterness. A doctor charged with revealing a diagnosis of mental retardation is quoted: "Most of all I dreaded being the one who would have to tell them that their fears were justified. I felt guilty in giving them the diagnosis, almost as if I were the creator of the defect" (Zuk, 1962, p. 406). These feelings in medical personnel can contribute to a brusqueness in manner of communication that contributes in turn to anger and hurt in parents: "So the doctor says, 'Yup, he's deaf, there's nothing anyone can do about it. That'll be twenty-five dollars, please.' Imagine that. All he did was hit a tuning fork and charged twenty-five dollars. You'd think he might at least say he was sorry about it" (Meadow, 1968a).

On the basis of her interviews with mothers of deaf children in England, Gregory says (1976, p. 151) that "the feeling of many mothers was that the doctors just did not want to know. In some cases the doctors were apparently unaware of the possibility, let alone the importance of early diagnosis."

DEALING WITH THE DIAGNOSIS OF DEAFNESS. The confirmation of a diagnosis of deafness in an infant or a young child is only the beginning of a family's struggle. There are many questions that parents need to have answered, and many feelings that continue to appear. One of the first questions that parents ask is the origin or cause of the handicap. Here, again, the nature of childhood deafness can foil an adequate answer to this basic question. In the study of parents of deaf children cited earlier (Meadow, 1967), over 80 percent of the parents interviewed had no definite information regarding the cause of the child's deafness. As one parent said, "I have always believed that some day we'll know why she doesn't hear. I think you always get an answer to everything, and I believe someday we'll know."

Zuk (1962, p. 407) observed the same concern for knowledge about etiology in his studies of parents of mentally retarded children. He suggests that this concern is related to an attempt to "shift anger and guilt." Until there is some definite reason to believe otherwise, parents may continue to feel that in some unknown way they were themselves responsible for their child's handicap.

The question of etiology and responsibility is particularly poignant in the case of congenital deafness, because there is always the possibility of genetic linkage. Perhaps one reason parents are anxious to "know" the cause of their child's deafness is the unspoken fear that it might have a hereditary basis, thus reflecting a stigma of imperfection on the parents and, in effect, making them responsible for the child's condition. Parents often believe that professionals with medical expertise *should* be able to provide this information. They may become angry and resentful with doctors or audiologists when the knowledge they want cannot be offered.

Another source of difficulty in adjusting to the diagnostic information is the natural or habitual assumption that medical problems (especially in children) "should" have solutions. Thus, some parents look for a cure, shopping from one physician to another.* Some may seek help from practitioners of acupuncture, from faith healers, or from other pseudo-medical sources. Unfortunately, there are few mental health professionals who are available to parents of deaf children, or who have been trained to deal with the specific problems related to the diagnostic crisis. Many professionals believe that until parents have had the opportunity to examine their feelings, and to express their guilt, anger, and sorrow in an accepting atmosphere, these feelings will continue to crop up from time to time. Until resolved, the negative feelings can interfere in their relationship with the deaf child, and can reduce the energy and the coping strengths available to parents in helping the child to overcome the consequences of the auditory handicap. Thus there are some families who continue to relive the diagnostic trauma throughout the life of the child.

DEALING WITH THE SPECIAL NEEDS OF THE DEAF CHILD. In addition to feelings about the diagnosis of deafness, parents need to deal, on a day-to-day basis, with the practical aspects of training and remediation for a hearing loss. These needs can put tremendous burdens and pressures on the family. Many visits to audiologists, to speech and

*Roger Freeman, in a personal communication, points out that most parents are looking for *adequate care*, and not looking for a *cure*. He suggests that the characteristic lag from the time of parental suspicions to the time of medical confirmation of deafness affects parental behavior where deafness is involved. This lag is much greater for deaf children than it is for blind children (Freeman, 1977: 284). Keirn (1971), in a study of mentally retarded children, concluded that "shopping parents" reflect the professionals' problems rather than the patients' problems.

hearing centers, and to hearing-aid dealers must be scheduled. New skills and new information must be learned, and often parents feel besieged from all sides. It is usual to think about all the audiological and educational needs of the deaf child, and to emphasize the effect on the child of the absence of proper educational and audiological intervention. It is less usual to consider these demands in terms of the drain they may make on parents' energy, their time, and their financial resources.

Freeman's data (1977, p. 284) indicate that deaf children are more likely to experience hospitalizations than are their hearing peers, especially during the first two years of life. (Blind children were even more prone to frequent hospitalizations than were the deaf children who were studied in the Vancouver area.) The deaf children had forty times the number of tonsillectomies as their hearing controls, and almost 15 percent had myringotomies. Freeman suggests that these children had more attention by otologists "and more vigorous therapy for the common middle ear disorders of childhood" (p. 283). The high rate of illnesses and conditions resulting in hospitalizations for deaf children creates possible trauma for the children, and strain and expense for their parents. In addition, Freeman points out (Quinton and Rutter, 1976) that several British studies have found an association between later behavior disorder and hospitalization in early life.

EFFECT OF DEAFNESS ON MARITAL STRESS. The presence of a handicapped child in the family can create stress, can serve as a focus for existing stress, or can provide a rallying ground for increasing family cohesion. The ways in which these possibilities will emerge in a given family depend on the marital history, the resources at its command, and other events that are impinging on the group. Freeman and others (1975) found that the divorce rate was no higher among families with deaf children who were interviewed than among comparison families without deaf children. However, many parents indicate that where conflict exists, the deaf child and his needs become the issues around which the battles are joined.

EFFECT OF DEAFNESS ON SIBLING RELATIONSHIPS. The area of sibling relationships is one that is generally neglected, so it is not surprising that very little information exists on the brothers and sisters of deaf children. Barsch asked 177 mothers of children with various kinds of handicaps to report on the extent of positive or negative attitudes of siblings toward the child with the handicap. These mothers believed that the siblings were generally positive in their feelings toward the handicapped child (about three-quarters reported positive attitudes). Of the five categories of handicap (cerebral palsy, organic damage, mongolism, blindness, and deafness) the siblings of deaf children showed a much larger proportion with negative attitudes: 20 percent of the children with deaf siblings were considered to have negative attitudes, compared to an average of about 10 percent for children whose siblings had other kinds of handicaps (Barsch, 1968, p. 196). Barsch reports that "resentments were defined as beliefs that the handicapped child was loved more, given more attention, or given more material things. The expressions of these resentments took the form of teasing, overt physical attack, embarrassment among peers, refusal to play with the handicapped child, etc." (Barsch, 1968, p. 197). As Freeman and his colleagues point out (1975, p. 401), "siblings may need explanations and parents may need counseling around the subject of differences or similarities in their management of a handicapped child when there are one or more non-handicapped siblings."

The issue of the limitation of family size has been addressed by Barsch also. He found that the presence of a handicapped child in the family might lead either to the decision to have no more children or to the decision to have additional children (p. 197).

Freeman, Malkin, and Hastings (1975, p. 395) report that the diagnosis of deafness in the handicapped child produced either a mild or a moderate reaction in 17 percent of the siblings. Over the course of time, the deafness produced some degree of negative impact on slightly less than half of the siblings.

Schwirian (1976) conducted an interesting study of the impact on siblings of a younger deaf child in the family. She interviewed mothers about the responsibilities given to older siblings of deaf children, about the independence granted the siblings, and about the kinds of social activities in which the siblings were allowed to engage. Contrary to her hypotheses "as well as to commonly held opinion" she found that the "presence of a hearing-handicapped preschool child has little effect on (1) child care responsibilities; (2) assumption of household responsibilities; (3) the independence and privileges granted; or (4) the level of social activities of older siblings with normal hearing." Schwirian suggests that one important factor in her results might be the age of the deaf children who were the focus of her research. As the children get older, they may create more disruptions in the lives of family members.

However, an obvious research need in this area is for some direct interview studies of the siblings of deaf children. Second-hand reports about ideas and attitudes are always problematic. In a sensitive area where social desirability could influence responses so heavily, it is even more of a problem. The general belief in the deaf community is that siblings tend either to become very much involved with deafness when they reach adulthood, or they pull away completely from contact with deaf adults. This would be an interesting hypothesis for investigation.

THE EXTENDED FAMILY. Extended family members can interact with the deaf child and his parents in two distinctly different ways. (1) They can provide additional support, creating a network of expressive and instrumental help. Thus, grandparents, aunts, and uncles may rally 'round a family experiencing the diagnostic crisis, enveloping them in a circle of affection and sympathetic support, and helping with babysitting at times of special stress. Or (2) the disappointment and grief of grandparents, especially if the deaf child is the first grandchild, may add to parental burdens, increasing the feelings of guilt and despair. Grandparents may hope to realize frustrated ambitions for themselves and their children in their grandchildren. Often, they see these hopes as impossible if the child is deaf.

## The Deaf Child and the School

Teachers and the educational system play an important role in the development of all children. Deaf children begin their education early, often experience a more intensive relationship with their teachers than do their hearing peers, and may be older than hearing peers when they complete secondary school. Thus teachers and other school personnel have an especially profound influence on the development of deaf children.

To illustrate the early time of school beginning for deaf children, we can turn to data collected by the Office of Demographic Studies. In the 1969–1970 school year, data were gathered on approximately 35,000 students enrolled in schools or classes for hearing-impaired students. About 18 percent of these students were younger than six years of age. Of the 1200 children for whom the data were available, it was reported that 11 percent had begun their education by the age of 12 months; 28 percent by the age of two years; 36 percent by the time they were three years old; and 25 percent by the age of four or five years (Murphy, 1972, p.

11). Among those children for whom the data were available, it was reported that about half their parents were receiving training as well as the children, and that about half attended school 16 hours or more per week (Murphy, 1972, p. 15). Educational arrangements at the younger age levels vary a good deal. As more and more states are providing education for very young deaf children, there are more public school districts that have hired teachers to go into homes to work with mothers and their deaf babies. Speech and hearing clinics very often provide services for deaf preschoolers and infants. Many residential schools for the deaf have added programs for very young children and their parents, and regular public schools house classes for young deaf children also. Of the 671 schools and classes reporting to the American Annals of the Deaf for the 1976 school year, 425 or 63 percent had preschool programs (Craig and Craig, 1977, p. 138). The Vancouver study found that 88 percent of the deaf children had been enrolled in a preschool program, compared to 77 percent of the hearing controls (Freeman, Malkin, and Hastings, 1975, p. 397).

When the parents and the young deaf child enroll in an educational program, parents generally do not know what to expect. They usually continue to suffer from the "diagnostic crisis," feeling bewildered about what has happened to them and unsure about what is expected of them. Too often, educators are not trained to deal with the feelings of parents during this period, and they add to parental burdens by expecting a great deal from mothers and fathers who are not ready to deal with all the advice they receive. When the child's education begins, there may be many prescriptions and proscriptions that are perceived to be overwhelming, conflicting, or incompatible by the parents. The tasks may be so numerous, so time-consuming, or so onerous that the parents become discouraged and feel incapable of ever doing everything required. They may, finally, give up altogether. The young deaf child must be fitted with hearing aids, and with ear molds for the aids. Often, the hearing aids break, requiring many trips to the hearing-aid dealer, or constant mailing of the aids to the manufacturer for repairs. Sometimes, deaf children have frequent ear infections, and this is a source of great worry since this condition can interfere with the child's use of residual hearing. Frequent recurrences may also damage any hearing that remains.

Professionals need to be aware that some behavior on the part of parents that appears to be careless or irresponsible (such as "forgetting" to have new glasses or hearing aids fitted) is in fact an emotional response to the sorrow surrounding the diagnosis. For example, a teacher may encounter a mother who insists that she encourages the use of the hearing aid, yet who often forgets to put the aid on the child before school, or who forgets to get repairs or new batteries. The financial burden imposed by hearing aids, ear molds, batteries, and repairs is not inconsiderable. These practical problems add to the emotional distress so many parents feel in the early years of their deaf child (Schlesinger and Meadow, 1976, p. 42).

THE MIDDLE YEARS AT SCHOOL. For some deaf children, the shift from preschool to primary education is a simple one, merely involving a different classroom or teacher in the same school. This is often the case for children living in metropolitan areas where numbers make preschool classes a reality in many school districts. Children living in more sparsely populated areas may not have had contact with a teacher before they reach the age of five. Many families, especially those in rural areas, use the correspondence course developed by the John Tracy Clinic. This clinic, located in Los Angeles, was founded by Mrs. Louise Tracy, the wife of the late actor Spencer Tracy. It is named for their son, who was deaf from childhood. Between 1943 and 1958, more than 8,000 families had enrolled in the correspondence course provided by the clinic. When deaf children reach the age of five or six and must attend school, many families face the difficult decision of sending the child to a state residential school which may have more facilities to provide for the child's special needs, or have him or her continue to live at home and attend the neighborhood school.

For a group of parents of residential school students, interviewed about their decision to send the student away to school, this decision was one of the most traumatic they had to face (Meadow, 1967, p. 291). One mother described her feelings about this experience as follows:

> Sam looked forward to taking the trip to school. The getting ready. Then he didn't know why he was being deserted. He was terribly homesick at first. . . . It was awfully hard to take (to have him away from home). It was a good thing I had to teach. I didn't want to *hurt* him on top of everything else. I felt I was *punishing* him for his handicap. . . . He never wants to go back to school, always begs not to. At Christmas he wouldn't get on the bus, then when I got him on, he braced his feet against the seats on each side of the aisle and wouldn't sit down (Meadow, 1967, p. 292).

For many years, the battle waged around oral and manual communication in deaf education was joined between the residential schools and the day schools. The residential schools were viewed as being attached to manual-only methods and the day schools were viewed as being attached to oral-only methods. Thus, for parents who had been urged to show a commitment to oral education (as most had been) it seemed an admission of defeat to send their deaf child to a school that permitted the use of sign language.

COMMUNICATION MODE IN EDUCATION. The question of what communication mode is best in teaching the deaf has been at the center of a long controversy in educational circles. It is worth looking briefly at the history of this controversy in an effort to understand its dimensions.

The first permanent school for the deaf in the United States was established in Hartford, Connecticut, in 1817. This school, originally called The Connecticut Asylum for the Education and Instruction of Deaf and Dumb Persons, eventually became today's American School for the Deaf (Brill, 1974, p. 9). The communication mode used by the school was manual, but this choice was greatly influenced by a series of accidental events that were to have a profound effect on the history of deaf education in the United States. The school's founder, Thomas Hopkins Gallaudet, went to England to learn about methods being used for teaching deaf children. The oral techniques used there were carefully guarded secrets. Apprentices to the school run by the Braidwood family were sworn not to reveal the methods. While Gallaudet was trying to gain access to Braidwood's confidence, with little success, he heard about a school for deaf children in Paris, founded by Abbé de l'Epée. This school used sign language. Gallaudet was invited to visit Paris and urged to learn the French methods and the sign language being used. He traveled to France, spent several months at the school, and then returned to the United States to found the Hartford school. His experience with Braidwood in England may have embittered him regarding oral techniques generally, since he eschewed all speech training as leading to "parlor tricks" with no meaning and "entitled to rank little higher than training starlings or parrots" (Bender, 1960, p. 127). In these early days, parents who were interested in having their deaf children receive an education that included or emphasized oral training found few friends. Eventually, in 1867, after a long struggle with the Massachusetts legislature, the Clarke School for the Deaf was established in Northampton, in spite of opposition from the American School in Hartford.

From then until now, a controversy around mode of communication—often called the Hundred Years War— has raged in the field of deaf education.* Basically, the conflict has focused on the use of spoken language as opposed to the use of signed language. However, this dichotomy masks many of the nuances of disagreement in what is actually a set of extremely complex arguments. The "oral method" or the "oral-aural method" stresses the use of speech, the application of hearing aids, and the encouragement of voice and lipreading skills through the discouragement of reliance on any visual cues other than the lip movements that accompany speech. For many years, the oral philosophy included the idea that deaf children who were allowed to rely on other visual cues would become dependent on these cues (signs) and would therefore not expend the additional effort to learn the more difficult skills of speech and lipreading. Children who succeeded in acquiring speech and lipreading through oral-aural means (usually those with considerable residual hearing) were used as examples of the benefits of the methods; children who were "oral failures" were then sent to residential

*Freeman suggests (1976, p. 112) that one reason for the enduring nature of this controversy, in the face of objective evidence that the oral-only method is optimal, is found in assumptions "about desirable norms and features of human behavior and communication, as defined by the majority group or culture." He draws on the history of treatment of other handicapping conditions to bolster this important insight. For example, many people are unaware that the use of Braille with blind children was the focus of controversy for one hundred years because "if the blind were not to be isolated, the type that they were to read should be one that the seeing could read also." In the initial treatment of thalidomide limb-deficient children, it was assumed that the early introduction of an upper-limb prosthesis would be the preferred treatment. Unexpectably, many of the children rejected the prostheses, preferring their own abnormal arms or to substitute the use of their legs. The third example offered by Freeman is that of persons with cerebral palsy. Professionals have fostered treatment to encourage a gait that would "look normal." However, patients themselves find their natural gait more adaptive. However, it has been found that "those children who do not begin to walk successfully start to encounter increasingly negative responses from physiotherapists and mothers" (p. 113).

schools where they were allowed to use the previously forbidden manual sign language—long after the optimum time for the acquisition of language. The process was a self-perpetuating one, almost guaranteed to foster bitterness and resentment among all the participants: teachers who were committed through training and conviction to do their best to further acquisition of spoken language; parents with no previous experience with deafness who followed the advice of professionals, often with disappointing results; and children who grew up to feel that they had been deprived of their right to early family communication.

Over the years, there were some efforts to find a middle ground, somewhere between the "oral only" and "manual only" approaches. These included the Rochester Method (Scouten, 1967) involving the use of fingerspelling with speech, enabling the precise translation of spoken English into a visual pattern; Cued Speech (Cornett, 1967), involving visual translation of phonetic symbols by hand signs; and the Simultaneous Method. The latter was used for instruction very often in residential schools. Teachers would speak while using the closest approximation to English from the signs of American Sign Language, or Ameslan. Beginning in about 1966, there were a variety of efforts to construct systems for expressing all the linguistic features of English in signs.

Wilbur (1976) describes eight of these artificial or constructed sign language systems or adaptations; Bornstein (1979) analyzes distinctive features of some of these that are used most frequently. With the development of some of these systems, and for many other reasons, a new "movement" in deaf education began, and was referred to as Total Communication. This term was coined by Roy Holcomb, who was then the director of a school program for deaf children in California (Brill, 1974, p. 272). The Maryland School for the Deaf was one of the first to adopt the concept (Denton, 1972). In spite of its popularity, there is no generally accepted definition of the term. This can be said even though a committee of the Conference of Executives of American Schools for the Deaf spent four years in a nationwide study culminating in the adoption of this definition: "Total Communication is a philosophy requiring the incorporation of appropriate aural, manual, and oral modes of communication in order to ensure effective communication with and among hearing impaired persons" (Conference of Executives of American Schools for the Deaf, 1976, p. 358).

This definition still leaves open many important questions, such as the use of fingerspelling, the type of manual communication to be used, and whether manual and oral modes are to be used alternately or simultaneously (Brill, 1974, p. 272). This lack of agreement about a precise definition of the approach enables many schools and classes to assert that they are using Total Communication. A survey of primary mode of communication used with classes at four age-levels reported responses of 796 school programs (82 percent of programs on the mailing list of the Office of Demographic Studies). When data are evaluated from the perspective of the total number of classes within programs using different modes of communication, the following results were found. Total Communication was used at the preschool level in 55 percent of the classes, at the elementary level in 62 percent of the classes, and at the junior high and senior high levels in 63 percent and 80 percent of the classes, respectively. The Oral-Aural mode was used by between 19 and 57 percent of the classes; the Rochester Method by between 1 and 3 percent; Cued Speech was reported used by even fewer classes (Jordan, Gustason, and Rosen, 1976, p. 529). These figures reflect changes in deaf education that are little short of revolutionary when one considers that Total Communication did not even exist as a term ten years earlier.

As in any revolutionary movement, the effort and the results of different Total Communication programs vary greatly. Teachers who had been oriented to oral communication for years suddenly were asked to learn and to teach by means of some form of sign language. Some resisted the idea or agreed reluctantly. Others jumped on the bandwagon and in their enthusiasm for the new mode discarded altogether their emphasis on speech and hearing training. True believers sprang up overnight, and a new cycle in educational history began.

EFFORTS TO EVALUATE VARIOUS EDUCATIONAL METHODS. Since Total Communication represents a relatively new emphasis on combining oral-aural techniques with one of the artificial sign languages aimed at a precise English gloss, there have been as yet few efforts at systematic program evaluation. One ambitious effort in this direction is the five-year study initiated in 1969 by Moores, Weiss, and Goodwin (1973). Despite numerous difficulties encountered by the researchers (including shifts in methodology after the research had begun and withdrawal of cooperation from some programs), some relevant results were reported. Seventy-four children from seven preschool programs for the deaf throughout the United States were involved in the study. For the 1972 test period, when the children had a mean age of about five years, a receptive communication test was administered with the following results. When speech alone was used to present the message, 34 percent of the content was understood. This increased to 56 percent with the addition of speechreading, 61 percent with the addition of fingerspelling, and 71 percent with the addition of signs. "Children with the highest scores in reception of speech plus speechreading were from programs using manual and oral communication from the time the children started their education, suggesting that instead of inhibiting the reception of spoken language, early manual communication probably facilitates it" (Moores, 1979, p. 268).

When Moores and his colleagues looked at school programs rather than at individual students, they found that the three more successful of the seven programs had five elements in common: (1) all had a pronounced heavy cognitive or academic orientation; (2) all used some form of manual as well as oral communication in the classroom; (3) classroom activities tended to be structured and organized; (4) auditory training activities were included in ongoing classroom events; and (5) parents viewed the program as a combination of oral and manual and were comfortable with the teachers' communicative mode (Moores, McIntyre, and Weiss, 1972).

One portion of the studies of deaf children undertaken at the University of California in San Francisco involved the intensive study of language acquisition of six children exposed to both signed and spoken language during the preschool years (Schlesinger and Meadow, 1972; Schlesinger, 1976; Meadow, 1976b, 1976c). These studies will be discussed in the following chapter. They point out the possible advantages of the early and optimum use of the combined visual and auditory modes of communication.

RESIDENTIAL SCHOOLS VS. HOME LIFE. Choice of communication mode is one of the important decisions in which the educational system has a profound effect on the life of the deaf child. Another and perhaps equally important life choice is made for the child and his family in relation to the availability of day programs as compared to residential programs. In this area, too, there have been many changes over the years. In 1900, 90 percent of deaf children were receiving their education in public residential schools. In 1966, 51 percent had residential school placements (Brill, 1974, p. 261). In 1976, 41 percent were in public

residential schools (Craig and Craig, 1977, p. 138). One reason for the decrease in the proportion of deaf children in
residential schools is pressure from parents for the establishment of more local day programs that will permit the
deaf child to continue to live at home. As this trend continued, it may have been one source of additional pressure
for the increased use of manual communication in day programs: parents became less willing for their children to
leave home in order to be given the kind of communication
or education that both parents and teachers agreed was
needed.

The state residential schools (61 were listed in the 1977
Directory published by the American Annals of the Deaf)
have been an important element in the lives of deaf people
for many years. Things are changing very rapidly today,
and modern educational and child development principles
are being adopted by most of these schools. In the past,
however, tradition reigned. Little freedom was given to
students, and discipline was strict. Privacy and individual
rights were subordinated to the needs of the institution.
These patterns were no different from those in other large
institutions where many children or adults were cared for.
Today, more and more residential schools are developing
programs of apartment living for groups of older students.
School administrators are insisting that most children go
home for weekends and holidays. Community visits are encouraged, and usual boy-girl relationships are permitted.

Quigley and Frisina (1961) completed the most carefully
designed study of the effects of residential school living on
the deaf child's development, and concluded that there
was no evidence that living in residential schools is detrimental to deaf children in terms of educational achievement and psycho-social adjustment.

INTEGRATION OR MAINSTREAMING. Another phenome-
non of change that is taking place is increasing pressure for

the integration of deaf children in classrooms with their hearing peers. This movement, of course, tends to weaken the residential school, since there is usually less opportunity for interaction with hearing children for deaf children in the residential school environment. The thrust toward "integration" has come to be called "mainstreaming" for handicapped children.

While the traditional use of the term "integration" referred to placement of a handicapped child in a setting that encouraged interaction with non-handicapped age-mates, the newer term, "mainstreaming," is used to denote full-time attendance of the handicapped child in a neighborhood school. Since the degree of "integration" can be seen on a continuum, I have used the two terms interchangeably here. Vernon and Prickett (1976) have called mainstreaming "the most crucial single issue in the education of deaf children today" (p. 5). Much of the impetus toward the integration of handicapped children into classrooms with their non-handicapped peers has come from questions raised by minority group members regarding methods of tracking students into special classes for mentally retarded students. However, the issues for students labeled as "mildly mentally retarded" are much different than for handicapped children who need many specialized services, and teachers especially trained to provide them. It seems ironic that parents and educators have been struggling for many years to improve the quality of education for deaf children by decreasing the pupil-teacher ratio in classrooms, and that suddenly the thrust has changed to placing a single deaf child in a classroom with twenty or more others.

There are several models for integration or mainstreaming. The most dramatic one involves that suggested above: a single child placed in a classroom with many hearing children, with few specialized services available. Another model that is more widespread is that in which a class of deaf children is located within a public school, with the deaf child attending classes with hearing children in subjects where he or she can maintain the pace. This has usually meant that deaf children participate with the others in such subjects as art, home economics, and physical education. A recently implemented model, called The Holcomb Plan, calls for deaf children to be placed in classrooms with hearing peers and with a tutor-interpreter who interprets into sign language what the regular classroom teacher says. At the same time, hearing students in the school are encouraged to learn fingerspelling and sign language (Vernon and Prickett, 1976, p. 10).

DEAF EDUCATION AND PUBLIC LAW 94–142. The Education for All Handicapped Children Act of 1975, or Public Law 94–142, has provided some of the impetus, or some of the rationale, for increased pressure for the mainstreaming of handicapped children. It has been called the "mainstreaming law," but this is actually a misnomer because the portion of the act relative to mainstreaming is a very minor aspect of the total law. The law was passed because it had been found that of the 7 million handicapped children in the U.S., 4 million were reported to be inadequately or inappropriately served. It has been called a "civil rights act for the handicapped" and delineates seven basic guarantees to handicapped children and their parents (excerpted from Rosen, Skinsi, and Pimentel, 1977, pp. 4–5):

1. Right to an education. P.L. 94–142 is based upon the premise that any child is capable of benefitting from an education; consequently there is no reason to exclude any child from educational opportunities.
2. Right to a free education. Public schools must bear the cost of any special services or programs needed for handicapped children in private or special schools if the public schools turn them away.
3. Right to an appropriate education. The law states

that an individualized educational program (IEP) should be developed for and provided to every handicapped child at no cost to the parents. This program will determine both the proper placement for the child and the special services that are needed.

4. Right to least restrictive environment (LRE). This guarantees the handicapped child equal accessibility opportunity to the environment that would be most appropriate and most conducive to his academic, social, and emotional maturity. This is the clause that has been associated with the mainstreaming mandate. Obviously, there can be much disagreement about what constitutes the "least restrictive environment," but it has been defined as the classroom with children who are not handicapped.

5. The right to due process. P.L. 94–142 says to parents, "You have the right to be heard, to be informed, and to be involved. You have the right to do so in your native tongue or with the assistance of an interpreter. . . . You have the right to be informed in writing in detail of the proposed action and the reasons for it. You have the right to examine records and evaluation results, and to have them explained to you. . . . You have the right to a hearing conducted by an impartial hearing officer."

6. The right to confidentiality. Confidential or identifiable data will not be shared inappropriately or without the written consent of parents or guardians.

7. The right to non-discriminatory testing. This includes the mandate to (use only) tests that do not discriminate on the basis of race, culture, language, or communication method. The implications are that tests must be appropriate and validated for the target population in question, that the evaluator must either be proficient in the child's native language, or use an interpreter, and that the evaluator must be certified and qualified for his job.

As can be seen, the provisions of this act have far-reaching implications for deaf education. The deadline for

compliance by schools was October 1, 1977. It remains to be
seen what enforcement procedures will be developed, and
what effect the regulations will have on deaf children and
their parents.

## The Deaf Child and the Community

The community in which she or he lives has a profound
influence on the deaf child, just as it does for any other
child. In the case of the deaf child, however, we must be
concerned not with one community, but with two: the deaf
community and the general community-at-large comprised of persons with normal hearing. Depending on the
deaf child's life history and situation, the structural features of these two separate groups, and the societal and
cultural attitudes and ideas expressed by and through their
members, will exert an influence on the child. Of course,
these ideas and attitudes are frequently expressed by and
filtered through the child's family and the educational systems that have been discussed previously. However, the
features of the deaf community and the hearing community help to create the context that leads to an understanding of the developmental environment in which the deaf
child grows.

THE DEAF COMMUNITY. "Profound deafness is much
more than a medical diagnosis: it is a cultural phenomenon
in which social, emotional, linguistic, and intellectual patterns and problems are inextricably bound together"
(Schlesinger and Meadow, 1972). These patterns are expressed through forms that have been summarized or defined as the deaf community (Schein, 1968), or subculture
(Stokoe and others, 1965; Meadow, 1972), or minority
group (Vernon and Makowsky, 1969). A number of distinctive features mark the existence of a self-conscious deaf
community, and reflect the cohesiveness that leads many

(but not all) profoundly deaf adults to identify themselves as members of it.

VOLUNTARY ASSOCIATIONS. The National Association of the Deaf, with 10,000 deaf persons on its membership rolls, has branches in every state and a permanent office in the suburbs of Washington, D.C. (Mindel and Vernon, 1971, p. 97). The N.A.D. serves as a social and political force in the deaf community, conducts and sponsors research (including the National Census of the Deaf), publishes materials on deafness, and supports parent education. The *Deaf American* is the official publication of the organization and is circulated widely throughout the world.* Most large cities and many smaller ones have social clubs for the deaf that sponsor sporting, social, and recreational activities. The World Deaf Olympics draws deaf athletes from many nations. Most of the major religious denominations have special facilities for deaf members, with increasing numbers of interpreters available for services.

MEDIA FOR MEMBERS OF THE DEAF COMMUNITY. More and more cities are responding to the special communication needs of the deaf community with news broadcasts in sign language on local television stations as a regular daily feature. Captioned films are available to most deaf clubs free of charge, funded through a federal agency. The National Theater of the Deaf is recognized nationally and internationally for its theatrical excellence and is enjoyed by deaf and hearing persons alike.

INSTITUTIONS AS CULTURE CARRIERS. The tradition of the state residential schools is important in defining the deaf

---

*There are parallel organizations and publications in other countries—for example, The Canadian Association of the Deaf which publishes *The Deaf Canadian,* and the British Deaf Association, which publishes *The British Deaf News.*

community. Alumnae from different schools continue to feel a loyalty and allegiance, a sense of comradeship with their fellow students, for many years after graduation. The state schools are in themselves "preservers" of the subculture, with pride in particular varieties of sign language and special idiomatic expressions known to belong to individual schools. Gallaudet College in Washington, D.C., is an institution with special meaning for the deaf community. Gallaudet was established in 1864, and has been supported by special Congressional funding throughout its existence. The Kendall Demonstration Elementary School and the Model Secondary School for the Deaf (MSSD) are also located on the Gallaudet campus. In 1977–1978, Kendall had about 185 deaf students, MSSD about 190. There were about 250 preparatory students, 900 undergraduate students, and 200 graduate students enrolled at Gallaudet in the 1977–1978 school year. The Gallaudet Alumni Association is very active, and graduates of the college are among the most influential leaders of the deaf community.

INTERMARRIAGE OF DEAF ADULTS. There is a marked tendency for deaf adults to marry deaf spouses. The National Census of the Deaf Population showed that 87 percent of the respondents had either deaf or hard of hearing spouses (Schein and Delk, 1974, p. 40). One interview study with deaf and hearing respondents showed marked discrepancies between the two groups in their ideas on this subject. When parents were asked whether they had any feelings about mixed marriages of deaf and hearing persons, the deaf parents were more likely to answer only in terms of the future marital happiness of the husband and wife, while the hearing parents might think of possible hereditary deafness for the children of deaf couples. Seventy percent of the deaf parents felt that it was "much better" for deaf persons to marry deaf spouses, compared to only 17 percent of the hearing parents of deaf children (Meadow, 1967, pp. 298–299).

AMERICAN SIGN LANGUAGE. Important as each of the features discussed above is in defining and marking the deaf community, the most outstanding visible and salient feature of the deaf community is its language. American Sign Language (Ameslan) is used perhaps most of the time but at least part of the time by 75 percent of deaf adults in the United States. This figure is in striking contrast to the proportion of hearing parents of deaf children. The New York State survey found that only 12 percent of deaf adults had any hearing family members who knew sign language (Rainer and others, 1969). However, as educational philosophies have changed, so have the numbers of hearing parents who learn sign language. Results from the Vancouver study (Freeman, Malkin, and Hastings, 1975) show that 22 percent of the parents of deaf children were learning sign language. Almost half of the group studied in the San Francisco Bay Area (Schlesinger and Meadow, 1976) were using sign language at home. Since most members of the deaf community do not learn sign language at home, their linguistic socialization (and therefore their socialization to the deaf community) takes place through persons other than their own parents. This is a major feature of the development of deaf children: the family of orientation is rarely the agent of linguistic socialization. The times at which linguistic socialization is accomplished reflect the times of entry into the deaf community.

1. Linguistic socialization from birth. Hearing status rather than family status is the crucial variable in the identity of the initial agent of socialization to the deaf linguistic community. True "native signers" are those who are the children of two deaf parents (about 8 percent of the population of deaf children). Hearing children of deaf parents

may be counted as native signers, especially if they are first-born. Not every deaf child of deaf parents is exposed to sign language. In some instances (probably very few) the deaf parents use spoken English exclusively within the home. In other cases, deaf parents have accepted the ban placed on manual communication by hearing educators, and avoid the use of signs with their children even though sign language may be the primary communicative mode between husband and wife. "Baby signs" are seen in young deaf children of deaf parents, and their language acquisition follows much the same pattern as that of hearing children acquiring spoken language (Schlesinger and Meadow, 1972). As more and more families with young deaf children are oriented to Total Communication, this pattern will be seen to change.

2. Linguistic socialization at school entry. A frequent pattern of linguistic socialization is for sign language to be acquired by the deaf children of hearing parents at the time they enroll in a residential school—most often at age six or at age thirteen. When they enroll, these children become friends with the deaf children of deaf parents, who teach them their own version of sign language. Thus we see the interesting and unusual phenomenon of a language that is transmitted primarily not from adult to child but instead from child to child. Some of the adults who teach or who serve as dormitory counselors in residential schools are themselves deaf and know sign language. However, until the general movement toward Total Communication, even many residential schools did not recognize and legitimize sign language by offering formal classes to students. According to a recent survey (Jordan, Gustason, and Rosen, 1976, p. 531), more than half of the school programs with Total Communication offer formal sign language classes for both students and parents. This in itself represents an astounding change in patterns of linguistic socialization for deaf children.

3. Linguistic socialization in adulthood. Finally, there is a group of deaf persons who enter the subculture of the deaf community after they reach adulthood. These are deaf people who have been educated in schools where oral-only methods were used, or who were integrated in the classroom with normally hearing children throughout their school years. Padden and Markowicz (1975) interviewed 21 such students at Gallaudet, and report some fascinating data about the experiences of these students.

The students learned that not only must they know Ameslan if they were to be accepted by the Gallaudet community, but that they were expected to conform with particular styles and codes of linguistic behavior. These included fairly obvious or observable mannerisms such as signing without speech or without non-vocal lip movements, but also included more subtle (and more difficult to learn) language patterns that are a part of the visual code of sign language, such as specific ways of using the eyes and the body in communication. Some of the oral deaf students, learning sign language at Gallaudet for the first time, were used as "cultural brokers" by their formerly socialized classmates. Their more proficient speech skills and their greater experience in the hearing community were seen as marks of "worldly wisdom." "One of these subjects remarked that the same girls who seek her advice ignore her when they see her outside of her dormitory room" (p. 10). Thus stigma cuts both ways, with the ethnocentrism of the deaf linguistic community operating as a basis for exclusion as well as inclusion, just as in any racial or ethnic minority group.

THE HEARING COMMUNITY. The cumulative impact that the hearing community or "society" has on the deaf community is a product of at least four separate factors: (1) the feelings, or ideas, or attitudes that have developed around physical handicaps generally and around deafness specifically; (2) the ways in which hearing people translate these feelings or attitudes into behavior in particular situations; (3) the ways that deaf people experience the behavior of hearing people in both personal and impersonal situations; and (4) the ways in which deaf people interpret or define or conceptualize behavioral interactions with those who have normal hearing. Also important in building a framework for looking at these considerations is the notion that the roles and the status of each individual involved in an interaction, or toward whom an expression of feeling is directed, will influence both the attitudes and behaviors of those involved. For example, the attitudes and behaviors of hearing adults toward very young deaf children may be quite different than those toward either deaf adolescents or deaf adults. The response of a deaf adult to behavior that he defines as discriminatory may be quite different if the hearing individual involved is a clerk in a department store or is a medical doctor charged with diagnosing severe symptoms of physical illness. With all the variations and situational differences, however, it is apparent that deaf children and deaf adults are a minority in a world that is geared to the needs of people with normal hearing, and that there are a variety of important ways in which the attitudes and behaviors of hearing people toward deaf people will influence the lives of the deaf group.

In discussing the status of sick and disabled people from a historical and cross-cultural viewpoint, Safilios-Rothschild (1970, pp. 4–5) identified seven factors that seem to influence the direction and degree of prejudice that is experienced by handicapped people:

(1) The degree of a country's socio-economic development and its rate of unemployment; (2) the prevailing notions about the origins of poverty and unemployment and sociopolitical beliefs concerning the proper role of the government in alleviating social problems; (3) the prevailing notions about the etiology of illness and the degree of individual "re-

sponsibility" involved in falling ill and remaining disabled; (4) the cultural values or stigmata attached to different physical conditions or characteristics; (5) illness or disability-connected factors, such as (a) the degree of visibility of the illness or disability, (b) whether or not the incapacitating illness is contagious, (c) the part of the body afflicted, (d) the nature of the illness (physical or mental) and the assumed "pervasiveness" of the disability, and (e) the severity of functional impairment and the degree of predictability of its course; (6) the effectiveness of the public relations groups representing the interests of a specific disability and the dramatic-sensational image attached to a particular illness (for example, polio); and (7) the degree of importance for the nation's welfare economy and security of such high-disability-risk undertakings as modern warfare and industrial work.

Safilios-Rothschild suggests (1970, p. 6) that most people are influenced by four separate strands of historical beliefs about the causes and consequences of disability: the ancient Hebrew notion that physical disabilities were the result of sin (either the individual's or his parents'); the old Greek notion associating illness and physical defects with social inferiority; the Christian doctrine that defined charity and the care of the sick as a major duty of all believers, and emphasized the dignity of human life and the equality of all in the eyes of God (although in the Middle Ages some of these were seen as "cursed by the Devil"); and the scientific view that defines disabilities as the result of amoral natural conditions that are beyond the will or control of the affected individual.

STIGMA SPECIFIC TO DEAFNESS. From earliest history, deaf persons have been viewed with a mixture of fear, scorn, awe, misunderstanding, and pity. They shared, with other physically handicapped persons, society's intolerance for those whose productive contributions were limited. Deaf babies probably escaped the fate of those with a gross physical deformity in Sparta or Athens, where they were left exposed on a mountainside to die, because their disability was invisible and undetectable at birth. Supposedly Romulus forbade the killing of children under the age of three. But when, at the age of three, a child appeared to be destined to become a liability to the state, it was killed. In those times the assumption was that deaf people had no intellect and thus were incapable of learning. Ancient Roman law included the "deaf and dumb" among those who had no legal rights. Both Aristotle and Galen assumed that deafness automatically precluded the ability to speak. Neither recognized the functional link between hearing and speaking.

As early as 534 A.D., Justinian's legal code recognized different categories of deafness: (1) Those who were "deaf and dumb from birth" were without legal rights or obligations. Guardians were appointed for them by the courts, who had complete charge of their affairs. (2) Those who became deaf from causes arising after birth: "if these people had acquired a knowledge of letters before their affliction, they were allowed to conduct their own affairs by means of writing." These were allowed to enter into a marriage contract, which was denied to those who were born deaf (Bender, 1960, p. 23). The fact that speech was considered to be the test of intellect and therefore of individual rights of inheritance and property before the law prompted some of the early efforts to teach deaf persons to speak. It is easy to understand how the belief in the inevitable linkage of deafness and absence of intelligence arose and was reinforced. If deaf people were seen as inherently uneducable, there was no reason for attempting to teach them. Without special efforts at instruction, language was unavailable to them, and the attributes associated with intelligence did not develop. Thus, the belief in the stupidity of deaf people was a self-fulfilling prophecy.

In addition to the traditional circular belief in the lack of intellectual potential of deaf persons, there has long been a superstitious notion that deafness was a consequence of supernatural punishment: "And Jehovah said unto him, Who hath made man's mouth? or maketh a man dumb or deaf, or seeing, or blind? Is it not I, Jehovah?" (Exodus 4:11). St. Augustine saw the birth of handicapped children as proof of man's natural depravity, a sign that children were punished for their fathers' sins: "from what source of culpability does it come that innocent ones deserve to be born sometimes blind, sometimes deaf, *which defect, indeed, hinders faith itself,* by witness of the Apostle, who says, *'Faith comes by hearing'* . . . Now truly, what bears out the assertion that the soul of the 'innocent' is in the image of God, inasmuch as the liberation of the one born foolish is by his rich gift, if not that the bad merited by the parents is transmitted to the children" (cited in Bender, 1960, p. 27, italics added).

While religious teachings propagated as well as reflected superstition and misinformation concerning the deaf, it was also religion that helped stimulate the first glimmers of interest in educating deaf children. In the sixteenth century, a Benedictine monk named Pedro Ponce de Leon succeeded in teaching several young deaf Spanish noblemen not only to read and to write, but also to speak. Ponce de Leon hoped to bring the deaf youths into the fold of Christianity by enabling them "to pray, to assist at the Mass, to know the doctrines of Christianity, and to know how to confess themselves by speech" (Levine, 1969a, p. xviii). The fact that Ponce de Leon's first pupils were noblemen is not without significance. Since speech was a prerequisite for legal rights, *including the right to own property,* the wealthy had not only the financial means but the financial motivation for finding teachers for their children. Even today, some of the most devoted workers in the field of deaf education are connected with the churches. Some denominations refer to their deaf parishes as part of a "home mission" program.

A French priest, Charles Michel de l'Epée, was the first to conduct a "class" for deaf children. His first pupils were two young deaf sisters. He is supposed to have said: "Believing that these two unfortunates would live and die in ignorance of religion if I made no effort to instruct them, my heart was filled with compassion, and I promised that if they were committed to my charge I would do all for them that I was able" (Ray, 1966, p. 9).

VISIBLE AND INVISIBLE ASPECTS OF DEAFNESS AND STIGMA. Perhaps one of the most important features of deafness influencing the response of the community to the deaf individual is the "invisible" nature of deafness. In this sense, hearing loss is quite different from an orthopedic handicap, both for the affected individual and for others. Davis (1963) found, in his study of child polio victims, that physical appearance is the first realm in which the handicapped child begins to take significant notice of how he differs from other children. The "literal looking-glass self" was the one these children found most difficult to accept as the likeness of who and what they were (p. 143). Richardson and his colleagues (1961) point out that a child with visible handicaps has constant opportunities to make negative comparisons between his appearance and that of other people. He compares the handicapped to a minority group in that they are devalued by themselves and by others. Furthermore, they believe that it is more likely that this "minority culture" will assimilate the values of the majority culture because it is more probable that handicapped people associate primarily with the non-handicapped, in comparison with associations between ethnic minority group members and non-group members (p. 246).

Although deafness is indeed invisible, the ability to remain invisible remains intact only until the deaf person begins to make use of the coping mechanisms that enable him to interact with other people, either deaf or hearing. These mechanisms that change deafness from an unknown to a recognizable condition—that make it either visible or audible—are of three different kinds: hearing aids, speech, and sign language (Meadow and Nemon, 1976, p. 7). The response of the hearing community to each of these mechanisms, and the deaf person's definition and interpretation of the responses of others, often determine that person's abilities to cope with the hearing world.

HEARING AIDS. The general community responds in a variety of ways to the sight of a hearing aid. To some, it is a signal to shout in the deaf person's ear, and to become perplexed when additional volume does not produce instant understanding. For others, the sight of a hearing aid worn by a deaf child produces incomprehension. Sometimes uninformed people believe that the child is wearing an earphone for a portable radio. The hearing aid may be the source of thoughtless comments that parents of deaf children find extremely painful. Often, relatives or friends believe that all deaf children can become hearing as soon as they are fitted with hearing aids. Deaf adults have differing ways of responding to the meaning which the hearing community places on hearing aids. Some refuse to wear a hearing aid even though it might give them some auditory contact with the environment. These may have had unfortunate experiences with hearing aids in their childhood years. Others scorn a hearing aid as a device designed to normalize a deaf person. Some few may wear a hearing aid without batteries because they have found that strangers are more comfortable with them if they have an explanation for what might otherwise be inexplicable behavior.

SPEECH. Many deaf people never use their voices in public because they have found that hearing people respond with fear or distaste to their vocal quality. Few profoundly deaf people have speech that is perfectly normal. Even if their spoken language is understandable, the use of it makes the hearing handicap audible, if not visible. The response of the hearing stranger to deaf speech is often extreme. Thus, we have met deaf mothers who will not use their speech with a hearing baby because they "know that it is ugly." (One mother also "knew" that it was "wrong" to use sign language with her hearing baby. Thus, she was left with no means of systematic communication at all.) It is a temptation to adults to pretend that they understand the speech of deaf children even when they do not. This, combined with the fact that patterns become more understandable with familiarity, can lead to a lack of awareness in deaf children that they are difficult to understand. When they reach adolescence and come into contact with strangers more often, this can be the basis for many bitter feelings. They feel as if their parents and teachers have been lying to them for years by "pretending" to understand or by "pretending" that their vocal quality was not deviant.

SIGN LANGUAGE. The third means by which deafness becomes "knowable" to the general community—that is, either visible or audible—is through the use of sign language. However, sign language identifies one with the deaf community, whereas the use of hearing aids and speech reflect an accommodation to the norms, values, and expectations of the larger hearing culture. This may be one reason for the long history of stigma that has been attached to sign language as a mode of communication for deaf children and for deaf adults.

Speech and speechreading enable the deaf person to "pass." In Goffman's (1963) terms, sign language is perceived as causing the deaf person to be discredited. Thus parents and educators have clung tenaciously to the goal of speech long after it has become evident that a particular deaf child will not realize the goal to any significant degree. The stigma attached to sign language by hearing parents and by teachers of deaf children may be one reason for its highly positive symbolic meaning for members of the deaf adult community. More than any other single feature, the use of sign language signifies membership in the deaf community. In Western societies, there is a generalized suspicion of body language, which adds to the negative reaction of some hearing people to manual communication. In the United States, there has long been a generally negative idea about bilingualism as well. In Europe, by way of contrast, it is generally felt that those who know several languages have an advantage. In America, it is more likely that one language is viewed as being competitive with another, or that all "good Americans" should speak homogenized, unaccented English. (However, some "unaccents" are better than others.)

Sign language is doubly stigmatized: it is only recently that serious students of linguistics have shown Ameslan to be a true language in its own right. One deaf adult has written about the role of sign language as follows: "Thanks to the militancy of the blacks, the Chicanos, the American Indians, and other minority groups, the large majority who hear have begun to be aware of the rights of deaf people as a minority group, and to realize that they have a vital message which has long been ignored by the hearing" (Jacobs, 1974, p. 27).

ATTITUDES REGARDING HANDICAPS AND DEAFNESS. One of the most important facts to remember, when discussing the attitudes of the general population toward deaf people, is that most hearing people have little or no contact with those who have a profound and prelingual hearing loss. The low incidence of deafness, combined with its low visibility, means that most hearing people have no opportunity for meeting and forming opinions—either positive or negative—about deaf people. This also means that the ideas held by a member of the general community may be quite at odds with reality, so that his first meeting with a deaf person may come as a surprise. Thus a generalized attitude survey may have little or no value in predicting either the feelings or the actual behavior of hearing people when they are confronted with a deaf person.*

There was one attempt made to survey a sample of persons in the general community to determine the degree to which deaf persons were known to them. The authors concluded that "the average (person) may know that a deaf couple lives down the street or that a deaf boy works in the stockroom at his place of employment, but that this is about all he knows of actual deaf people" (Furfey and Harte, 1968, p. 89). This lack of contact undoubtedly contributes to other research findings that most people in the general population are "indifferent" to deaf people: that is, they have neither positive nor negative attitudes toward them. This was in marked contrast to the stated favorable attitudes toward very old people, "cripples," foreigners, and blind people (Barker and others, 1953, p. 221).

Efforts to correlate attitudes regarding disabled persons with various personality variables have indicated that acceptance of handicapped people is related to low rigidity, low authoritarianism, and low aggressiveness (Siller and Chipman, 1964, p. 832). One of the most valuable results of this attitude research is its indication of some important determinants of differences in attitudes: "For example, persons having difficulty in communication for psychological reasons may have particular distress with the deaf";

*Change is taking place in this area, too, as more deaf actors are cast in television programs, as sign language news is carried on more television stations, and as the media generally is used by the deaf community for their own needs.

and "quality of contact with the disabled is more crucial than amount" (Siller and others, 1967, p. iv).

> The sense of profound loss associated with blindness was rarely noted with deafness. Compared to the other seven, this disability was the most blandly reacted to. Despite this, annoyance with the practical difficulties of communication was universally stressed, and irritation with the deaf was apparent. Many subjects confused total deafness with varying degrees of hearing deficit. The possibility was raised that lack of immediate visual cues about the condition may cause the public to react as if the deaf are willfully setting up a communication barrier (Siller and others, 1967, p. 77).

The extent to which children with handicaps experience negative responses from their non-handicapped peers is a somewhat different issue. A recent literature review summarized the research findings on this question as follows:

1. Non-handicapped children first become aware of physical handicaps in other children at about age four. It is likely that awareness of other, less obvious types of handicaps occurs somewhat later.

2. Non-handicapped children tend to have a negative attitude toward the handicapped. In the case of the physically handicapped, this attitude seems to make its first appearance at about age five. Emergence of this attitude toward other types of handicaps would presumably be dependent on a prior ability to perceive such handicaps.

3. Older children have a more negative attitude toward the handicapped than younger children do.

4. Contact with handicapped children does not necessarily reduce negative attitudes toward them. In some instances this contact may intensify rather than diminish these attitudes (Levitt and Cohen, 1976, p. 173).

One study (or series of studies) has been completed in Minnesota dealing with the social status of hearing-impaired children who were in regular classrooms (Kennedy and Bruininks, 1974; Kennedy and others, 1976). Eleven children with hearing impairments were followed over a three-year period after being assigned to regular classrooms (grades one through three). Sociometric instruments were used to determine the level of social acceptance these children enjoyed. During the first year of their integrated experience, they were selected by classmates significantly more often than chance; in the second year there was no difference; in the third year the hearing-impaired children were chosen significantly less often (Kennedy and Bruininks, 1974, p. 76). Observations of peer interactions were also collected for these children and their classmates. These data seem to point to the fact that hearing-impaired children rely to a greater degree on their teachers as a source of giving and receiving rewarding social interactions in the classroom. In comparison, their classmates with normal hearing derived most of their socially satisfying interactions with classmates.

Richardson has completed a series of studies aimed at understanding the attitudes of children toward handicapped peers. He shows children a set of drawings depicting a child with a variety of handicaps, with the request that the drawing "liked best" be selected. These pictures are usually ranked in the following order: (1) a child with no physical handicap; (2) a child with crutches and a brace on the left leg; (3) a child seated in a wheel chair with both legs covered with a blanket; (4) a child with a left forearm amputation; (5) a child with a slight facial disfigurement on the left side of the mouth; (6) a child who is obese. One study, conducted in New York City, showed physical handicap to be more salient than race in predicting preferences. A second study, conducted in a Southern city and using black children as subjects, showed the reverse (Richardson and Emerson, 1970).

RESPONSES OF DEAF PERSONS TO OTHERS' EVALUATIONS. Just as the responses of hearing persons to deafness vary with the situation and the individual, there is wide variation in the responses of deaf persons to the evaluations of others. Twenty-seven percent of deaf respondents in the New York State study indicated that they believed that hearing people had negative feelings toward deaf people (Rainer and others, 1969, p. 129). Those deaf respondents with additional years of schooling tended to be more moderate in their opinions, perceiving the "attitudes of the non-deaf in less emotional terms" (p. 130). A questionnaire study of graduates of schools for the deaf indicated that deaf people felt as though they were treated like "furniture" by hearing people (Barker and others, 1953, p. 221). A woman who lost her hearing as an adult says this about her reactions to hearing friends as her own hearing loss became progressively more severe: "When I saw two of my friends with their heads together, talking, I grew tense with suspicion. They must be talking about me because they seemed to be taking care that I should not hear what was said. Sometimes keeping up became so difficult for me that I, who used to laugh and chuckle all day long, became short-tempered and snappish—a crab!" (Heiner, 1949, p. 47).

Heider and Heider (1941) found that the deaf perceived the hearing as having the following attitudes: (1) they are impatient with the deaf person's slowness to understand; (2) they whisper about private matters in front of the deaf; (3) they believe that since the deaf cannot hear speech, they cannot understand, and are thus inferior; (4) they pity the deaf; (5) the deaf are overprotected by, and lose their freedom to, the hearing; (6) the hearing slight and take advantage of the deaf; (7) hearing people tease and make fun of the deaf; (8) hearing people misunderstand the deaf.

The most intensive contemporary study of deaf persons'

beliefs about hearing persons' attitudes toward deafness was conducted by Sussman (1973) as part of a general investigation of the self-concepts of deaf adults. Using the Disability Factor Scale for Deafness developed by the Siller group (described in the preceding section), and the Tennessee Self-Concept Scale, Sussman concluded that the self-concepts of his 129 subjects were significantly more negative than the norms developed for hearing persons, and that their perceptions of the attitudes of hearing persons toward deafness were much more negative than the actual responses of hearing persons surveyed. As Sussman points out, however, it is much more likely that the deaf respondents were answering the questions based on their own direct personal experiences. While hearing people have little or no direct experience with deaf people, the deaf respondents knew how a fairly broad sampling of hearing individuals had responded to them in real-life situations.

Although attitude surveys give us interesting data about how people believe they feel, it is clear that these data are inferred, and cannot be assumed to predict the ways in which people—either deaf or hearing—may actually behave when confronted by a situation requiring action or interaction. Deaf people have only recently begun to act as though they were a self-conscious minority group, to band together with members of other disability groups, and to vocalize their complaints and demands for equal treatment under the law. These activities reflect a burgeoning development of group pride. The activities of many disability groups and disabled individuals in protest marches and demonstrations, which led eventually to the signing into law of Section 504 of the Rehabilitation Act of 1973, were of great importance. Section 504 requires that all institutions receiving federal monies take steps to insure that disabled persons have equal access to buildings and to services that are provided to non-disabled persons. Where deaf persons are concerned, this will most often be reflected in increasing demands for interpreters on television and in hospitals, libraries, and other public places where communication is a prerequisite for equal access. These kinds of activities, reflecting self-conscious determination, are the best indexes of self-confidence and positive response to the attitudes and behaviors of the hearing community.

*Summary*

The deaf child's development can be viewed in terms of the individual areas in which growth and development take place: that is, in the areas of language, cognition, social behavior, and psychological functioning. However, if development is to be understood, it must be seen in the context of the child's environment. The environment includes the significant others in the child's world, beginning with his immediate family, extending to peers, teachers, and members of the various communities that impinge on his life, and finally to his society, with its norms and values, its institutions and laws. In this chapter, we have looked at many of the special elements which contribute to the deaf child's environment, and which make it different from the environment experienced by children without a hearing impairment.

CHAPTER SEVEN

# Policy Implications
# of the Research Findings

I N the preceding chapters, a sustained effort has been
made to present research findings as objec-
tively as possible. Facts rather than opinions have been
collected, and social-science findings rather than anecdotal
evidence have been offered for the reader's consideration.
The time must come, however, when every individual involved with deaf children must make some hard decisions.
Policy questions influencing the treatment of individual
deaf children, their families, and their teachers; school systems; social institutions; legislation—all may hinge on the
interpretation of research findings. These interpretations,
in turn, must be colored by personal experiences, by
theoretical orientations, and by individual value systems.
In these final pages, I propose to offer my own assessment
of the contemporary issues that I consider central to the
education and habilitation of deaf children. My selection of
these issues, as well as my approach to their resolution, is
based not only on my interpretation of the research findings presented in the preceding chapters, but on my experience, orientation, and value system as well.

*Choice of Communication Mode*

Despite the thousands of pages that have been written,
the hundreds of arguments that have been joined, the
dozens of research studies that have been conducted, the
central issue in the treatment of deafness continues to be

the selection of the preferred mode of communication. Should the communication mode be oral, manual, or some combination of both? Depending on the response to this central question, there is a whole series of sub-questions that can be listed as flowing from the initial response. Those of us who work in some way with deaf children or adults tend to believe that the question has been resolved—in the direction of our preference—until we are caught up abruptly, time and again, with the realization that indeed the argument rages on in both new and recurring forms.

My own conviction is that deaf children with hearing parents* should be exposed, as soon as their hearing deficit is discovered, to the combined (simultaneous) usage of spoken and signed English (often referred to as Total Communication). This would seem to be a simple statement, but it has innumerable ramifications, and needs a good deal of explanation in order to cover the many questions and reservations raised by it.

My reading of the literature on deafness and child development leads me to the conclusion that almost all the deficits related to deafness are created by deficiencies related to language and communication. For the deaf child with normal intellectual potential, educational achievement should be at grade level if communication or language are adequate. There is nothing inherent in a hearing deficit that should create additional social or psychological problems. Deficiencies in communication that create lowered understanding of social norms *and* lowered expectations of significant others lead to additional problems in these areas as well.

The major argument against the early addition of signed language to the oral-language input that has been traditionally prescribed by educators has been the notion that

*The treatment of deaf children with deaf parents should be considered as a separate issue, for reasons that I will give later.

deaf children would fail to expend the effort to acquire the more difficult skills of speech and speechreading if they were allowed to rely on the easier language of signs. This is a powerful argument for parents who are anxious that their hearing-impaired children be given every opportunity for normal adult participation in a world that relies on spoken communication for most interpersonal exchanges.

It was this question about the possible interference of the early use of sign language in the acquisition of spoken language that led to my own initial research into the development of deaf children (Meadow, 1967, 1968). A decade ago, when that research was conceived and executed, there were no educational programs using signs with young deaf children. Thus, no experimental design was possible in the comparison of the effects of oral-only and oral-plus methods. The best design that could be devised was one where deaf children with deaf parents (exposed to manual language alone or in combination with spoken language) were compared in terms of educational achievement and social and language development to deaf children with hearing parents (exposed to oral language only in the early years). This research, along with similar research by others (Quigley and Frisina, 1961; Quigley, 1968; Stuckless and Birch, 1966; Vernon and Koh, 1970), demonstrated that deaf children with deaf parents performed at least on the same level as deaf children of hearing parents. While these findings do *not* demonstrate the positive value of the addition of the visual mode, they do indicate that the use of sign language does not have a negative effect on the development of linguistic, social, and educational skills.

As these various studies became more widely known in the field of deaf education, many professionals relaxed their formal strictures against any use of sign language. Some began to prescribe sign language for deaf children who had handicaps in addition to a hearing impairment, or to reserve sign language for children who had not successfully acquired oral skills by the time they were six or eight or ten years old, or to set some limit on the decibel loss for which the addition of sign language would be seen as appropriate. These approaches have some built-in dangers and pitfalls. They define oral language—speech and speechreading—as always superior and preferred to the use of signed language. Thus, any child who is shifted from an "oral track" to a "combined" or "simultaneous" track is defined as an "oral failure." If the parents have been oriented and are committed to the idea that oral language is both preferred and seen as being in opposition to signed language rather than as complementary to it, then the parents, too, see both themselves and their child as failures. No matter how early the decision to make a "shift" in educational program comes, parents and child see or feel the change as a reflection of their inability to perform in the optimum modality. The definition of signed language as reserved for the less adequate deaf child has profound and far-reaching effects.

Thus far, I have addressed only the question of answering criticisms of the early use of sign language—of eliminating the stigma against sign language for young deaf children. This, however, is not sufficient. There are positive reasons for the early introduction of the visual mode. The most important, perhaps, is that children who must rely primarily on their vision for learning language will obviously respond more quickly to language in the visual mode. They will understand their parents more quickly *and* will be able to respond appropriately to the messages their parents are transmitting. The early parent-child bond, increasingly seen as essential for optimal development of social and psychological skills, can grow and develop in the absence of spoken communication. Even deaf children who are eventually defined as "oral successes" lag in their acquisition of language. They and their parents experience frustration stemming from decreased communication until the speech skills are developed. If a child does not receive normal auditory contact with his environment, either naturally or through the use of amplification, this lag *must* be present. Otherwise, we would be considering a child who is neither deaf nor hard-of-hearing. The younger the child at the time of diagnosis the less likely it is that parents will have felt the press of the communication deficit. If the basis for communication is not established early, during this period when messages can easily be transmitted with ordinary gestures or simple, idiosyncratic codes, the family cannot hope to continue to communicate adequately for very long. Soon parents and child need to refer to absent objects, to past or future events, to feelings and emotions that cannot be referenced concretely.

Parents and children who are introduced to sign language initially, at the time of diagnosis, as a means of coping with a hearing handicap (just as a hearing aid is introduced as a means of coping with a hearing deficit) seem to take it as a matter of course. If there is some question—or some withholding by professionals—sign language becomes a dreaded symbol of lack of success, rather than a potential avenue to mutual understanding, pragmatic coping, and aid to future development of spoken language. This approach answers two questions that are frequently voiced in terms of the introduction of sign language: when should it be introduced, and for which hearing-impaired children? If sign language is viewed as a support to parent-child interaction, and as an additional means to the acquisition of inner language, it will be introduced to any child with a hearing impairment that requires remediation, and as early as possible.

THE RECOMMENDED FORM OF VISUAL LANGUAGE. Since sign language has begun to be more accepted in some quarters of deaf education, new arenas for controversy have appeared in the varieties of sign that have developed. My preference—and again, I am thinking of children from families where spoken English is the norm for communication—is one of the several forms of sign that make possible a precise gloss of English. With the basic assumption that the child's exposure or input determines the forms that his expressive language will eventually take, it seems logical that we should expose children to the linguistic form that will make English their native language. There are many ramifications to this issue, however. Strictly speaking, there are two systems that give the most precise gloss for English. One is the Rochester Method, which consists of fingerspelling each and every word that is spoken. The other is Cued Speech, where each syllable or phoneme is represented by a discrete hand movement. Some parents and children have used each of these methods successfully, and I have no real theoretical objection to either of them. However, in dealing with very young children, their ability to make the small and precise distinctions in hand and finger movements that are necessary for differentiating between many similar hand configurations that have differing meanings is limited. This difficulty in expressive formulations (and perhaps in receptive differentiation as well) make these two approaches seem to me to be less useful in providing initial linguistic input for the very young deaf child first acquiring language. Again, this means a delay for parents in receiving feedback from the child that serves as reinforcement for their further linguistic productions.

It is true that this objection (that the complexity of the systems creates difficulties for users) can also be raised to some of the systems of signed English. A very long array of signs denoting different tenses, endings, possessives, and so forth, can become a burden for both parents and children in the process of learning.

Another thing to consider in the selection of a system of

signed English is the attitudes of deaf adults. Again, this can become a ticklish business—one of balancing the needs of deaf children, their parents, and the deaf community. Some deaf adults feel that a system that tampers with "their" language, that distorts the basic rationale that American Sign Language follows, poses an insult and a threat to their identity as expressed in their language. While I do not believe that deaf adults should ultimately be the ones to decide upon the language form to which deaf children are exposed (that decision is, in the final analysis, one for the children's parents to make), they have a feel for visual language that should be tapped. Congruence between artificial and natural sign languages will help the deaf child to move back and forth between the deaf and the hearing communities when he grows older.

One of the determining factors in the selection of a sign language system by the parents of deaf children is, simply, the availability of classes for teaching sign language. Many educational programs provide teachers of sign language, and the form of sign language taught is that selected for use in the educational program. It makes good sense for parents to learn the sign language form that has been selected by the school system their child will attend. Some of these comments regarding optimal visual language are certainly relevant for teachers and administrators responsible for making this decision for an entire system.

Other questions can be raised about the form of sign language to be used with deaf children. There are a number of professionals who have suggested that Ameslan may be the best form, and that hearing parents should be taught Ameslan at the time of diagnosis. Their arguments in some cases are an extension of the points that I made when I compared the use of the Rochester Method or Cued Speech to the use of signed English. That is, Ameslan is a shorter, more compact, and more easily expressed and understood form of language. Ideas can be expressed more quickly and less laboriously, the argument goes. Facial expression and body language are more likely to be incorporated into communication with Ameslan. My response to these suggestions is again based on my essential or core idea that the "best" form of sign language is the one that hearing parents can learn most quickly and easily and feel most comfortable in using with their children. Thus, I would suggest that the sign language that conforms best to their own native language (signed English) will conform to those specifications most easily.

Proponents of Ameslan would be most vocal in insisting that it is truly a language, with all the components that other languages have. I am convinced of this also, but I believe that we are only at the threshold of understanding what these linguistic features are. Although there have been a number of advances in the analysis of Ameslan in recent years, the ability to systematize all the features and teach parents to incorporate them into their language productions with their young children is a very complex task. Thus, we could predict that the hearing parents, learning Ameslan as a second language themselves, might well be using a pidgin sign that was quite idiosyncratic. In contrast, the "rules" for some of the artificial signed English systems are quite simple. Once they are internalized, it is a question of practice. Compared to learning an entirely different language, this is a much simpler process.

There is no reason why some of the desirable features of Ameslan related to facial and body expressiveness could not be encouraged in the use of artificial sign language. Another notion that seems to me to be important is that when hearing parents are just beginning to learn sign, they will have incomplete vocabularies and an incomplete grasp of the "rules" of the artificial system. Thus, when "telescopic" or incomplete sentences and language are most appropriate—that is, during the early months or years of the child's language learning—the parents will, by necessity, be using a telescopic kind of communication. However, by the time the child "needs" more complete sentence input, the parents could be equipped to provide it.

THE IMPORTANCE OF EARLY LANGUAGE INTERVENTION. There are a number of reasons for my emphasis on the importance of early language acquisition. Arguments over the "critical age" for the acquisition of language, in terms of biological development, have waxed and waned over the past ten years. Deaf children who have been exposed to consistent language after the age of three years and have successfully acquired fluency would tend to provide negative evidence for the biological theory. However, even if we assume that children who acquire language late *can* "catch up," both linguistically and cognitively, there is still the question of their need to "catch up" on the social and emotional tasks that are gained through symbolic interaction (the use of language) with their parents.

Even if deaf children could be given those social and emotional skills in the absence of language (and there are those who argue that they could not), we must still deal with the question of parental expectations and orientations toward ways of dealing with their young children. If parents are accustomed to dealing with young children verbally, and expect language to be a major channel for play and enjoyment, for socialization and the setting of limits, and for the expression of affection and pleasure, the parents may be less able than the children to shift to nonverbal communication. Just as there may be an optimum age or stage for a child to acquire language, there may be an optimum age or stage of parenthood for language to be transmitted to a child. Obviously this is in terms of emotional expectations about parenthood, and expectations about a child's response to the parents.

Another reason for emphasizing the importance of early

language here is that parents are more likely to be motivated to learn sign if they begin when their children are still
very young. Sign language skills do not develop overnight.
While it is probably easier to learn sign language that is
based on English than it is to learn a completely different
second language, it usually takes several years for an individual to become highly fluent, unless he or she has daily
contact with adult signers. Thus, if parents begin to learn
after their children are fluent, they may feel inadequate
and lose their motivation for learning.

THE NEED FOR EARLY PARENT COUNSELING. At various
places in the preceding chapters, we have referred to the
emotional impact on parents of having their child diagnosed as deaf. Grief, anger, guilt, sorrow, and despair are
emotions that parents often experience in the early stages
of their encounters with a handicap. People who are suffer-
ing from these kinds of emotions frequently are unable to
function at top efficiency. Professionals who are attempting
to orient parents to the need for learning sign language, as
well as fitting hearing aids, providing speech training, and
other needed habilitation efforts, must be prepared to deal
with parents' feelings about the child's handicap. Perhaps
one of the major ingredients of a successful early education
program is a staff of people trained in coping with the
emotional responses of parents. Some parents are unable
to "hear" the educational prescriptions of teachers for
weeks or even months, until they have begun to sort out
their thoughts and emotions about the diagnosis. Unless
teachers are trained to expect this reaction and are prepared to deal with it (often by waiting until parents are
really ready to hear what is being said about language),
both parents and teachers will be frustrated in their efforts
to establish an optimum environment for the deaf child's
development. Some of the most successful preschool
teachers of deaf children are those who are willing to listen

week after week to parents expressing their disappointment, anger, and sadness. Only then can the speech and
language lessons proceed. Some educators feel that this
listening process should be fulfilled by a trained counselor.
Even if the supply of counselors were great enough to meet
the needs of parents, there would still be some question in
my mind about the desirability of splitting completely the
functions of preschool teaching and parent counseling. I
would prefer to see mental health professionals available to
teachers to help them in handling situations in the best
possible way, and also to provide the teachers with needed
relief for their own emotions after dealing with the pain
and sorrow of parents.

TOTAL COMMUNICATION: WHAT IS IT, WHAT SHOULD IT
BE? Total Communication means many different things to
different people. To some, it appears to be the old "simultaneous method" in a new guise. To others, it promises the
dawning of a new day in deaf education, which will result
in miraculous language and educational achievement for
all deaf children. Some prefer to call it a "philosophy"
rather than a "method." In recommending Total Communication as the preferred approach to the education of
deaf children, I consider it to mean the early, consistent,
simultaneous use of spoken and signed English by all
significant others in the deaf child's environment. This
definition sets Total Communication apart from the old
"simultaneous approach" because it uses one of the
newer sign language systems with English grammatical
and syntactical markers; it is introduced during the
early months or years of the deaf child's life (rather than
at age six or age thirteen, as in residential schools); and
because it assumes that parents and siblings as well as
teachers will use this means of communication with the
deaf child. The inclusion of "consistent" in this definition
implies that *all* communication addressed to the child,

or made in his or her presence, will be bimodal. The communication can be simplified, but not by dropping one or the other modality. Simplified language might take the form of shortened phrases or "baby talk," but at all times, and for every message, the child must be given the opportunity to respond to either speech or sign or both. This approach does not rule out the addition of gesture, or pantomime, or writing if these are useful in stimulating understanding and communication. However, the major thrust is toward providing a systematic language model that will enable and encourage the deaf child to use any and all of his or her capabilities in acquiring language and meaning.

This approach and recommendation have developed from observing children at the University of California, San Francisco (as described in Chapter Two). The children who were exposed to this "optimum" language environment—which included the introduction of signs with spoken language no later than three years of age, and as early as eighteen months of age, consistent and careful amplification, a program of counseling for parents, and intensive support services—acquired language in much the same way as hearing children do, and at very similar rates. Parent-child interaction was marked by enjoyment and by the communication of meaning. It must be noted that these children had varying degrees of residual hearing (from moderate to profound hearing loss) but that none had handicapping conditions in addition to deafness. All had received adequate medical attention and were fortunate in having parents who were very much involved in their development and committed to working closely with them and with the helping professionals.

In contrast, deaf children who enter kindergarten or first grade with no meaningful linguistic system, with additional handicapping problems, with busy or non-involved parents, present a picture which already calls for remediation—for rehabilitation rather than habilitation. Whether this same kind of language approach is optimum for these children is an open question. If they are bright and aware of their environment, they may well have developed their own esoteric language or gestural system. They may have focused on a "set" modality that makes bimodal communication distracting rather than helpful for them. Or they may be so far past the optimal age for language learning that grossly reduced goals must be accepted for them. These are researchable questions, and should receive attention by professionals interested in the welfare of deaf children.

LANGUAGE FOR DEAF CHILDREN OF DEAF PARENTS. Earlier, it was suggested that signed English rather than American Sign Language was the preferred approach for deaf children with hearing parents. One reason for this was the greater ease with which English-speaking parents could be expected to learn signed English. Another reason is that parents should not be asked or expected to socialize their children in a language that is "foreign" to them. One's language is very much a part of one's identity. If we ask parents to communicate an identity different from their own, it is tantamount to suggesting that their identities are inferior, or that their children are destined to be foreign to them. The same kind of reasoning holds for deaf parents. If they normally use American Sign Language at home in communicating with each other and with other family members, they should not be asked or expected to use a different language form—that is, signed English—with a deaf son or daughter. The ease of parent-child communication, the increased possibilities for pleasure in parent-child interaction, should take precedence over any possible suggestion of the value of signed English for later educational achievement.

Some deaf parents will be interested in adding signed English to their family's repertoire in the interest of giving their child a "head start" in the language that will probably be used in the classroom. Teachers need to handle requests to and from deaf families with care. Probably the most beneficial advice that can be given to deaf families is to encourage them to communicate *more* with their deaf child, rather than "differently." It is my impression that old attitudes about American Sign Language will continue to plague deaf adults for many years to come. American Sign Language (Ameslan) has come into its own in the recent past. Attention from linguists has given it a mantle of respectability as a complex and subtle language with a grammar and syntax appropriate for the visual modality. The growing sense of pride within the deaf community has increased the official respect that Ameslan commands. However, for many deaf adults who grew up with a deep sense of inferiority about their communication mode, old attitudes and values die hard. They continue to apologize for their linguistic system, and to feel that the use of Ameslan will damage the future ability of their deaf children to acquire English and to succeed academically.

Erting (1978) suggests that the presence of a deaf adult in the educational setting gives deaf children "an opportunity to learn and use a variety of communicative skills that will be important to them in settings outside the classroom, especially those that involve members of the deaf ethnolinguistic group" (p. 147). She emphasizes that this is particularly important for deaf children of deaf parents, who are accustomed to the use of Ameslan at home. Observations in a preschool classroom indicated that both the children and the deaf teacher's aide used code-switching, from Ameslan to signed English, depending on the formality or informality of the situation. Erting suggests the use of a bilingual model in approaching the education of deaf children. The presence of the native signer in the classroom enabled more accurate interpretations of the children's signed language productions.

> While the hearing teacher supplied information in signed English during the structured lessons, the deaf children whose native language was Ameslan were able to conduct extended interchanges with the deaf aide, providing them with a clarification of the subject matter, with language experience and practice, and with the possibility of a greater satisfaction in terms of the interpersonal functions of communication. At the same time, all of the children were being exposed to an adult model who identified herself as deaf too and functioned as a member of the deaf ethnolinguistic group—as well as functioning, with the hearing teacher, as a member of the wider society through her use of signed English (Erting, 1978, p. 148).

It is my guess that we neither understand nor appreciate the extreme influence that linguistic attitudes play in creating the linguistic environments of the deaf children of deaf parents, because of the way their parents have learned to devalue their own language. That the systematic comparisons of groups of deaf children with deaf and with hearing parents have continually favored those with deaf parents probably represents a much greater achievement than we realize. Many of these parents did not themselves experience a rich linguistic environment when they were small, and therefore may well be blocked in establishing this with their own children because they do not have the experience—either conscious or unconscious—on which to draw in their interaction with their own children.

Finally, for all deaf children, whether their parents be hearing or deaf, my interpretation of the research findings on linguistic development suggests that the best applied language approach is the one that creates the greatest possibilities for early, relaxed, meaningful communication between the children and their parents. Furthermore, it seems to me that for hearing parents, this goal can best be achieved through Total Communication. For deaf parents, more individualized recommendations are needed, depending on families' most comfortable linguistic style. In this way, I believe that optimal cognitive, social, and psychological development are more likely to be achieved.

## Deaf Education and Social Change

Change seems to come very slowly to deaf education. The same might be said of the field of education generally, but what is true for the general field is doubly true where hearing-impaired children are concerned. Many changes that are seen in the general field may appear ten years later in deaf education. This could be beneficial if educators of deaf children learned from the mistakes made in earlier developments among the general population, but, sadly, this does not seem to be the case. What are some of the reasons for this state of affairs? The oral-manual controversy in deaf education has been called the Two Hundred Years War. In my opinion, the bitterness with which this battle has raged (and it still continues) has sapped the energies of deaf educators. If teachers must continue to justify their methods, if administrators are constantly on the defensive with each new generation of students and parents, there is that much less energy available to go toward the investigation of new educational developments, to the consideration of new research findings, and to creative thinking for the improvement of current programs.

THE HISTORICAL ISOLATION AND INBREEDING OF RESIDENTIAL SCHOOLS. For many years, the state residential schools for the deaf exerted great influence on the field of deaf education. A small clique controlled the selection of new school superintendents, who wielded great power.

Sometimes these administrative offices were even passed from father to son. Change does not come easily in this kind of traditional situation, where a very small group makes many major decisions. The major center for the training of teachers (who eventually become administrators) was for many years Gallaudet College. Graduation from the college was an acknowledged prerequisite for advancing in the field of deaf education, and many hiring decisions were influenced by officials in the college.

Slowly, this situation is changing, and with the changes come new developments in deaf education generally. The picture is instructive both for understanding deaf education and for gaining insight to the nature of social change as well.

In the early days, very few hearing people knew sign language. Most of those who did were the children or siblings of deaf people. Knowledge of sign language was necessary for a teacher or administrator of a residential school, and therefore the pool from which these officials could be selected was very small. Great power was held in the hands of a few. Today, sign language is becoming more and more popular. Classes are taught in metropolitan areas, and in many smaller urban and even rural settings as well. The pool for possible administrators has expanded, and no longer does a very small group control the business of deaf education.

In earlier times, residential schools, and even Gallaudet College, were organized as systems of benevolent paternalism. Decisions were made about the education of deaf children by hearing adults rather than by deaf adults. To some extent, this situation has been self-perpetuating: those who are not allowed to make decisions become deficient in that ability. Thus the situation in deaf education was a reflection of the sheltered position of deaf people generally. The general situation of the deaf community has improved in recent years. The quality of education has increased; more deaf persons have become qualified as professionals in all fields, including education. Each small improvement in the general position of the deaf community has lessened the isolation of the residential schools and of deaf education generally.

As deaf people have become their own spokesmen for social change, the speed of legislative change has increased. Gallaudet College is no longer the only place where deaf students can acquire higher education. They may now attend the National Technical Institute for the Deaf in Rochester, New York, programs at California State University, Northridge, or numerous smaller programs scattered across the country. This dispersion of resources would seem to be a healthy development.

THE "BENEVOLENT MOTIVATION" OF DEAF EDUCATORS. Historically, work with handicapped people has been viewed as spiritual service. It is no accident that the early teachers of the deaf (such as Abbé de l'Epée) were priests who saw their ministry as an attempt to shepherd the "heathen" into the fold of the Lord. Many churches today see their deaf parishes as "missions." The social work with the deaf in Britain is primarily accomplished by Missioners through the Church of England. This service orientation has negative as well as positive effects on the educational scene. Among the positive aspects are, obviously, the selfless dedication that many teachers and administrators have to their work. Traditionally, salaries for teachers in special education have been lower than for teachers in ordinary classrooms, and deaf children have gained the benefit of the dedication that their teachers have been willing to exert for lower than average pay. However, in the long run, this orientation can result in less obvious disadvantages. After a certain period of time, people who are underpaid, even if their initial choice was made with the full knowledge and understanding of the relative com-

pensation scale, may feel slighted or even exploited. The
most ambitious (and possibly most highly qualified) professionals may move to positions where the work is
less frustrating, more highly paid, and less difficult.
There is a tendency for everyone in the field to have at
least a covert attitude that work with handicapped children should involve a higher level of commitment than
other kinds of work. Eventually these higher expectations
can lead to bitterness and lack of job satisfaction.

CONTINUING LOW EDUCATIONAL ACHIEVEMENT OF DEAF
CHILDREN. One of the most frequently cited facts about
deaf students is their persistent achievement far below the
levels of age mates without hearing impairments. Language deprivation with attendant social and emotional
(experiential) handicapping is recognized as the basis for
the lower achievement. However, for teachers who work
daily with children, with the purpose of helping them to
become academically equipped to take their places in a
career world that is geared to high educational achievement, the situation of low achievement becomes frustrating, discouraging, and depressing. It is my belief that this
low achievement level can lead to "professional depression" for teachers, and to a climate where change is less
welcome because so many things have been tried "to no
avail." Thus there is a circular effect: low achievement leads
to low expectations that lead to lowered acceptance of new
ideas. In spite of this pessimistic analysis, I feel that many
recent developments have begun to break this self-
defeating cycle. Movements toward community action led
by deaf persons, increasing opportunities for deaf persons
in high-status positions, greater attention to the deaf
community by federal agencies—any and all of these developments can break into the cycle and help to turn deaf
education into a new and more promising direction.

MAINSTREAMING FOR DEAF CHILDREN: THE PROS AND CONS. Mainstreaming, which means the inclusion of deaf children (and children with other handicapping conditions) in classrooms with non-handicapped peers, has been called the most important issue in deaf education today. The passage of Public Law 94-142 has brought much attention to it recently, but in deaf education the issue was raised long ago, and today's arguments have been discussed for many years in relation to day schools versus residential schools and "segregated settings" versus "integrated settings." There are many versions of mainstreaming policies, and it is important to separate them in any consideration of pros and cons of the question.

There are two extremes, in contrasting educational settings: one consists of full-time placement in a residential school for deaf children where all students are deaf, and where the deaf child lives in a dormitory and attends classes with other deaf students, seeing hearing family members and peers no more frequently than during weekend visits home. The other extreme is full-time placement in the neighborhood school closest to the deaf child's home, where he or she may be the only child with a hearing impairment in his or her classroom, or indeed in the entire school. Some variations of this arrangement might include visits from itinerant specialists for tutoring or speech therapy, and the provision of a full-time interpreter if the deaf child depends on Total Communication. An older variant of "integration" for deaf children is the provision of a trained teacher of the deaf for a small group of deaf children in a special classroom within an ordinary school. This "day class" arrangement is a model that has been extant for many years. Deaf children would often participate with hearing peers in non-academic classes such as home economics, physical education, and art. They would have opportunities to interact with non-deaf students at lunchtime and during recess. Small class size and individualized attention were possible. However, the age range in these classrooms, as well as the range in ability or academic achievement level, is often very wide. This can mean that the deaf child has no true peers against whom to measure or pit his skills or to look for intellectual stimulation or companionship. In the larger age pools of day schools *or* residential schools, it is possible to group students on the basis of age or ability or both, thus using teaching time and student self-help models more successfully than in settings where numbers of deaf students are very small.

There is still another kind of educational prescription available to some deaf children. This is found in the experience of the deaf child who is mainstreamed and who is the only handicapped child in his neighborhood school. For some parents and educators, this model is the ideal—the goal toward which early education and training are directed from infancy onward. It is true that this situation most nearly approximates the appearance of normalization. The deaf child can live at home rather than traveling to a residential school, where he must live in a dormitory rather than growing up in a full-time family setting. He does not have the tiring experience of traveling long distances on a schoolbus in order to get to the special school. Classmates live nearby rather than being scattered throughout an urban or a metropolitan area. This means that after-school playmates are more readily at hand. Neighborhood children of the same age are known through the classroom and supposedly are more available for after-school play. The deaf child has the positive experience of sharing school and teachers with older and younger siblings. Parents can devote all their energies to one school rather than dividing time and effort between schools where deaf and hearing brothers and sisters attend. The deaf child is not singled out for special treatment and made to feel different from neighborhood friends and siblings. These are some of the advantages of mainstreaming or integration, if it works in the ideal manner envisaged by its proponents. Unfortunately, however, reality is frequently very different from the ideal.

In the real situation, the deaf child is often overwhelmed in a large group of classmates. For many years, educators of deaf children have been working to reduce the size of classes in which deaf youngsters are taught. A class size of ten was once considered to be a goal toward which to work; then seven became the norm in most states. Now six or even five deaf children are considered to be the most that a special education teacher can handle comfortably. The mainstreamed deaf child is deposited in a classroom with 25 or 30 other children. Instead of a teacher who has been specifically trained to work with children with hearing handicaps, the teacher in the mainstreamed child's classroom may never have seen a deaf child before, and may have had absolutely no orientation in what to expect or how to respond. Integration of any kind requires communication. Acceptance is based on more than good will. It comes from comfortable interaction. Too often, this easy interaction between a deaf child and hearing classmates is a difficult and perhaps unrealized dream. For younger deaf children, this interaction may come more easily, especially if the deaf child is outgoing. The games and activities of younger children are less likely to be based on language. As children become older, their activities are less physical, and deaf children have a more difficult time keeping up. Interaction becomes more and more difficult, communication more and more strained. The difficulties that deaf children feel in a situation where there is only one child who is "different"—because he wears a hearing aid, has unusual speech, and does not understand spoken messages as quickly as others—can create extreme difficulties of self-image and social development.

The thrust toward mainstreaming has come primarily from the effort to provide mildly mentally retarded children with needed opportunities for placement in regular classes. This thrust, in turn, came to some extent from persons who were concerned (and rightly so) with the large numbers of ethnic and racial minority children who were labeled retarded because they were culturally different and because they received low scores on intelligence tests that were designed for children from the middle-class majority culture. The efforts to encourage greater opportunities for these children should not have the unintended consequences of forcing deaf children into classrooms where they cannot get the special help they need from teachers who have been trained in special methods to help them to overcome their handicap. It should not be assumed automatically that the classroom in the neighborhood school with a single handicapped youngster is the "least restrictive environment." For some handicapped children this is in fact the "most restrictive environment."

BUILDING SOCIAL SKILLS IN DEAF CHILDREN. One of the most encouraging developments on the contemporary scene of deaf education is the growing realization by teachers and administrators that one of the major needs of deaf children is help in making up their experiential deficiencies, and the provision of opportunities for developing social skills that are necessary for happy and productive lives. For many years this area was neglected, at the expense of "pouring in" language in a structured way. There is some movement away from this heavily structured approach today, and some additional possibilities for creative work in classrooms are being offered to deaf children. Perhaps as much as anything else, these developments show promise of helping to close the gap between deaf and hearing children in adjustment to modern living. Although there are exciting programs being offered in many schools across the country, I am most familiar with those at the Kendall Demonstration Elementary School of Gallaudet College, and will use them to illustrate briefly some of the concepts that show great promise for the future.

One program that has created a great deal of positive comment is based on group counseling for young deaf children. Often, the youngsters have had few opportunities to interact in a structured give-and-take discussion outside the classroom. Counselors have experimented with the development of group skills, stressing constructive discussions that encourage the expression of feelings (Gawlick, McAleer, and Ozer, 1976). Based on a series of materials created by Dinkmeyer called Developing Understanding of Self and Others (DUSO), one theme that is stressed is an appreciation of differences and positive feelings about the self. The growing abilities of six- to ten-year-old students to use the group sessions, to ask for more exposure to "DUSO" the talking dolphin, and to sign up for individual counseling sessions, attests to the success of this kind of program.

Another approach to the development of social skills is the use of Career Education materials. While in older age groups these materials are vocational or pre-vocational, for younger children they are geared toward teaching children they can exert an influence on their own lives by consciously choosing between alternatives and working toward a goal. These materials have been developed and tried in the classroom by groups of Kendall teachers in conjunction with staff members at Ohio State University.

A third project that has exciting possibilities for increasing social development has been labeled "survival skills" and emphasizes helping deaf children to manage well in the community by giving them practice in interaction with strangers.

Projects encouraging deaf students to take responsibility for others less fortunate than themselves, to participate in community affairs, and to take responsibility for providing some of their own funds for class trips through money-raising projects are other examples of ways in which teachers and schools can help to establish a sense of social responsibility that comes from experience.

SOME FORGOTTEN SUB-GROUPS OF DEAF CHILDREN. The language and educational problems of the majority of deaf children are so great, and have remained unsolved for so long, that there is a tendency among those involved with deaf education and rehabilitation to be less concerned with more difficult sub-groups than might otherwise be the case. Another reason for this lack of concern is the small-ness of the total numbers of children involved. When the total number of deaf children is only 1 percent of the school-age population, providing specialized services for smaller numbers of special groups *within* the total deaf group becomes even more difficult.

I am thinking of deaf children who come from homes where the language spoken is Spanish, Chinese, or some other non-English spoken system. I am thinking of deaf children who have some other physical handicap, such as blindness or cerebral palsy, in addition to their auditory handicap—or who are mentally retarded or emotionally disturbed. I am thinking of children whose families do not belong to the majority white middle-class culture, or who come from isolated rural areas, or from families whose re-sources are extremely limited. It is these families who are most likely to be excluded from the advantages of adequate medical care, and their children who are least likely to be diagnosed for congenital handicapping conditions. Thus, the first and most helpful program for these children would be a truly effective "child find" to identify babies with auditory handicaps in the first months of life. Public Law 94-142 was aimed primarily at these kinds of children, and we hope that they will begin to get the additional attention they need as a result of its provisions.

Another group of deaf children that is neglected consists of the gifted. Gifted deaf children are those who perform at or above the level of their hearing peers. They may be capable of these elevated performances because of superior intelligence, or because they were exposed to language very early (either because their parents are deaf or because their hearing parents provided input in a visual mode). At the present time, these children are so few in numbers that they do not fit into existing programs for hearing-handicapped children. Thus, another discouraging and frustrating experience that parents have is that of trying to find an appropriate school program for a deaf child who does *too* well. Hopefully, we will begin to see new ways of dealing with these kinds of sub-groups in the future.

THE INFLUENCE OF DEAF ADULTS AS ROLE MODELS. It is my bias that life is richer for people who are capable and comfortable in interacting with many different kinds of groups, for people who can move easily from one community or subculture to another. This is true for deaf persons as well as for hearing persons. It is my impression that the most effective leaders in the deaf community—those who have the most influence and have been the most successful in promoting change that leads to greater opportunities for deaf persons—are those deaf persons who have fluent command of spoken and signed English and Ameslan. Many of these talented persons have achieved positions of great influence, and deaf leaders are increasingly taking precedence over hearing persons in affairs that are important to the deaf community. This is a sign of the coming of age of the deaf community and has all kinds of positive reverberations. As more and more deaf persons achieve eminence through their own efforts and through increasing opportunities for participation in the majority culture, there are more and more deaf adults who are available to young deaf students as role models. And so, in spite of the many discouraging obstacles to the linguistic, cognitive, social, and psychological development of deaf children, the future of these children begins to look brighter.

# References

Altshuler, K. Z. The social and psychological development of the deaf child: problems, their treatment and prevention. *American Annals of the Deaf*, 1974, *119*, 365–376.

————. Identifying and programming for the emotionally handicapped deaf child. In D. W. Naiman (ed.), *Needs of Emotionally Disturbed Hearing Impaired Children*. N.Y.: Deafness Research and Training Center, New York University, 1975, 3–12.

Altshuler, K. Z., W. E. Deming, J. Vollenweider, J. D. Rainer, and R. Tendler. Impulsivity and profound early deafness: a cross cultural inquiry. *American Annals of the Deaf*, 1976, *121*, 331–345.

Altshuler, K. Z., and J. D. Rainer. Distribution and diagnosis of patients in New York State mental hospitals. In J. D. Rainer, K. Z. Altshuler, F. J. Kallmann (eds.), *Family and Mental Health Problems in a Deaf Population* (2nd ed.). Springfield, Ill.: C C Thomas, 1969, 195–203.

Anderson, H., B. Barr, and E. Wedenberg. Genetic disposition—prerequisite for maternal rubella deafness. *Archives of Otolaryngology*, 1970, *91*, 141–147.

Anderson, R. J., and F. Y. Sisco. *Standardization of the WISC-R Performance Scale for Deaf Children*. Washington, D.C.: Office of Demographic Studies, Gallaudet College, 1977.

Anthony, D. A. Signing essential English. Unpublished M.A. thesis, Eastern Michigan University, 1966.

Avery, C. The social competence of pre-school acoustically handicapped children. *Journal of Exceptional Children*, 1948, *15*, 71–73.

Balow, I. H., and R. G. Brill. An evaluation study of reading and academic achievement levels of sixteen graduating classes of the California School for the Deaf, Riverside. Mimeo report, Contract #4566 with the State of California, Department of Education, 1972.

Barker, R. G., in collaboration with B. A. Wright, L. Meyerson, and M. R. Gonick. *Adjustment to Physical Handicap and Illness: A Survey of the Social Psychology of Physique and Disability.* New York: Social Science Council Bulletin 55, rev. 1953.

Barsch, R. H. *The Parent of the Handicapped Child.* Springfield, Illinois: C. C. Thomas, 1968.

Barton, M. E., S. D. Court, and W. Walker. Causes of severe deafness in school children in Northumberland and Durham. *British Medical Journal*, 1962, *1*, 351–355.

Basilier, T. Surdophrenia, the psychic consequences of congenital or early acquired deafness. Some theoretical and clinical considerations. *Acta Psychiatrica Scandinavica*, 1964, Supplementum 180, *40*, 362–372.

Bell, R. Q. The effect on the family of a limitation in coping ability in the child: a research approach and a finding. *Merrill-Palmer Quarterly*, 1964, *10*, 129–142.

Bellugi, U. The acquisition of negation. Unpublished Ph.D. dissertation, Harvard University, 1967.

———. Studies in sign language. In T. J. O'Rourke (ed.), *Psycholinguistics and Total Communication: The State of the Art.* Washington, D.C.: American Annals of the Deaf, 1972, 68–74.

Bellugi, U. and E. S. Klima. Aspects of sign language and its structure. In Kavanagh, J. F. and J. E. Cutting (eds.), *The Role of Speech in Language.* Cambridge, Mass.: M.I.T. Press, 1975, 171–205.

————. The roots of language in the sign talk of the deaf. *Psychology Today*, 1972, *76*, 61–64.

Bender, R. E. *The Conquest of Deafness.* Cleveland: The Press of Western Reserve University, 1960.

Berlin, I. N. Preventive aspects of mental health consultation to schools. *Mental Hygiene*, 1967, *51*, 34–40.

Best, B. Development of classification skills in deaf children with and without early manual communication. Unpublished Ph.D. dissertation, University of California, Berkeley, 1970.

Bindon, D. M. Personality characteristics of rubella-deaf children: implications for teaching of the deaf in general. *American Annals of the Deaf*, 1957, *102*, 264–270.

Black, J. W., P. P. O'Reilly, and L. Peck. Self-administered training in lipreading. *Journal of Speech and Hearing Disorders*, 1963, *28*, 183–186.

Blair, F. X. A study of the visual memory of deaf and hearing children. *American Annals of the Deaf*, 1957, *102*, 254–263.

Blank, M. Use of the deaf in language studies: A reply to Furth. *Psychological Bulletin*, 1965, *63*, 442–444.

————. Cognitive functions of language in the preschool years. *Developmental Psychology*, 1974, *10*, 229–245.

Blank, M., and W. H. Bridger. Conceptual cross-modal transfer in deaf and hearing children. *Child Development*, 1966, *37*, 29–38.

Blanton, R. L., and J. C. Nunnally. Retention of trigrams by deaf and hearing subjects as a function of pronunciability. *Journal of Verbal Learning and Verbal Behavior*, 1967, *6*, 428–431.

Blanton, R. L., J. C. Nunnally, and P. B. Odom. Graphemic, phonetic, and associative factors in the verbal behavior of deaf and hearing subjects. *Journal of Speech and Hearing Research*, 1967, *10*, 225–231.

Bonvillian, J. D., V. R. Charrow, and K. E. Nelson. Psycholinguistic and educational implications of deafness. *Human Development*, 1973, *16*, 321–345.

Boothroyd, A. Some aspects of language function in a group of lower school children. Sensory Aids Research Project Report #6, C. V. Hudgins Diagnostic and Research Center, Clarke School for the Deaf, Northampton, Mass., 1971.

Bornstein, H. A description of some current sign systems designed to represent English. *American Annals of the Deaf*, 1973, *118*, 454–463.

———. Systems of sign. In L. J. Bradford and W. G. Hardy (eds.), *Hearing and Hearing Impairment*. New York: Grune and Stratton, 1979.

Bower, E. M. A process for early identification of emotionally disturbed children. *Bulletin of the California State Department of Education*, *27*, 1958.

Boyd, J. Comparison of motor behavior in deaf and hearing boys. *American Annals of the Deaf*, 1967, *112*, 598–605.

Brasel, K. E., and S. P. Quigley. Influence of certain language and communication environments in early childhood on the development of language in deaf individuals. *Journal of Speech and Hearing Research*, 1977, *20*, 81–94.

Brill, R. G. A study in adjustment of three groups of deaf children. *Exceptional Children*, 1960, *26*, 464–466.

———. *Education of the Deaf, Administrative and Professional Developments*. Washington, D.C.: Gallaudet College Press, 1974.

Brown, R. *A First Language, The Early Stages*. Cambridge: Harvard University Press, 1973.

Bruininks, R. H., and C. Clark. Auditory and visual learning in first-grade educable mentally retarded and normal children. Research Report #13, Research, Development and Demonstration Center in Education of Handicapped Children. University of Minnesota, November, 1970.

Brunschwig, L. A study of some personality aspects of deaf children. Contributions to Education No. 687, New York: Teachers College Press, Columbia University, 1936.

Bryan, T. Peer popularity of learning disabled children. *Journal of Learning Disabilities*, 1974, 7, 261–268.

Burchard, E. M. L., and H. R. Myklebust. A comparison of congenital and adventitious deafness with respect to its effect on intelligence, personality, and social maturity. *American Annals of the Deaf*, 1942, 87, 140–154; 342–360.

Butt, D., and F. M. Chreist. A speechreading test for young children. *Volta Review*, 1968, 70, 225–235.

California, State of. *Mental Health Survey of Los Angeles County*. Sacramento: Department of Mental Hygiene, 1960.

Charrow, V. R., and J. D. Fletcher. English as the second language of deaf children. *Developmental Psychology*, 1974, 10, 463–470.

Chess, S., S. J. Korn, and P. B. Fernandez. *Psychiatric Disorders of Children with Congenital Rubella*. New York: Brunner-Mazel, 1971.

Clausen, J. A. Family structure, socialization, and personality. In Hoffman, L. W. and M. L. Hoffman (eds.), *Review of Child Development Research*, New York: Russell Sage Foundation, 1966, 2, 1–53.

Cohen, S. R. Predictability of deaf and hearing story paraphrases. *Journal of Verbal Learning and Verbal Behavior*, 1967, 6, 916–921.

Collins, J. L. Communication between deaf children of pre-school age and their mothers. Unpublished Ph.D. dissertation, University of Pittsburgh, 1969.

Conference of Executives of American Schools for the Deaf. Definition of Total Communication. *American Annals of the Deaf*, 1976, 121, 358.

Conrad, R. Short-term memory processes in the deaf. *British Journal of Psychology*, 1970, 61, 179–195.

———. The effect of vocalizing on comprehension in the

profoundly deaf. *British Journal of Psychology*, 1971, *62*, 147–150.

———. Lip-reading by deaf and hearing children. *British Journal of Educational Psychology*, 1977a, *47*, 60–65.

———. Reading ability of deaf school-leavers. *British Journal of Educational Psychology*, 1977b, *47*, 138–148.

———. Facts and fantasies about the verbal abilities of deaf school-leavers. *British Deaf News*, 1977c, *11*, 145–147.

Cooper, R. L., and J. Rosenstein. Language acquisition of deaf children. *Volta Review*, 1966, *68*, 58-67.

Cornett, R. Cued speech. *American Annals of the Deaf*, 1967, *112*, 3–13.

Craig, H. B. A sociometric investigation of the self-concept of the deaf child. *American Annals of the Deaf*, 1965, *110*, 456–478.

Craig, W. N. Effects of pre-school training on the development of reading and lipreading skills of deaf children. *American Annals of the Deaf*, 1964, *109*, 280–296.

Craig, W. N., and H. B. Craig. Programs and services for the deaf in the United States. *American Annals of the Deaf*, 1977, *122*, 53–296.

Craig, W. N., H. B. Craig, and A. DiJohnson. Pre-school verbotonal instruction for deaf children. *Volta Review*, 1972, *74*, 236–246.

Cummings, S. T., H. C. Bayley, and H. E. Rie. Effects of the child's deficiency on the mother. A study of mothers of mentally retarded, chronically ill and neurotic children. *American Journal of Orthopsychiatry*, 1966, *35*, 595–608.

Davis, F. Deviance disavowal: the management of strained interaction by the visibly handicapped. *Social Problems*, 1961, *9*, 120–132.

———. *Passage through Crisis. Polio Victims and Their Families*. Indianapolis: Bobbs-Merrill, 1963.

Denton, D. M. A rationale for total communication. In T. J. O'Rourke (ed.), *Psycholinguistics and Total Communica-*

*tion: The State of the Art.* Silver Spring, Md.: American Annals of the Deaf, 1972, 53–61.

DiCarlo, L. M. *The Deaf.* Englewood Cliffs, New Jersey: Prentice-Hall, 1964.

DiCarlo, L. M., and J. Dolphin. Social adjustment and personality development of deaf children: A review of literature. *Exceptional Children,* 1952, *18,* 111–118.

DiFrancesca, S. *Academic Achievement Test Results of a National Testing Program for Hearing Impaired Students, United States: Spring 1971.* Series D, Number 9. Washington, D.C.: Office of Demographic Studies, Gallaudet College, 1972.

DiFrancesca, S., and S. Carey. *Item Analysis of an Achievement Testing Program for Hearing Impaired Students, United States: Spring 1971.* Series D, Number 8. Washington, D.C.: Office of Demographic Studies, Gallaudet College, 1972.

Doehring, D. G., and J. Rosenstein. Visual word recognition by deaf and hearing children. *Journal of Speech and Hearing Research,* 1960, *3,* 320–326.

Doll, E. A. *Vineland Social Maturity Scale: Condensed Manual of Directions.* Circle Pines, Minn.: American Guidance Service, Inc., 1965.

Donnelly, K. An investigation into the determinants of lipreading of deaf adults. *International Audiology,* 1969, *8,* 501–508.

Downs, M. P., and G. M. Sterritt. A guide to newborn and infant hearing screening programs. *Archives of Otolaryngology,* 1967, *85,* 15–22.

Edelstein, T. J. Educational treatment programs for emotionally disturbed deaf children. In R. J. Trybus (ed.), *Mental Health in Deafness,* 1977, *1,* 30–37.

Elliott, L. L., and Y. B. Armbruster. Some possible effects of the delay of early treatment of deafness. *Journal of Speech and Hearing Research,* 1967, *10,* 209–224.

Erber, N. P. Evaluation of special hearing aids for deaf children. *Journal of Speech and Hearing Disorders*, 1971, *36*, 527–537.

———. Auditory-visual perception of speech. *Journal of Speech and Hearing Disorder*, 1975, *40*, 481–492.

Erting, C. Language policy and deaf ethnicity in the United States. *Sign Language Studies*, 1978, *19*, 139–152.

Ewoldt, C. K. A psycholinguistic description of selected deaf children reading in sign language. Unpublished Ph.D. dissertation, Wayne State University, 1977.

Farber, B. Family organization and crisis: Maintenance of integration in families with a severely mentally retarded child. *Monographs of the Society for Research in Child Development*, 1960, *25*, No. 1.

Farwell, R. M. Speechreading, a review of the research. *American Annals of the Deaf*, 1976, *121*, 19–30.

Fellendorf, G. W., and I. Harrow. Parent counseling, 1961–1968. *Volta Review*, 1970, *72*, 51–57.

Fiedler, M. F. Developmental studies of deaf children. *ASHA Monographs Number 13*, Washington: American Speech and Hearing Association, 1969.

Fitzgerald, M. D., A. B. Sitton, and F. McConnell. Audiometric, development and learning characteristics of a group of rubella-deaf children. *Journal of Speech and Hearing Disorders*, 1970, *35*, 218–228.

Fraser, G. R. Profound childhood deafness. *Journal of Medical Genetics*, 1964, *1*, 118–151.

Freedman, D. A., C. Cannady, and J. A. Robinson. Speech and psychic structure: a reconsideration of their relation. *Journal of the American Psychoanalytic Association*, 1971, *19*, 765–779.

Freeman, R. D. Some psychiatric reflections on the controversy over methods of communication in the life of the deaf. In *Methods of Communication Currently Used in the Education of Deaf Children*. London: Royal National Institute for the Deaf, 1976, 110–118.

Freeman, R. D. Psychiatric aspects of sensory disorders and intervention. In Graham, P. J. (ed.), *Epidemiological Approaches in Child Psychiatry*. New York: Academic Press, 1977, 275–304.

Freeman, R. D., S. F. Malkin, and J. O. Hastings. Psychosocial problems of deaf children and their families: a comparative study. *American Annals of the Deaf*, 1975, *120*, 391–405.

Fry, D. B. The development of the phonological system in the normal and the deaf child. In F. Smith and G. A. Miller (eds.), *The Genesis of Language: A Psycholinguistic Approach*. Cambridge: M.I.T. Press, 1966, 187–206.

Furfey, P. H., and T. J. Harte. *Interaction of Deaf and Hearing in Baltimore City, Maryland*. Studies from the Bureau of Social Research, No. 4. Washington, D.C.: The Catholic University of America Press, 1968.

Furth, H. G. Visual paired-associates task with deaf and hearing children. *Journal of Speech and Hearing Research*, 1961a, *4*, 172–177.

———. Influence of language on the development of concept formation in deaf children. *Journal of Abnormal and Social Psychology*, 1961b, *63*, 386–389.

———. Classification transfer with disjunctive concepts as a function of verbal training and set. *Journal of Psychology*, 1963a, *55*, 477–485.

———. Conceptual discovery and control on a pictorial part-whole task as a function of age, intelligence, and language. *Journal of Educational Psychology*, 1963b, *54*, 191–196.

———. Research with the deaf: Implications for language and cognition. *Psychological Bulletin*, 1964, *62*, 145–164.

———. *Thinking Without Language. Psychological Implications of Deafness*. New York: The Free Press, 1966a.

———. A comparison of reading test norms of deaf and hearing children. *American Annals of the Deaf*, 1966b, *111*, 461–462.

————. Linguistic deficiency and thinking: Research with deaf subjects 1964–1969. *Psychological Bulletin*, 1971, 76, 58–72.

————. *Deafness and Learning: A Psychosocial Approach.* Belmont, Ca.: Wadsworth Publishing Company, Inc., 1973.

Furth, H. G., and N. A. Milgram. The influence of language on classification: A theoretical model applied to normal, retarded, and deaf children. *Genetic Psychology Monographs*, 1965, 72, 317–351.

Fusfeld, I. S. How the deaf communicate—written language. *American Annals of the Deaf*, 1958, 103, 255–263.

Gawlik, R., M. McAleer, and M. N. Ozer. Language for adaptive interaction. *American Annals of the Deaf*, 1976, 121, 556–559.

Gentile, A., and S. DiFrancesca. *Academic Achievement Test Performance of Hearing Impaired Students, United States: Spring 1969.* Series D, Number 1. Washington, D.C.: Office of Demographic Studies, Gallaudet College, 1969.

Gentile, A., and B. McCarthy. *Additional Handicapping Conditions Among Hearing Impaired Students, United States: 1971–72.* Series D, Number 14. Washington, D.C.: Office of Demographic Studies, Gaullaudet College, 1973.

Getz, S. *Environment and the Deaf Child.* Springfield, Illinois: C C Thomas, 1953.

Gilbert, J., and R. F. Levee. Performances of deaf and normally hearing children on the Bender Gestalt and the Archimedes Spiral Tests. *Perceptual and Motor Skills*, 1967, 24, 1059–1066.

Gillies, J. Variations in drawings of "a person" and "myself" by hearing-impaired and normal children. *British Journal of Educational Psychology*, 1968, 38, 86–88.

Glorig, A. Routine neonate hearing screening: summary and evaluation. *Hearing and Speech News*, 1971, 39, 4–7.

Goetzinger, C. P., and T. C. Huber. A study of immediate and delayed visual retention with deaf and hearing adolescents. *American Annals of the Deaf*, 1964, 109, 297–305.

Goetzinger, C. P. and C. L. Rousey. A study of the

Wechsler Performance Scale (Form II) and the Knox Cube Test with deaf adolescents. *American Annals of the Deaf*, 1957, *102*, 388–398.

Goffman, E. *Stigma: Notes on the Management of Spoiled Identity*. Englewood Cliffs, N.J.: Prentice-Hall, Inc., 1963.

Goldberg, B., H. Lobb, and H. Kroll. Psychiatric problems of the deaf child. *Canadian Psychiatric Association Journal*, 1975, *20*, 75–83.

Goldstein, R., and C. Tait. Critique of neonatal hearing evaluation. *Journal of Speech and Hearing Disorders*, 1971, *36*, 3–18.

Goodman, K. Miscue analysis: Theory and reality in reading. In *New Horizons in Reading*. Newark, Delaware: International Reading Association, 1976.

Goodman, Y. M., and C. Burke. *Reading Miscue Inventory*. New York: Macmillan, 1970.

Gordon, J. E. Relationship among mother's achievement, independence training attitudes, and handicapped child's performance. *Journal of Consulting Psychology*, 1959, *23*, 207–213.

Goss, R. N. Language used by mothers of deaf children and mothers of hearing children. *American Annals of the Deaf*, 1970, *115*, 93–96.

Goulder, T. J. Mental health programs for the deaf in hospitals and clinics. In R. J. Trybus (ed.), *Mental Health in Deafness*, 1977, *1*, 13–17.

Goulder, T. J., and R. J. Trybus. *The Classroom Behavior of Emotionally Disturbed Hearing Impaired Children*. Series R, Number 3. Washington, D.C.: Office of Demographic Studies, Gallaudet College, 1977.

Graham, E. E., and E. Shapiro. Use of the Performance Scale of the W.I.S.C. with the deaf child. *Journal of Consulting Psychology*, 1953, *17*, 396–398.

Graham, P., and M. Rutter. Organic brain dysfunction and child psychiatric disorder. *British Medical Journal*, 1968, *3*, 695–700.

Greenberg, M. T. Attachment behavior, communicative

competence and parental attitudes in preschool deaf children. Unpublished Ph.D. dissertation, University of Virginia, 1978.

Gregory, S. *The Deaf Child and His Family.* London: George Allen and Unwin, 1976.

Gustason, G., D. Pfetzing, and E. Zawolkow. *Signing Exact English.* Rossmoor, California: Modern Signs Press, 1972.

Harris, R. I. Impulse control and parent hearing status in deaf children. Paper presented at the VIIth World Congress of the World Federation of the Deaf, Washington, D.C., August 1975.

Heider, F., and G. M. Heider. Studies in the psychology of the deaf, No. 1. Psychological Division, Clarke School for the Deaf. *Psychological Monographs,* 1940, *52,* No. 232.

———. Studies in the psychology of the deaf. *Psychological Monographs,* 1941, *53,* No. 242.

Heider, G. M. Adjustment problems of the deaf child. *Nervous Child,* 1948, *7,* 38–44.

Heiner, M. H. *Hearing is Believing.* Cleveland: The World Publishing Co., 1949.

Herren, H., and D. Colin. Implicit language and cooperation in children: comparative study of deaf and hearing children. *Enfance,* 1972, *5,* 325–337 *(Psych. Abstracts,* 50:9192).

Hess, W. Personality adjustment in deaf children. Unpublished Ph.D. dissertation, University of Rochester, 1960.

Hicks, D. E. Comparison profiles of rubella and non-rubella deaf children. *American Annals of the Deaf,* 1970, *115,* 86–92.

Hirsh, I. J. Teaching the deaf child to speak. In F. Smith and G. A. Miller (eds.), *The Genesis of Language.* Cambridge, Mass.: M.I.T. Press, 1966, 207–216.

Hiskey, M. C. A study of the intelligence of deaf and hearing children. *American Annals of the Deaf,* 1956, *101,* 329–339.

Hobbs, N. *The Futures of Children: Categories, Labels, and Their Consequences.* San Francisco, Ca.: Jossey-Bass, Inc., 1975.

Hodgson, K. W. *The Deaf and Their Problems, A Study in Special Education.* London: C. A. Watts and Company, Ltd., 1953.

Hoemann, H. W., C. E. Andrews, V. A. Florian, S. A. Hoemann, and C. J. Jensema. The spelling proficiency of deaf children. *American Annals of the Deaf,* 1976, *121,* 489–493.

Hoffmeister, R. J., and D. F. Moores. The acquisition of specific reference in the linguistic system of a deaf child of deaf parents. Research Report #53, Research, Development, and Demonstration Center in Education of Handicapped Children, University of Minnesota, August 1973.

Jackson, A. D. M., and J. Fisch. Deafness following maternal rubella: results of a prospective investigation. *Lancet,* 1958, *2,* 1241–1244.

Jacobs, L. M. *A Deaf Adult Speaks Out.* Washington, D.C.: Gallaudet College Press, 1974.

Jensema, C., and R. J. Trybus. *Reported Emotional-Behavioral Problems Among Hearing-Impaired Children in Special Educational Programs: United States, 1972–73.* Series R, Number 1. Washington. D. C.: Office of Demographic Studies, Gallaudet College, 1975.

Joint Commission on Mental Health of Children. *Crisis in Child Mental Health: Challenge for the 1970's.* New York: Harper and Row, 1970.

Jones, P. A. An educational comparison of rubella and non-rubella students at the Clarke School for the Deaf. *American Annals of the Deaf,* 1976, *121,* 547–553.

Jordan, I. K. A referential communication study of signers and speakers using realistic referents. *Sign Language Studies,* 1975, *6,* 65–103.

Jordan, I. K., G. Gustason, and R. Rosen. Current communication trends at programs for the deaf. *American Annals of the Deaf,* 1976, *121,* 527–532.

Jordan, T. E. Research on the handicapped child and the family. *Merrill-Palmer Quarterly,* 1962, *8,* 243–260.

Kannapell, B. M., L. B. Hamilton, and H. Bornstein. *Signs for Instructional Purposes.* Washington, D.C.: Gallaudet College Press, 1969.

Kates, S. L., L. Yudin, and R. K. Tiffany. Concept attainment by deaf and hearing adolescents. *Journal of Educational Psychology,* 1962, *53,* 119–126.

Keirn, W. C. Shopping parents: patient problem or professional problem? *Mental Retardation,* 1971, *9,* 6–7.

Kennedy, P., and R. H. Bruininks. Social status of hearing impaired children in regular classrooms. *Exceptional Children,* 1974, *40,* 336–342.

Kennedy, P., W. Northcutt, R. McCauley, and S. M. Williams. Longitudinal sociometric and cross-sectional data on mainstreaming hearing-impaired children: Implications for preschool programming. *Volta Review,* 1976, *78,* 71–81.

Kent, M. S. Differential educational needs in the habilitation and rehabilitation of the deaf. *American Annals of the Deaf,* 1962, *107,* 523–529.

Keogh, B. K., M. Vernon, and C. E. Smith. Deafness and visuo-motor function. *Journal of Special Education,* 1970, *4,* 41–47.

Kirk, H. D. *Shared Fate: A Theory of Adoption and Mental Health.* New York: Free Press, 1964.

Kitano, M. K., J. Stiehl, and J. T. Cole. Role taking: implications for special education. *Journal of Special Education,* 1978, *12,* 59–74.

Klima, E. S., and U. Bellugi. *The Signs of Language.* Cambridge, Mass.: Harvard University Press, 1979.

Kloepfer, H. W., J. Laguaite, and J. W. McLaurin. Genetic aspects of congenital hearing loss. *American Annals of the Deaf,* 1970, *115,* 17–22.

Konigsmark, B. W. Genetic hearing loss with no associated

abnormalities: a review. *Journal of Speech and Hearing Disorders*, 1972, 37, 89–99.

Lach, R., D. Ling, A. H. Ling, and N. Ship. Early speech development in deaf infants. *American Annals of the Deaf*, 1970, 115, 522–526.

Lenneberg, E. H. *Biological Foundations of Language.* New York: Wiley and Sons, Inc., 1967.

Lenneberg, E. H., F. G. Rebelsky, and I. A. Nichols. The vocalizations of infants born to deaf and to hearing parents. *Human Development*, 1965, 8, 23–37.

Lesser, S. R., and B. R. Easser. Personality differences in the perceptually handicapped. *Journal of the American Academy of Child Psychiatry*, 1972, 11, 458–466.

Levine, E. S. Psychoeducational study of children born deaf following maternal rubella in pregnancy. *American Journal of Diseases of Children*, 1951, 81, 627–635.

———. *Youth in a Soundless World, A Search for Personality.* New York: New York University Press, 1956.

———. *The Psychology of Deafness, Techniques of Appraisal for Rehabilitation.* New York: Columbia University Press, 1960.

———. Historical review of special education and mental health services. In J. D. Rainer, K. Z. Altshuler, and F. J. Kallmann (eds.), *Family and Mental Health Problems in a Deaf Population* (2nd ed.), Springfield, Ill.: C C Thomas, 1969a, xvii–xxvi.

———. Psychological testing: development and practice. In J. D. Rainer, K. Z. Altshuler, and F. J. Kallmann (eds.), *Family and Mental Health Problems in a Deaf Population* (2nd ed.). Springfield, Illinois: C C Thomas, 1969.

———. Psychological contributions. *Volta Review*, 1976, 78, 23–33.

Levine, E. S., and E. E. Wagner. Personality patterns of deaf persons: An interpretation based on research with the Hand Test. *Perceptual and Motor Skills*, Monograph Supplement 4-V39, 1974, 1168–1236.

Levitt, E., and S. Cohen. Attitudes of children toward

their handicapped peers. *Childhood Education*, 1976, 52, 171–173.

Lewis, D. N. Lipreading skills of hearing-impaired children in regular schools. *Volta Review*, 1972, 74, 303–311.

Lewis, M. M. *Language and Personality in Deaf Children*. National Foundation for Educational Research. Occasional Publication Series No. 20. Slough, England, 1968.

Ling, D. Conventional hearing aids: an overview. *Volta Review*, 1971, 73, 343–352, 375–383.

————. Amplification for speech. In D. R. Calvert and S. R. Silverman, *Speech and Deafness, A Text for Learning and Teaching*. Washington, D.C.: Alexander Graham Bell Association for the Deaf, 1975, 64–88.

McCall, E. A generative grammar of signs. Unpublished M.A. thesis, University of Iowa, 1965.

MacDougall, J. C., and M. S. Rabinovitch. Early auditory deprivation and sensory compensation. *Developmental Psychology*, 1971a, 5, 368.

————. Imagery and learning in deaf and hearing children. *Psychonomic Science*, 1971b, 22, 347–349.

————. Early auditory deprivation and exploratory activity. *Developmental Psychology*, 1972, 7, 17–20.

McIntire, M. A modified model for the description of language acquisition in a deaf child. Unpublished M.A. thesis, California State University, Northridge, 1974.

McNeill, D. The capacity for language acquisition. In *Research on Behavioral Aspects of Deafness*, Proceedings of National Research Conference on Behavioral Aspects of Deafness, New Orleans, May 1965, Vocational Rehabilitation Administration.

Meadow, K. P. The effect of early manual communication and family climate on the deaf child's development. Unpublished Ph.D. dissertation, University of California, Berkeley, 1967.

————. Parental responses to the medical ambiguities of deafness. *Journal of Health and Social Behavior*, 1968a, 9, 299–309.

————. Early manual communication in relation to the deaf child's intellectual, social, and communicative functioning. *American Annals of the Deaf*, 1968b, *113*, 29–41.

————. Self-image, family climate, and deafness. *Social Forces*, 1969, *47*, 428–438.

————. Sociolinguistics, sign language, and the deaf subculture. In T. J. O'Rourke (ed.), *Psycholinguistics and Total Communication: The State of the Art*. Washington, D.C.: American Annals of the Deaf, 1972, 19–33.

————. Behavioral problems of deaf children. In H. S. Schlesinger and K. P. Meadow (eds.), *Studies of Family Interaction, Language Acquisition, and Deafness*. San Francisco: University of California, S.F. Final Report, Office of Maternal and Child Health, Bureau of Community Health Services, 1976a, 257–293.

————. Psychosocial aspects of language development in deaf children. In H. S. Schlesinger and K. P. Meadow (eds.), *Studies of Family Interaction, Language Acquisition, and Deafness*. San Francisco: University of California, S.F. Final Report, Office of Maternal and Child Health, Bureau of Community Health Services, 1976b.

————. A developmental perspective on the use of manual communication with deaf children. In *Methods of Communication Currently Used in the Education of Deaf Children*. London: Royal National Institute for the Deaf, 1976c, 87–98.

————. Name signs as identity symbols in the deaf community. *Sign Language Studies*, 1977, *16*, 237–246.

Meadow, K. P., and A. Nemon. Deafness as stigma. *American Rehabilitation*, 1976, *2*, 7–9; 19–22.

Meadow, K. P., and H. S. Schlesinger. The prevalence of behavioral problems in a population of deaf school children. *American Annals of the Deaf*, 1971, *116*, 346–348.

Meadow, K. P., and R. J. Trybus. Behavioral and emotional problems of deaf children: An overview. In L. J. Bradford and W. G. Hardy (eds.), *Hearing and Hearing Impairment*. N.Y.: Grune and Stratton, Inc., 1979, 395–403.

Mindel, E. D., and M. Vernon. *They Grow in Silence–The Deaf Child and His Family.* Silver Spring, Md.: National Association of the Deaf, 1971.

Mira, M. P. The use of the Arthur Adaptation of the Leiter International Performance Scale and Nebraska Test of Learning Aptitude with pre-school deaf children. *American Annals of the Deaf*, 1962, *107*, 224–228.

Montgomery, G. W. G. The relationship of oral skills to manual communication in profoundly deaf students. *American Annals of the Deaf*, 1966, *111*, 557–565.

Moores, D. F. An investigation of the psycholinguistic functioning of deaf adolescents. *Exceptional Children*, 1970a, *36*, 645–654.

———. Oral vs. manual; "Old prejudices die hard, but die they must." *American Annals of the Deaf*, 1970b, *115*, 667–669.

———. Current research and theory with the deaf: educational implications. In L. S. Liben (ed.), *Multidisciplinary Perspectives on the Development of Deaf Children: Theoretical and Applied Issues.* N.Y.: Academic Press, 1979.

Moores, D. F., C. K. McIntyre, and K. L. Weiss. Evaluation of programs for hearing impaired children: Report of 1971–72. Research Report #39, Research, Development and Demonstration Center in Education of Handicapped Children, University of Minnesota, September 1972.

Moores, D. F., K. L. Weiss, and M. W. Goodwin. Receptive abilities of deaf children across five modes of communication. *Exceptional Children*, 1973, *40*, 22–28.

Murphy, N. J. *Characteristics of Hearing Impaired Students Under Six Years of Age. United States: 1969–70.* Washington, D.C.: Office of Demographic Studies, Gallaudet College, 1972.

Myklebust, H. R. *The Psychology of Deafness, Sensory Deprivation, Learning, and Adjustment.* New York: Grune and Stratton, 1960.

Myklebust, H. R., A. Neyhus, and A. M. Mulholland. Guidance and counseling for the deaf. *American Annals of the Deaf*, 1962, *107*, 370–415.

Neyhus, A. The social and emotional adjustment of deaf adults. *Volta Review*, 1964, *66*, 319–325.

———. Speechreading failure in deaf children. Washington, D.C.: Office of Education, Department of Health, Education and Welfare, 1969.

Odom, P. B., and R. L. Blanton. Phrase-learning in deaf and hearing subjects. *Journal of Speech and Hearing Research*, 1967, *10*, 600–605.

Odom, P. B., R. L. Blanton, and C. K. McIntyre. Coding medium and word recall by deaf and hearing subjects. *Journal of Speech and Hearing Research*, 1970, *13*, 54–58.

Odom, P. B., R. L. Blanton, and C. Laukhuf. Facial expressions and interpretation of emotion-arousing situations in deaf and hearing children. *Journal of Abnormal Child Psychology*, 1973, *1*, 139–151.

Oleron, P. Conceptual thinking of the deaf. *American Annals of the Deaf*, 1953, *98*, 304–310.

Oleron, P., and H. Herren. L'acquisition des conservations et langage: étude comparative sur des enfants sourds et entendants. *Enfance*, 1961, *14*, 203–219.

O'Neill, J. J., and J. L. Davidson. Relationship between lipreading and five psychological factors. *Journal of Speech and Hearing Disorders*, 1956, *21*, 478–481.

O'Rourke, T. J. *A Basic Course in Manual Communication.* Silver Spring, Md.: National Association of the Deaf, 1970.

Padden, C., and H. Markowicz. Cultural conflicts between hearing and deaf communities. Washington, D.C.: Linguistics Research Laboratory, Gallaudet College, 1975 (mimeo).

Phillips, L., J. G. Draguns, and D. P. Bartlett. Classification of behavior disorders. In N. Hobbs (ed.), *Issues in the Classification of Children*, San Francisco, Ca.: Jossey-Bass, 1975, *1*, 26–55.

Pintner, R. Emotional stability of the hard of hearing. *Journal of Genetic Psychology*, 1933, *43*, 293–311.

Pintner, R., J. Eisenson, and M. Stanton. *The Psychology of the Physically Handicapped*. New York: F. S. Crofts and Company, 1941.

Pintner, R., and D. G. Paterson. The ability of deaf and hearing children to follow printed directions. *Pediatric Seminary*, 1916, *23*, 477–497.

Pintner, R., and J. F. Reamer. A mental and educational survey of schools for the deaf. *American Annals of the Deaf*, 1920, *65*, 451.

Pollack, D. Acoupedics: a unisensory approach to auditory training. *Volta Review*, 1964, *66*, 400–409.

Porter, T. A. Hearing aids in a residential school. *American Annals of the Deaf*, 1973, *118*, 31–33.

Prugh, D. G., M. Engel, and W. C. Morse. Emotional disturbance in children. In N. Hobbs (ed.), *Issues in the Classification of Children*. San Francisco, Ca.: Jossey-Bass, 1975, *1*, 261–299.

Quigley, S. P. *The Influence of Fingerspelling on the Development of Language, Communication, and Educational Achievement in Deaf Children*. University of Illinois, Institute for Research on Exceptional Children, 1968.

Quigley, S. P., and D. R. Frisina. Institutionalization and psychoeducational development of deaf children. *Council for Exceptional Children Research Monographs*, Series A, No. 3, 1961.

Quinton, D., and M. Rutter. Early hospital admissions and later disturbances of behaviour: an attempted replication of Douglas' findings. *Developmental Medicine and Child Neurology*, 1976, *18*, 447–459.

Rainer, J. D., and K. Z. Altshuler. *Comprehensive Mental Health Services for the Deaf*. New York: New York State Psychiatric Institute, Columbia University, 1966.

———. *Expanded Mental Health Care for the Deaf: Rehabilita-*

*tion and Prevention*. Washington, D.C.: USGPO, 1971.

Rainer, J. D., K. Z. Altshuler, and F. J. Kallmann (eds). *Family and Mental Health Problems in a Deaf Population* (2nd ed.). Springfield, Illinois: C C Thomas, 1969.

Rains, P., J. I. Kitsuse, T. Duster, and E. Freidson. The labeling approach to deviance. In N. Hobbs (ed.), *Issues in the Classification of Children*, San Francisco, Ca.: Jossey-Bass, 1975, *1*, 88–100.

Rawlings, B. *Characteristics of Hearing Impaired Students by Hearing Status, United States: 1970–71*. Series D, Number 10. Washington, D.C.: Office of Demographic Studies, Gallaudet College, 1973.

Ray, L. The Abbé de l'Epée. *Deaf American*, 1966, *18*, 9–11.

Reid, G. W. A preliminary investigation of the testing of lipreading achievement. *Journal of Speech and Hearing Disorders*, 1947, *12*, 77–82.

Reivich, R. S., and I. A. Rothrock. Behavior problems of deaf children and adolescents: a factor-analytic study. *Journal of Speech and Hearing Research*, 1972, *15*, 84–92.

Richardson, S. A., and P. Emerson. Race and physical handicap in children's preference for other children: A replication in a southern city. *Human Relations*, 1970, *23*, 31–36.

Richardson, S. A., N. Goodman, A. H. Hastorf, and S. M. Dornbusch. Cultural uniformity in reaction to physical disabilities. *American Sociological Review*, 1961, *26*, 241–247.

Ries, P., R. Trybus, P. Sepielli, and C. Buchanan. *Further Studies in Achievement Testing, Hearing Impaired Students, United States: Spring 1971*. Series D, Number 13. Washington, D.C.: Office of Demographic Studies, Gallaudet College, 1973.

Rosen, R., E. Skinski, and A. Pimentel. P.L. 94–142: An analysis of its evolution, features, and implications. Special issue of *Gallaudet Alumni Newsletter*, 1977.

Rosenstein, J. Tactile perception of rhythmic patterns by normal, blind, deaf, and aphasic children. *American Annals of the Deaf,* 1957, *102,* 339–403.

———. Cognitive abilities of deaf children. *Journal of Speech and Hearing Research,* 1960, *3,* 108–119.

———. Perception, cognition, and language in deaf children. *Exceptional Children,* 1961, *27,* 276–284.

Rosenzweig, M. R. Environmental complexity, cerebral change, and behavior. *American Psychologist,* 1966, *21,* 321–332.

Ross, M., M. E. Kessler, M. E. Phillips, and J. W. Lerman. Visual, auditory, and combined mode presentations of the WIPI Test to hearing-impaired children. *Volta Review,* 1972, *74,* 90–96.

Ross, M., and N. D. Matkin. The rising audiometric configuration. *Journal of Speech and Hearing Disorders,* 1967, *32,* 377–382.

Rutter, M. Brain damage syndromes in childhood: concepts and findings. *Journal of Child Psychology and Psychiatry,* 1977, *18,* 1–21.

Rutter, M., J. Tizard, and K. Whitmore (eds.). *Education, Health and Behavior. A Psychological and Medical Study of Childhood Development.* New York: Wiley, 1970.

Rutter, M., J. Tizard, W. Yule, P. Graham, and K. Whitmore. Isle of Wight Studies, 1964–74. *Psychological Medicine,* 1976, *6,* 313–332.

Safilios-Rothschild, C. *The Sociology and Social Psychology of Disability and Rehabilitation.* N.Y.: Random House, 1970.

Sank, D. Genetic aspects of early total deafness. In J. D. Rainer, K. Z. Altshuler, and F. J. Kallmann (eds.), *Family and Mental Health in a Deaf Population* (2nd ed.). Springfield, Illinois: C C Thomas, 1969, 28–68.

Schaefer, E. S., and R. Q. Bell. Development of a parental attitude research instrument. *Child Development,* 1958, *29,* 339–361.

Schein, J. D. *The Deaf Community. Studies in the Social*

*Psychology of Deafness.* Washington, D.C.: Gallaudet College Press, 1968.

———. Deaf students with other disabilities. *American Annals of the Deaf,* 1975, *120,* 92–99.

Schein, J. D., and M. T. Delk, Jr. *The Deaf Population of the United States.* Silver Spring, Md.: National Association of the Deaf, 1974.

Schiff, W., and R. S. Dytell. Tactile identification of letters: a comparison of deaf and hearing children's performances. *Journal of Experimental Child Psychology,* 1971, *11,* 150–164.

Schlesinger, H. S. Beyond the range of sound. *California Medicine,* 1969, *110,* 213–217.

———. Prevention, diagnosis, and habilitation of deafness: a critical look. In D. Hicks (ed.), *Medical Aspects of Deafness,* Proceedings, National Forum IV, Council of Organizations Serving the Deaf, Atlantic City, New Jersey, 1971, 19–30.

———. Meaning and enjoyment: language acquisition of deaf children. In T. J. O'Rourke (ed.), *Psycholinguistics and Total Communication: The State of the Art.* Washington, D.C.: American Annals of the Deaf, 1972, 92–102.

———. The acquisition of sign language. In H. S. Schlesinger and K. P. Meadow (eds.), *Studies of Family Interaction, Language Acquisition, and Deafness.* San Francisco: University of California, S.F. Final Report, Office of Maternal and Child Health, Bureau of Community Health Services, 1976, 302–353.

———. Treatment of the deaf child in the school setting. In R. J. Trybus (ed.), *Mental Health in Deafness,* 1977, *1,* 93–95, 96–105.

———. The acquisition of bimodal language. In I. M. Schlesinger and L. Namir (eds.), *Sign Language of the Deaf. Psychological, Linguistic, and Sociological Perspectives.* N.Y.: Academic Press, 1978, 57–93.

———. Hearing and vision problems. In I. Berlin and J.

Noshpitz (eds.), *Basic Handbook of Child Psychiatry*. N.Y.: Basic Books, in press.

Schlesinger, H. S., and K. P. Meadow. *Deafness and Mental Health: A Developmental Approach*. San Francisco: Langley Porter Neuropsychiatric Institute (multilithed report), 1971.

———. *Sound and Sign: Childhood Deafness and Mental Health*. Berkeley: University of California Press, 1972.

———. Emotional support for parents. In D. L. Lillie, P. L. Trohanis, and K. W. Goin (eds.), *Teaching Parents to Teach*. N.Y.: Walker and Co., 1976, 35–47.

Schneidman, E. S. *Manual for the Make a Picture Story Method*. New York: Society for Projective Techniques and Rorschach Institute, 1952.

Schroedel, J. G. Variables related to the attainment of occupational status among deaf adults. Unpublished Ph.D. dissertation, New York University, 1976.

Schwirian, P. M. Effects of the presence of a hearing-impaired preschool child in the family on behavior patterns of older "normal" siblings. *American Annals of the Deaf*, 1976, *121*, 373–380.

Scouten, E. L. The Rochester method, an oral multisensory approach for instructing prelingual deaf children. *American Annals of the Deaf*, 1967, *112*, 50–55.

Seidel, U. P., O. Chadwick, and M. Rutter. Psychological disorders in crippled children: a comparative study of children with and without brain damage. *Developmental Medicine and Child Neurology*, 1975, *17*, 563–573.

Shaffer, D. Brain injury. In M. Rutter and L. Hersov (eds.), *Child Psychiatry: Modern Approaches*. Oxford: Blackwell Scientific, 1977, 185–215.

Shaffer, D., N. McNamara, and J. H. Pincus. Controlled observations on patterns of activity, attention, and impulsivity in brain-damaged and psychiatrically disturbed boys. *Psychological Medicine*, 1974, *4*, 4–18.

Sigel, I. E. The attainment of concepts. In M. L. Hoffman

and L. W. Hoffman (eds.), *Review of Child Development Research*. New York: Russell Sage Foundation, 1964, *1*, 209–248.

Siller, J., and A. Chipman. Factorial structure and correlates of the attitudes toward disabled persons scale. *Educational and Psychological Measurement*, 1964, *24*, 831–840.

Siller, J., A. Chipman, L. Ferguson, and D. H. Vann. *Attitudes of the Nondisabled Toward the Physically Disabled. Studies in Reactions to Disability: XI*. N.Y.: New York University, School of Education, 1967.

Silverman, R. T. Categorization behavior and achievement in deaf and hearing children. *Exceptional Children*, 1967, *34*, 241–250.

Silverman, S. R. Rehabilitation for irreversible deafness. *Journal of the American Medical Association*, 1966, *196*, 843–846.

Simmons, A. A. Factors related to lipreading. *Journal of Speech and Hearing Research*, 1959, *2*, 340–352.

Springer, N. N. A comparative study of behavior traits of deaf and hearing children of New York City. *American Annals of the Deaf*, 1938, *83*, 255–273.

Stein, L. A cure for deafness: reality or myth. *American Annals of the Deaf*, 1973, *118*, 670–671.

Sterritt, G. M., B. W. Camp, and B. S. Lipman. Effects of early auditory deprivation upon auditory and visual information processing. *Perceptual and Motor Skills*, 1966, *23*, 123–130.

Stevenson, E. A. A study of the educational achievement of deaf children of deaf parents. *California News*, 1964, *80*, 1–3.

Stinson, M. S. Maternal reinforcement and help and the achievement motive in hearing and hearing-impaired children. *Developmental Psychology*, 1974, *10*, 348–353.

———. Effects of deafness on maternal expectations about child development. *Journal of Special Education*, 1978, *12*, 75–81.

Stokoe, W. C., Jr. *Sign Language Structure: An Outline of the Visual Communication Systems of the American Deaf.* Studies in linguistics, occasional papers, 8, Department of Anthropology and Linguistics, University of Buffalo, New York, 1960.

Stokoe, W. C., Jr., and R. Battison. Sign language, mental health, and satisfactory interaction. Unpublished paper, Linguistics Research Laboratory, Gallaudet College, Washington, D.C., 1975.

Stokoe, W. C., Jr., D. C. Casterline, and C. G. Croneberg. *A Dictionary of American Sign Language on Linguistic Principles.* Washington, D.C.: Gallaudet College Press, 1965.

Streng, A., and S. A. Kirk. The social competence of deaf and hard of hearing children in a public day school. *American Annals of the Deaf,* 1938, *83,* 244–254.

Stuckless, E. R., and J. W. Birch. The influence of early manual communication on the linguistic development of deaf children. *American Annals of the Deaf,* 1966, *111,* 452–460; 499–504.

Sussman, A. E. An investigation into the relationship between self concepts of deaf adults and their perceived attitudes toward deafness. Unpublished Ph.D. dissertation, New York University, 1973.

———. Preventive mental health services in the deaf community. In R. Trybus (ed.), *Mental Health in Deafness,* 1977, *1,* 106–108.

Templin, M. *The Development of Reasoning in Children with Normal and Defective Hearing.* Minneapolis: University of Minnesota Press, 1950.

———. Methodological variations in language research with deaf subjects. *Proceedings of International Conference on Oral Education of the Deaf,* Washington, D.C.: Alexander Graham Bell Association, 1967, *11,* 1428–1440.

Tervoort, B. T. Esoteric symbolism in the communication behavior of young deaf children. *American Annals of the Deaf,* 1961, *106,* 436–480.

Titus, E. S. The self-concept and adjustment of deaf teenagers. Unpublished Ph.D. dissertation, University of Missouri, Columbia, 1965.

Todd, Peyton H. A case of structural interference across sensory modalities in second-language learning. *Word,* 1971, *27,* 102–118 *(Child Language, 1975).*

Trybus, R., C. Buchanan, and S. DiFrancesa. *Studies in Achievement Testing, United States: Spring 1971.* Series D, Number 11. Washington, D.C.: Office of Demographic Studies, Gallaudet College, 1973.

Trybus, R. J., and M. A. Karchmer. School achievement scores of hearing-impaired children: National data on achievement status and growth patterns. *American Annals of the Deaf,* 1977, *122,* 62–69.

U.S. Census. *The Deaf-Mute Population of the United States, 1920.* Department of Commerce, Bureau of the Census. Washington, D.C.: U.S. Government Printing Office, 1928.

———. *The Blind and Deaf-Mutes in the United States, 1930.* Department of Commerce, Bureau of the Census. Washington, D.C.: U.S. Government Printing Office, 1931.

Upshall, C. C. *Day Schools vs. Institutions for the Deaf.* Teachers College, Columbia University Contributions to Education, No. 389. New York: Bureau of Publications, Teachers College, Columbia University, 1929.

Van Lieshout, C. F. M. The assessment of stability and change in peer interaction of normal hearing and deaf pre-school children. Paper presented at the 1973 biennial meeting of the International Society for the Study of Behavioral Development, Ann Arbor, Michigan, August 21–25, 1973.

Vernon, M. Characteristics associated with post-rubella children: psychological, educational, and physical. *Volta Review,* 1967a, *69,* 176–185.

———. Prematurity and deafness: the magnitude and nature of the problem among deaf children. *Exceptional Children,* 1967b, *34,* 289–298.

———. Rh factor and deafness: the problem, its psychological, physical, and educational manifestations. *Exceptional Children*, 1967c, *34*, 5–12.

———. Current etiological factors in deafness. *American Annals of the Deaf*, 1968, *113*, 1–12.

———. *Multiply Handicapped Deaf Children: Medical, Educational, and Psychological Considerations*. CEC Research Monograph. Washington, D.C.: Council for Exceptional Children, 1969a.

———. Sociological and psychological factors associated with hearing loss. *Journal of Speech and Hearing Research*, 1969b, *12*, 541–563.

———. The final report. In R. R. Grinker, Sr. (ed.), *Psychiatric Diagnosis, Therapy, and Research on the Psychotic Deaf*. Chicago: Institute for Psychosomatic and Psychiatric Research and Training, Michael Reese Hospital, 1969c, 13–37.

Vernon, M., and Brown, D. W. A guide to psychological tests and testing procedures in the evaluation of deaf and hard-of-hearing children. *Journal of Speech and Hearing Disorders*, 1964, *29*, 414–423.

Vernon, M., and S. D. Koh. Early manual communication and deaf children's achievement. *American Annals of the Deaf*, 1970, *115*, 527–536.

Vernon, M., and B. Makowsky. Deafness and minority group dynamics. *Deaf American*, 1969, *21*, 3–6.

Vernon, M., and H. Prickett, Jr. Mainstreaming: issues and a model plan. *Audiology and Hearing Education*, 1976, February–March, 5–6; 10–11.

Vernon, M., and D. A. Rothstein. Prelingual deafness, an experiment of nature. *Archives of Genetic Psychiatry*, 1968, *19*, 361–369.

Vonderhaar, W. F., and J. F. Chambers. An examination of deaf students' Wechsler Performance Subtest scores. *American Annals of the Deaf*, 1975, *120*, 540–544.

Wagner, E. E. *Hand Test: Manual for Administration, Scoring and Interpretation*. Los Angeles: Western Psychological Services, 1962.

Warren, D. *Blindness and Early Childhood Development*. New York: American Foundation for the Blind, 1977.

Wechsler, D. *Manual for the WISC-R*. N.Y.: The Psychological Corp., 1974.

Welles, H. H. Measurement of certain aspects of personality among hard of hearing adults. *Teachers College, Columbia University Contributions to Education*, No. 545, 1932.

Wilbur, R. B. The linguistics of manual language and manual systems. In L. L. Lloyd (ed.), *Communication Assessment and Intervention Strategies*. Baltimore: University Park Press, 1976, 423–500.

Williams, C. E. Some psychiatric observations in a group of maladjusted deaf children. *Journal of Child Psychology and Psychiatry*, 1970, *11*, 1–18.

Wittgenstein, L. *Tractatus Logico-Philosophicus*. London: Routledge and Kegan Paul, 1921.

Wrightstone, J. W., M. S. Aronow, and S. Moskowitz. Developing reading test norms for deaf children. *American Annals of the Deaf*, 1963, *108*, 311–316.

Zink, G. D. Hearing aids children wear: a longitudinal study of performance. *Volta Review*, 1972, *74*, 41–51.

Zuk, G. H. The cultural dilemma and spiritual crisis of the family with a handicapped child. *Exceptional Children*, 1962, *28*, 405–408.

# Index of Subjects

Achievement test results for deaf children, 50–56; effects of low scores, 190

Acoupedics, 26

Acting out. *See* Impulsivity

Adopted handicapped children, 14

American Annals of the Deaf, 139, 148

American School for the Deaf, 142

American Sign Language: derivation, 18; linguistic status, 18–19; acquisition by children from parents, 19–22; importance, 18–19, 155–157. *See also* Sign language

Analogy difficulty and deaf persons, 59, 64–65

Annual Survey of Hearing Impaired Children and Youth, 105–108

Aristotle, 160

Attainment of concepts. *See* Concepts

Attitudes toward deafness, 160–161, 165–168. *See also* Deaf community; Social development

Audiogram, 2–3; interpretation, 3–5

Behavioral problems of deaf children: classification, 99–104, 108–109, 113–116; examples, 108, 112, 116–120; etiology, 109, 119, 121–126; treatment programs, 102, 104, 126–127; observation and diagnosis, 107–108, 112–115, 120–123; prevalence, 109, 112–113, 117–118, 120; correlation with multiple handicaps, 119–120

Behavior Symptom Checklist, 116, 118

Bender Gestalt Test, 68

Bimodal English, 22–26. *See also* Language modes

Birth order and treatment of handicapped children, 14–15

Body language, 83, 179

Braidwood family, 142

Brain damage, 10, 68–69, 121–122.

Bureau of Education for the Handicapped, 1

Census data, 7

Clarke School for the Deaf, 34, 52–53, 84, 142

Classification tests, 59–60, 64–65. *See also* Concepts

"Cloze" technique, 35–37

Concepts: role in thought processes, 58–59; attainment by deaf children, 59–60; necessity of language in understanding, 60; transfer, 61; conservation, 63–64

Cued Speech, 24, 144

Deaf community, 152–153; institutions of, 153–154; role of language in, 155–157; interaction with hearing community, 157–158, 162–165; perception of others' attitudes, 169–171

Deafness: incidence, 1–2; degrees, 2–5; etiology, 8–10, 54, 121–122; as deprivation of language, 17; diagnosis in infants, 123, 130–131; recognition by general community, 163–165

de Leon, Pedro Ponce, 161

de l'Epée, Charles Michel, 142, 162

Donaldson Lipreading Test, 39

Education for All Handicapped Children Act of 1975, 150–151

Education for the deaf: numbers involved, 1–2; preschool programs, 138–140; colleges, 33, 188–189; correspondence course for parents, 140–141; early history, 142, 161–162; educators' motivations, 189–190; laws regarding, 150–152

Erikson, Erik, 123–124

Experience and cognitive development, 64–65

Eye-contact avoidance, 118–119. *See also* Behavioral problems

Family environment: parents' hearing status, 12–14; attitudes toward child's deafness, 12–14; fathers' roles, 82; extended family, 138; relation to linguistic socialization, 155–157. *See also* Parent-child interaction

Fingerspelling, 22, 25, 38–39; relation to spelling achievement, 53

Frequencies necessary for understanding speech, 3

*Futures of Children, The*, 99

Future time references, 83–85

Galen, 160

Gallaudet College, 33, 50–51, 105, 154, 188, 189, 195. *See also* Office of Demographic Studies

Gallaudet, Thomas Hopkins, 142

Goodenough Draw-a-Man Test, 48

Handedness in deaf children, 69

Handicaps. *See* Multiple handicaps

Hand Test, 94, 96, 115

Heath Railwalking Test, 69

Hearing aids, 3, 13, 40; response by hearing persons, 163; attitudes of the deaf, 163

Holcomb Plan, 150

Holcomb, Roy, 144

Holophrasis, 20

Hospitalization of deaf children, 135

Hyperactivity of rubella-deaf children, 9

Impulsivity, 93–95, 120, 125–126. *See also* Behavioral problems

IQ tests: correlation with speechreading ability, 30; characteristics and results, 47–50; correlation with language skills, 47–50, 61–63; meaning of "deficit," 57

Isle of Wight Study, 110–111

John Tracy Clinic, 140

Joint Commission on Mental Health of Children, 112–113

Knox Cube Test, 66

Language acquisition and development: sign language, 19–22; role of affect, 20; "bimodalism," 22–26; oral only, 27–28; relation to speechreading, 29–31; critical period, 28, 180; written language, 33–35; reading, 35–37; parental expectations, 79–80; role in social development, 82–86; relation to memory, 37, 67–68. *See also* Language modes, Sign Language

Language modes: studies of effectiveness, 38–42, 53–55, 146–147, 174; debate over relative merits, 143–147, 172–176

Learning-disabled children, 83

Learning theories, 2, 44

McClelland's Thematic Apperception Test, 77

Magazines for the deaf, 153

"Mainstreaming," 148–150; debate over, 191–194

Make-a-Picture Story Test, 91–92

Marriage: affected by deaf children, 135–136; among deaf adults, 154

Memory, 65–68

Memory-for-Designs Test, 66

Mental health. *See* Behavioral problems

Methodological problems: in speechreading studies, 30–31; in second language acquisition, 32; in cognitive development, 44–46; in testing attainment of concepts, 60–61, 63–65; regarding self-concept, 87; in diagnosis of behavioral problems, 120–121

Metropolitan Achievement Test, 50, 54

Michael Reese Hospital, 126

Miscue analysis, 55–56

Multiple handicaps, 7, 10; with hereditary deafness, 8; with Rh deafness, relation to language development, 29; relation to behavioral problems, 119–120

National Association of the Deaf, 153

National Census of the Deaf, 23

National Theater of the Deaf, 153

Noise-making by deaf children, 118–119

Office of Demographic Studies, 50–51, 113, 138–139, 145

Oral-only communication, 143 n. *See also* Language modes

Oseretsky Scale for Evaluation, 69

Parental Attitude Research Inventory, 81

Parent-child interaction: affect and language acquisition, 20; attachment, 41; differential treatment, 78–82; protectiveness, 77–82; discipline, 78–80; limited communication, 125

Parents of deaf children: attitudes toward handicap, 78–82, 117, 122, 133–134; pressure for special programs, 102–103; diagnosis of children, 104; "diagnostic crisis," 129–134, 139–140; special demands of child's deafness, 134–135

Perceptual and motor functioning: relevance to learning, 68–69; test results, 70–71

Personality inventories, 90

Physician's diagnosis of deafness, 130–133

Piaget, Jean, 46, 57, 59

Play, imaginary, 85

Pointing action, 22

Ponce de Leon, Pedro, 161

Prelingual deafness, 7

Psycholinguistics: holophrasis, 20; approach to reading, 55–56

Public Law 94–142, 150–151, 191, 196–197

Public schools. *See* Residential schools

Raven's Progressive Matrices, 52

Reading comprehension of deaf children: tests, 50–51; longitudinal studies, 51–53; factors in, 51–55; psycholinguistic approach, 55–56

Reasoning: role of language, 58–60; relation to school environment, 64–65. *See also* Concepts

Rehabilitation Act of 1973, 170

Residential schools, 11–12, 187–189; compared to day schools, 11–12, 64–65, 76, 88–90, 147–148; language modes used, 141, 145; cultural role, 153–154

Residual hearing in oral English programs, 26–27

Rh deafness, 9, 107

Rochester Method, 24, 144

Rorschach Test, 91, 93, 115

Rubella deafness, 9–10, 53; behavioral problems, 119, 124–125

St. Augustine, 161

St. Elizabeth's Hospital, 126

Schools. *See* Education; Residential schools

Second language, defined, 31

Self-concept, 86–90; of children with other handicaps, 162–163; of deaf adults, 170. *See also* Deaf community; Social development

Sensory compensation: studies on animals, 69–70; in children, 70–71

Sex differences, relative to behavioral problems, 117–118, 120

Sibling relationships of deaf children, 79, 136–137

Sign language: debate over value, 18–19, 23, 26–27, 32, 39, 143–147, 172–176; pivot grammar, 20–21; systems, 23–24, 177–180; idiosyncratic development, 31–32; rate of communication, 60 n.; facilitates speechreading, 146–147; societal attitudes toward, 164–165; for deaf parents and children, 184–187

Social development of deaf children, 194–198; maturity defined, 74–76; factors, 76–82; observations, 81; relation to language, 82–86; facial expression, 83

Speech: important frequencies for understanding, 3; in communication with deaf children, 26–31; development, 28–29; use by deaf persons, 164

Speechreading, 29–31, 146–147. *See also* Total communication

Spelling achievement, 53

Tests. *See titles and by area tested*

Thematic Apperception Test, 77

Total communication, 23, 38–42, 144–146, 182–184; correlation with IQ, 62–63

Tracy Clinic, 140

Traditional beliefs concerning the deaf, 158–161

Vancouver Study, 111–112, 139

Videotapes and films in research on deafness, 22, 24–25, 31, 56, 75, 84

Vineland Social Maturity Scale, 74, 75, 77, 115

Wechsler Intelligence Scale for Children, 47–49

Winterbottom's Independence Training Attitude Questionnaire, 77

World Deaf Olympics, 153

Written language of deaf children, 33–38; samples, 33

# Index of Authors

Altshuler, K. Z., 8, 12, 18, 104, 113, 114, 120, 122, 126, 169
Anderson, H., 9
Anderson, R. J., 49
Andrews, C. E., 53
Anthony, D. A., 24
Armbruster, Y. B., 6
Aronow, M. S., 50
Avery, C., 74, 115

Balow, I. H., 54
Barker, R. G., 11, 76, 89, 166, 169
Barr, B., 9
Barsch, R. H., 136
Bartlett, D. P., 100, 104
Barton, M. E., 8
Bayley, H. C., 12
Bell, R. Q., 81
Bellugi, U., 19, 21, 22, 32
Bender, R. E., 17, 142, 161
Berlin, I. N., 104
Best, B., 61, 64
Bindon, D. M., 9, 91
Birch, J. W., 12, 39, 54, 174
Black, J. W., 30
Blair, F. X., 65
Blank, M., 45, 60, 71
Blanton, R. L., 37, 66, 67, 83
Bonvillian, J. D., 17–18
Boothroyd, A., 37
Bornstein, H., 23, 24
Bower, E. M., 104
Boyd, J., 69
Brasel, K. E., 54
Bridger, W. H., 71
Brill, R. G., 13, 54, 142, 144, 145, 147
Brown, R., 26, 47

Bruininks, R. H., 66–67, 168
Brunschwig, L., 87
Bryan, T., 83
Buchanan, C., 50
Burchard, E. M. L., 74, 75, 90–91, 115
Burke, C., 56
Butt, D., 30

California, State of, 108
Camp, B. W., 70
Cannady, C., 124, 125
Carey, S., 50
Casterline, D. C., 19
Chadwick, O., 10
Chambers, J. F., 49
Charrow, V. R., 17, 32
Chess, S., 9, 28, 77, 119, 120, 121, 125
Chipman, A., 166–167
Chreist, F. M., 30
Clark, C., 66, 67
Clausen, J. A., 14
Cohen, S. R., 36, 167
Cole, J. T., 82, 83
Colin, D., 86
Collins, J. L., 12, 81
Conference of Executives of American Schools for the Deaf, 145
Conrad, R., 30, 52, 68
Cooper, R. L., 17
Cornett, O., 24, 144
Court, S. D., 8
Craig, H. B., 1, 27, 87, 139, 148
Craig, W. N., 1, 27, 30, 139, 148
Croneberg, C. G., 19
Cummings, S. T., 12

Davidson, J. L., 30
Davis, F., 8, 122, 162
Delk, M. T., 7, 8, 154
Denton, D. M., 145
DiCarlo, L. M., 27, 28, 74
DiFrancesca, S., 50
DiJohnson, A., 27
Doehring, D. G., 65
Doll, E. A., 74, 115
Dolphin, J., 74
Donnelly, K., 30
Downs, M. P., 6
Draguns, J. G., 100, 104
Duster, T., 101
Dytell, R. S., 71

Easser, B. R., 125
Edelstein, T. J., 127
Eisenson, J., 47, 69
Elliott, L. L., 6
Emerson, P., 168
Engel, M., 99
Erber, N. P., 6, 67
Erting, C., 185, 186
Ewoldt, C. K., 55, 56

Farber, B., 12, 14
Farwell, R. M., 30
Fellendorf, G. W., 6, 104
Ferguson, L., 167
Fernandez, P. B., 9, 28, 77, 119, 120, 121, 125
Fiedler, M. F., 52
Fisch, J., 6, 9
Fitzgerald, M. D., 9
Fletcher, J. D., 32
Florian, V. A., 53
Fraser, G. R., 8
Freedman, D. A., 124, 125
Freeman, R. D., 14, 36, 104, 111, 112, 121, 132, 134 n., 135–137, 139, 143, 155
Freidson, E., 101
Frisina, D. R., 11, 39, 148, 174
Fry, D. B., 5, 7, 28
Furfey, P. H., 166
Furth, H. G., 27, 50, 57–59, 61, 63, 65, 66, 114
Fusfeld, I. S., 33

Gawlik, R., 195
Gentile, A., 7, 8, 50, 106

Getz, S., 91
Gilbert, J., 68
Gillies, J., 87
Glorig, A., 6
Goetzinger, C. P., 49, 65
Goffman, E., 164
Goldstein, R., 6
Goodman, K., 55
Goodman, Y. M., 56
Goodwin, M. W., 146
Gordon, J. E., 77
Goss, R. N., 81
Goulder, T. J., 104, 126
Graham, E. E., 48
Graham, P., 10, 110
Greenberg, M. T., 41
Gregory, S., 79, 132
Gustason, G., 24, 145, 156

Hamilton, L. B., 24
Harrow, I., 6, 104
Harte, T. J., 166
Hastings, J. O., 10, 111, 113, 121, 137, 139, 155
Heider, F., 30, 34, 84, 169
Heider, G. M., 30, 34, 84, 85, 169
Heiner, M. H., 169
Herren, H., 63, 86
Hess, W., 49, 91, 114
Hicks, D. E., 8, 9
Hirsh, I. J., 5
Hiskey, M. C., 47
Hobbs, N., 2, 98, 99, 104, 121
Hodgson, K. W., 27
Hoemann, H. W., 53
Hoemann, S. A., 53
Hoffmeister, R. J., 19, 22
Huber, T. C., 65

Jackson, A. D. M., 6, 9
Jensema, C., 53, 113
Jones, P. A., 53
Joint Commission on Mental Health of Children, 112–113
Jordan, I. K., 60, 145, 156
Jordan, T. E., 12, 82

Kallmann, F. J., 8, 12, 18, 104, 126, 169
Kannapell, B. M., 24
Karchmer, M. A., 51, 52
Kates, S. L., 59

Keirn, W. C., 124 n.
Kennedy, P., 168
Kent, M. S., 10
Keogh, B. K., 68
Kessler, M. E., 67
Kirk, H. D., 14, 74
Kitano, M. K., 82, 83
Kitsuse, J. I., 101
Klima, E. S., 19, 22, 23, 32
Kloepfer, H. W., 8
Knobloch, H., 104
Koh, S. D., 39, 54, 174
Korn, S. J., 9, 28, 77, 119, 120, 121, 125
Konigsmark, B. W., 8

Lach, R., 29
Laguaite, J., 8
Laukhuf, C., 83
Lenneberg, E. H., 7, 20, 29
Lerman, J. W., 67
Lesser, S. R., 125
Levee, R. F., 68
Levine, E. S., 9, 17, 47, 49, 91, 114, 115, 161
Levitt, E., 167
Lewis, D. N., 30
Lewis, M. M., 114
Ling, D., 6, 29
Ling, A. H., 29
Lipman, B. S., 70

McAleer, M., 195
McCall, E., 19
McCarthy, B., 7, 8, 106
McConnell, F., 9
MacDougall, J. C., 69, 70
McIntire, M., 19
McIntyre, C. K., 66, 85, 147
McLaurin, J. W., 8
McNamara, N., 10
McNeill, D., 28
Makowsky, B., 152
Malkin, S. F., 10, 111, 113, 121, 137, 139, 155
Markowicz, H., 157
Matkin, N. D., 5
Meadow, K. P., *many references throughout*
Mindel, E. D., 12, 121, 123, 153
Mira, M. P., 47
Montgomery, G. W. G., 39

Moores, D. F., 19, 22, 35, 38, 85, 146, 147
Morse, W. C., 99
Moskowitz, S., 50
Mulholland, A. M., 69
Murphy, N. J., 138
Myklebust, H. R., 30, 34, 35, 47, 69, 74, 75, 90–91, 114, 115

Nelson, K. E., 17–18
Nemon, A., 163
Neyhus, A., 30, 69, 92
Nichols, I. A., 29
Nunnally, J. C., 66, 67

Odom, P. B., 37, 66, 83
Oleron, P., 63
O'Neill, J. J., 30
O'Reilly, P. P., 30
O'Rourke, T. J., 24
Ozer, M. N., 195

Padden, C., 157
Paterson, D. G., 33
Peck, L., 30
Pfetzing, D., 24
Phillips, L., 67, 100, 104
Pimentel, A., 103, 150
Pincus, J. H., 10
Pintner, R., 11, 33, 47, 69, 90
Pollack, D., 27
Porter, T. A., 6
Prickett, H., 149, 150
Prugh, D. G., 99

Quigley, S. P., 11, 38, 39, 54, 148, 174
Quinton, D., 135

Rabinovitch, M. S., 69, 70
Rainer, J. D., 8, 12, 18, 104, 120, 126, 169
Rains, P., 101
Rawlings, B., 8
Ray, L., 162
Reamer, J. F., 11
Rebelsky, F. G., 29
Reid, G. W., 30
Reivich, R. S., 115
Richardson, S. A., 162, 168
Rie, H. E., 12
Ries, P., 50

Robinson, J. A., 124, 125
Rosen, R., 103, 145, 150, 156
Rosenstein, J., 17, 44, 59, 65, 70
Rosenzweig, M. R., 69, 70
Ross, M., 5, 67
Rothrock, I. A., 115
Rothstein, D. A., 44
Rousey, C. L., 49
Rutter, M., 10, 110, 112, 135

Safilios-Rothschild, C., 158, 159
Sank, D., 8
Schein, J. D., 6–8, 104, 152, 154
Schiff, W., 71
Schlesinger, H. S., *many references throughout*
Schneidman, E. S., 91
Schroedel, J. G., 23
Schwirian, P. M., 137
Scouten, E. L., 24, 144
Seidel, U. P., 10
Sepielli, P., 50
Shaffer, D., 10
Shapiro, E., 48
Ship, N., 29
Sigel, I. E., 46
Siller, J., 166, 167
Silverman, R. T., 61
Silverman, S. R., 5
Simmons, A. A., 30
Sisco, F. Y., 49
Sitton, A. B., 9
Skinski, E., 103, 150
Smith, C. E., 68
Springer, N. N., 91
Stanton, M., 47, 69
Stein, L., 6
Sterritt, G. M., 6, 70
Stiehl, J., 82, 83
Stinson, M. S., 79
Stokoe, W. C., 19, 123
Streng, A., 74

Stuckless, E. R., 12, 19, 39, 54, 174
Sussman, A. E., 127

Tait, C., 6
Templin, M., 59, 63, 64
Tervoort, B. T., 31–32
Tiffany, R. K., 59
Titus, E. S., 87
Tizard, J., 10, 110, 112
Todd, P. H., 19
Trybus, R. J., 50, 51, 52, 104, 106, 113

U. S. Bureau of the Census, 7
Upshall, C. C., 11

Van Lieshout, C. F. M., 86
Vann, D. H., 167
Vernon, M., 8–10, 12, 39, 44, 47, 54, 57, 68, 104–109, 121, 123, 149, 150, 152, 153, 174
Vonderhaar, W. F., 49

Wagner, E. E., 47, 115
Walker, W., 8
Warren, D., 71
Wechsler, D., 49
Wedenberg, E., 9
Weiss, K. L., 85, 146, 147
Welles, H. H., 90
Whitmore, K., 10, 110, 112
Wilbur, R. B., 144
Williams, C. E., 119, 123, 124
Wittgenstein, L., 17
Wrightstone, J. W., 50

Yudin, L., 59
Yule, W., 10

Zawolkow, E., 24
Zink, G. D., 6
Zuk, G. H., 12, 132, 133

| | |
|---|---|
| Designer: | Randall Goodall |
| Compositor: | Viking Typographics |
| Printer: | Vail-Ballou Press |
| Binder: | Vail-Ballou Press |
| Text: | VIP Palatino |
| Display: | VIP Olive Antique |
| Cloth: | Holliston Roxite B53590 |